The Economics of Social Security

Studies in Social Policy and Welfare
Edited by R. A. Pinker

The Economics of
Social Security

L. D. McClements

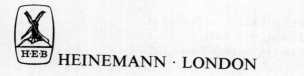

HEINEMANN · LONDON

For L, M and N

London Edinburgh Melbourne Auckland Toronto
Hong Kong Singapore Kuala Lumpur New Delhi
Nairobi Johannesburg Lusaka Ibadan
Kingston

ISBN 0 435 82598 4
Paperback ISBN 0 435 82599 2
© L. D. McClements 1978
First published 1978

Published by Heinemann Educational Books Ltd
48 Charles Street, London W1X 8AH
Printed in Great Britain by Butler & Tanner Ltd,
Frome and London

Preface

Poverty, and social security questions generally, have received little attention from the economics profession. Yet to someone beginning to work on these issues in late 1972 it seemed that there were numerous potentially useful areas of economics. In many ways this study is a fuller statement of the belief that economic analysis has a major contribution to make to decision-making in this important sector of the economy.

Like many other titles *The Economics of Social Security* may promise more than it delivers. The reader is forewarned that the study is neither comprehensive nor definitive. Although it has attempted to cover the main areas some, like the role of social security as an automatic stabilizer, have been omitted. Despite its shortcomings the book will have served its purpose if it encourages others to extend and improve on the ground which it covers.

At one stage, when there was little prospect of writing this book, B. Abel-Smith, I. C. R. Byatt, A. J. G. Crocker, D. Donnison and V. H. Hemming interceded to make it possible. I am also indebted to DHSS for three months' study leave and for a further three months' leave of absence. Much of my time was spent at the Institute for Research on Poverty, University of Wisconsin, which also supported me for part of the period and I am grateful to the Director, I. Garfinkel, for making the project possible. The German Marshall Fund of the United States also provided financial support which enabled me to meet many people concerned with social policy problems in the US. I am indebted to the Fund and the many individuals, especially M. C. Barth and L. Rainwater, who gave freely of their time to explain their work.

A large number of people contributed to the study in various ways. My greatest intellectual debt is to A. G. Coverdale: Chapters 6 to 8 draw freely on a number of unpublished papers which we had written jointly, and he produced the tables on a consistent basis for a single year. E. Armstrong helped with the numerous calculations summarized in Chapter 5 and much of the text has benefited from discussion with J. T. Macrae. In revising the penultimate draft I was aided by helpful comments from A. B. Atkinson, L. E. Bixby, A. E. Bowtell, T. F. Crawley, B. J. Ellis, A. J. Harrison, D. Piachaud, and F. Sutton although mainly for reasons of space it was not always possible to follow their counsel. Many others, especially in DHSS, have contributed to the work by posing problems, clarifying the intricacies of the social security system and questioning my logic. I am grateful to them all. Needless to say the final text is the responsibility of the author alone: it does not necessarily reflect the views of DHSS, the Institute for Research on Poverty, the German Marshall Fund or any of the individuals referred to above.

For the production of a typed manuscript with unfailing accuracy and good humour I am grateful to Joyce Collins, Mary Gallagher, Carol Graebert, Gail Mayer, Barbara Radowski, Debbie Radtke, Mary Ellen Rodriguez, Julie Roh, Diane Van de Hei and Judy Zick.

Finally, my greatest debt is to my wife and children. They not only allowed me to default on my parental duties for two lengthy periods in a foreign place but also helped in numerous other ways. I can only promise them that it will not happen again.

March 1978   L. D. McClements

Contents

*Denotes sections which the general reader may wish to omit.

*Denotes sections which the general reader may wish to omit.

*Denotes sections which the general reader may wish to omit.

Tables

Figures

Abbreviations

AER	*American Economic Review*
AFDC	Aid to Families with Dependent Children
DHSS	Department of Health and Social Security
EJ	*Economic Journal*
FES	Family Expenditure Survey
FIS	Family Income Supplement
GB	Great Britain
HMSO	Her Majesty's Stationery Office
ISP	Income Security Program
JPE	*Journal of Political Economy*
NI	National Insurance
NIT	Negative Income Tax
OECD	Organisation for Economic Cooperation and Development
PPI	Pensioner Price Indices
1PPI	One-Person Pensioner Price Index
2PPI	Two-Person Pensioner Price Index
QJE	*Quarterly Journal of Economics*
RP	Retirement Pension
RPI	Retail Price Index
SB	Supplementary Benefit
TC	Tax Credit
UK	United Kingdom
US	United States

1. The Economics of Social Security

1.1 Introduction

The economics of social security is neither a distinct nor a well-developed discipline. Yet as Chapter 2 shows the social security sector in the United Kingdom (UK) accounts for roughly one-tenth of national income and one-fifth of public expenditure. In other developed countries including the United States (US) social security is also important: in some cases it absorbs up to twice the British share of national income (OECD, 1976). Paradoxically social security (which is also referred to as income maintenance, or social insurance and welfare) has received much less attention from the economics profession than smaller sectors like agriculture or transport. The present study is therefore devoted to the application of economics to an important but neglected area of the British economy.

Economics is the science of choice. It is concerned with the allocation of scarce resources among competing uses in production and with the distribution of the resulting income. The distribution of income involves both the division between factors like capital or labour and, within the personal sector, between individuals. Allocation *and* distribution choices are important because together they determine the welfare or standard of living of the population.

Social security is largely concerned with maintaining the living standards of individuals or groups of persons. Thus it is chiefly involved with distribution among, and the economic welfare of, persons. The main focus of this study will accordingly be on questions of equity and the division of the national cake. But distribution cannot be considered in isolation: the division of the national cake can influence its overall size. Lampman (1966) and Okun (1975) provide a general discussion of the trade-off between equity and efficiency although in addition to income they also consider equality in health, education, judicial and political spheres. A good illustration of the dilemma between equity and efficiency is provided by the level of social security benefits. These are generally below what recipients could earn in the labour market but if they were not then many people would be better off on benefit. Given prevailing allocative mechanisms whereby factors respond to market stimuli there would be a tendency for workers to switch from employment to benefits. Greater equity could only be achieved at the expense of a reduction in output and a fall in economic efficiency. Thus questions of economic efficiency also need to be considered when analysing social security issues.

1.2 Objectives

The aims of this study are twofold. The first objective is to outline areas of economic theory which are useful in analysing practical problems of social security. Secondly, a corpus of theory having been identified, it is applied to some important questions posed by the social security sector in Britain. But what do we mean by the social security sector? And what sort of questions do we wish to answer?

In a narrow sense the social security sector is defined by national accounting and public expenditure conventions. It embraces income transfers like Retirement Pensions or Supplementary Benefit but excludes occupational pensions, health care or other benefits-in-kind. Thus the study must be concerned with the level of benefits and their relativities for different household types. However, Section 2.8 argues that the primary objective of social security in Britain is to provide a minimum standard of living. Therefore factors which influence living standards, especially those of the poor, also form the subject matter of this study. But stated in such general terms our inquiry covers practically every aspect of economic activity. The emphasis will be on taxes, subsidies, consumer prices generally and on those benefits-in-kind which are thought to have a more direct or important influence on living standards.

Having delimited the subject area it may be helpful to illustrate the sort of questions which we would like to answer: they can be divided into three broad categories.

(1) *Conceptual problems*. These involve some abstract and fundamental issues. How do we measure living standards? Can the method take account of families which differ in size and composition? Are living standards absolute or relative? Does social security influence labour supply and saving? How do we measure and judge the trade-off between equity and efficiency?

(2) *Empirical problems*. The answers to these conceptual questions lead to a range of more practical issues. What relative incomes are required by families of different size and composition to obtain similar standards of living? Are some categories like pensioners and one-parent families living exclusively in poverty? How do income transfers including taxes, social security contributions and benefits affect the distribution of living standards? To what extent do changes in relative prices and in benefits-in-kind like free school meals influence matters? Does social security lead to marked changes in labour supply and saving? Is household formation and splitting affected by policy measures?

(3) *Wider issues*. These practical matters in turn contribute to a number of more momentous issues. What are the objectives of the system? Can they be better achieved by cash payments or by benefits-in-kind? Are categorical benefits for unemployment, sickness, retirement and similar contingencies preferable to more general income maintenance of the negative income tax type? Perhaps some forms of income support are more efficient at achieving the objectives of the sector than others?

These are important questions and the ultimate aim of this study is to provide answers to them. Unfortunately, as Atkinson (1977) notes, they have been a minority interest to the economics profession. Much time and thought has been devoted to allocative efficiency while personal distribution has been largely ignored (Atkinson, 1975; Gordon, 1976; and Rivlin, 1975). This may be due, in part, to the need to make explicit ethical judgements when analysing distributional questions. But as Koopmans (1957) and Ward (1972) point out, studies of allocative efficiency implicitly embody distributional judgements: by ignoring the welfare implications of the personal distribution of income that arises when output is maximized they adopt, by default, the ethical position that whatever division of income occurs is desirable and acceptable.

The neglect of personal distribution may explain the limited attention which has been devoted to the economics of social security. One consequence of this state of affairs is that economic questions have been largely overlooked in formulating and implementing social security measures. The objectives of the various instruments are not well defined, alternative means of achieving these aims are not explored and the relative effectiveness of the options is not assessed.[1]

---

[1] Lindblom (1959) has argued that 'muddling through' or 'disjointed incrementalism' is an inevitable feature of the decision-making process which promotes flexibility in the face of uncertainty and disagreement about the objectives of policy: Hill (1974) pursues this line of argument in the context of welfare reform. However, there may

As a result the measures are less successful in obtaining objectives than they might be. Instruments often embody unrecognized inconsistencies or undermine the purpose of other measures and the overall outcome differs from the original intent. This general lack of knowledge generates myth and dogma: ideology takes the place of fact and analysis (Donnison, 1972).

In attempting to develop the economics of social security this study is primarily addressed to economists. But others also have responsibilities for the conduct and efficiency of the social security system. In the hope that some of the material will be accessible to non-economists technical economic terms have been avoided where possible. As an aid to the general reader the more technical sections are marked with an asterisk and the main ideas are recapitulated at the beginning of the ensuing non-technical section.

1.3 Economic analysis and judgements

The stress will be on economic analysis rather than the description of the main benefit programmes, client groups and institutions of the social security system. Focusing on a particular benefit or group of benefits does not, of course, preclude an analytical approach as Pechman *et al.* (1968) and Ross and Sawhill (1975) demonstrate. But it does concentrate attention on one set of institutional arrangements at the expense of inter-relationships with, and parallel problems in, other areas. A wider analytical approach also has a number of other advantages. It provides a way of looking at and understanding questions which is more general than the *ad hoc* consideration of current issues and can be applied to a range of problems many of which cannot be foreseen. Thus it is of more lasting interest than a catalogue of current problems and solutions. An analytical framework also provides the conceptual basis for further work. It shows how problems are connected to one another and allows new research to be integrated into the existing body of knowledge. Relating questions to one another will not only lead to more informed, consistent and better answers but may also highlight new and hitherto unrecognized issues.

The indifference curve analysis of Section 3.3 provides a good illustration of these advantages. It enables living standards to be measured in households of different size, composition or other cir-

---

be more effective strategies for dealing with uncertainty, disagreement and lack of information.

cumstances and as such is applicable to most social security benefits. It can also be used to demonstrate the impact of changing relative prices, allows the poor to be identified and so on. The application of this conceptual apparatus across the social security sector highlights differences in benefit relativities, the definition of the benefit unit in the various measures and many other important economic issues.

Very briefly, economic theory and its application involves the following process. On the basis of simple but approximate assumptions or axioms about economic behaviour the theory derives qualitative and sometimes quantitative statements, hypotheses or predictions. In Section 3.2 the indifference curve model predicts that an increase in price will, *ceteris paribus* (in this case real income held constant), lead to the substitution of the cheaper for the dearer commodity. By assuming that households maximize utility we predict that, holding real income constant, an increase in price will reduce demand for the dearer commodity and increase consumption of the cheaper good. The behavioural assumption that households maximize utility can be used to generate a wide range of useful hypotheses about expenditure behaviour in homogeneous and heterogeneous households.

The application of theory therefore involves behavioural assumptions or judgements. In characterizing expenditure behaviour the utility-maximising model incorporates ethical judgements about how consumers ought to allocate their income or how an extra unit of consumption ought to influence living standards. Hence applied economic analysis is not value-free or objective in any absolute sense. At best, if the predictions of theory are supported by empirical evidence it can only be argued that they are more objective than predictions which have no such basis. For example, the commodity and income scales estimated from household expenditure data and summarized in Section 5.7 are more objective than those in Section 5.8 because the latter, which are based on the Beveridge subsistence budgets, involve a much greater element of judgement.

The simplicity and objectivity of theories is furthered by minimizing the number and strength of the assumptions on which they are based—according to the maxim of Occam's razor 'entities are not to be multiplied without necessity' (Russell, 1946). The fewer and weaker the assumptions the more general and powerful the theory in terms of encompassing a wider range of phenomena. The rejection by economists of interpersonal comparisons of utility and cardinal measurement in favour of compensation tests and ordinality contributed to this process as, for many purposes, these assumptions were unnecessary. But this quest for theoretical elegance can also limit the application of theory (Stigler, 1950). In the case of personal distribution, inter-household type utility comparisons, cardinal measurement and distributional judgements are required. If these are ruled out then important aspects of personal distribution lie beyond the scope of economic analysis. The redundancy of assumptions in one branch of theory spilled over into another where they were required and contributed to the neglect of distribution by economists. It may be vain to do with more what can be done with fewer, but it is also purposeless to attempt to do with fewer what can only be done with more.

Thus economic analysis involves value judgements and these are of special importance in distributional studies. Judgements arise at many points in what follows but differ in nature with some being less crucial than others. Three broad categories of judgements can be identified.

(1) *Conscious judgements.* Some value judgements are made where the true situation is known but societal norms are consciously judged to be unacceptable. They correspond to what Myrdal (1969) terms valuations, or what should be. An illustration is provided in Section 5.9 where it is shown how the expenditure behaviour of men and women differs, implying that in society they are not treated as equals. Yet some aspects of the social security system incorporate the basic ethical judgement that men and women are equal. Thus value judgements are sometimes made in situations where we do know something of what is going on but consider it undesirable—it ought to be changed. This first category of judgements would appear to be the clear responsibility of the political process: the role of economics would be to explore the implications of ethical edicts from above.

(2) *Behavioural judgements.* Then there are the ethical judgements which are embodied in the behavioural and other assumptions of economic theory which were touched on in the previous section. The assumption that households maximize utility is one example of this category which Ng (1972) terms 'subjective judgements of fact'. Where there is a wide measure of professional consensus and no prospect of direct verification it might be appropriate to regard these as basic scientific truths. But in other cases there will be less agreement. Perhaps the clearest illustration of this sub-category are the distributional weights discussed in Section 4.5. Studies of allocative efficiency often ignore this problem and in so doing implicitly embody one set of distributional weights. In effect, they incorporate the judgement that an extra £1 of income adds as much to the living

standard of a poor household as to that of a rich household and as much to the welfare of a large family as to that of a small family. Others would judge that the marginal utility of income declines with increasing income and increases with family size. But by how much does it decline? Although estimates can be made on the basis of certain assumptions it is not possible to give any fully objective answer to this question because utility or living standards are unobserved. Direct measurement is, therefore, difficult and reliance has to be placed on indirect evidence like changes in expenditure patterns. Thus the second type of behavioural judgement arises in situations where we do not know what the true situation is and have little prospect of finding out. Where there is broad agreement it would seem sufficient to state the judgement clearly and proceed with the analysis. But if there is disagreement a more circumspect approach is required. Ideally these judgements should be laid down for economists by society through, for example, the political process, and Section 4.5 indicates how distributional judgements may be gleaned from existing measures. If this is not possible then a range of explicit judgements can be made and the implications of the alternatives explored.

(3) *Uniformed judgements.* The final category of judgements is associated with the myth and dogma mentioned in Section 1.2. Very strong and deeply held opinions are often expressed on social security matters without any factual basis or with only partial or limited evidence: the relationship between myth and rhetoric has been explored by Edelman (1975a). Unlike the second category of judgements the situation can be readily ascertained: and when determined, unlike the first category, the facts would not necessarily be considered undesirable. On the basis of casual experience it may be held that all pensioners and one-parent families are poor and, therefore, income support ought to be concentrated on these groups. But if some pensioners and one-parent families are in fact rich then this conclusion would not necessarily follow. Taussing (1973) provides another illustration of how myth and ideology can lead to ineffective poverty measures. It is popularly held that lack of education and unwillingness to work are major causes of poverty in the US. However, Harrison (1972) has demonstrated that additional education has a limited effect on the earnings or employment prospects of the poor, while Goodwin (1972) provides evidence that their work and life-style aspirations are as strong as those of the more affluent. Neither education nor work incentives will provide effective anti-poverty measures. Empirical evidence and logical analysis can transform judgements or opinions of the third type into factual statements and consistent positions.

While there is considerable overlap between the three categories of judgement—conscious, behavioural and uninformed—the distinction is nevertheless useful. The first group is beyond the domain of economic analysis, the second falls within it but the judgements involved should be clearly stated, while the third type is the antithesis of economic analysis and should be reduced in scope and number by the application of economic techniques.

1.4 Outline

A number of questions were posed in Section 1.2 and they were grouped into conceptual, empirical and wider issues. The remainder of the study follows the same broad outline. Before embarking on the economic analysis proper, Chapter 2 describes the social security sector in Britain. Chapters 3 and 4 develop most of the theoretical basis used in later parts of the work. The empirical results and evidence constitute the main body of the study and are covered in Chapters 5 to 10. The closing chapter considers a few big questions, which draw on the rest of the study and which are likely to be recurring issues.

2. Social Security in Britain

2.1 Introduction

This chapter reviews some of the more important institutional features of the social security system in the UK. As the sector is continually changing and evolving this description is inevitably obsolescent in certain respects. Where benefit levels and similar magnitudes are quoted they represent the amounts prevailing in November 1977. The focus is on economic aspects of the system and the account is not a comprehensive and detailed description which can only be obtained from current legislation, rules and regulations: a more detailed account is given in Lister (1976) or HMSO (1977), *Social Security in Britain*.

2.2 Population

Social security measures are primarily aimed at the personal sector of the UK economy. Thus demographic characteristics have a major influence on the size and importance of the sector and on the balance of expenditure between programmes.

The total UK population, of 56 million people, is at present relatively static from year to year. The small margin of births over deaths is largely offset by net migration. Nevertheless, changes are occurring in the age structure which have important implications for social security provision. Table 2.1 shows that in 1974 16·8 per cent of the population was over pension age while 25·2 per cent was below the school-leaving age. This compares with 14.5 per cent over pension age in 1961 and a projected 17·4 per cent in 1981, after which the proportion levels out and then declines somewhat. The proportion below the current school-leaving age of 16 years has also increased and projections suggest that it will fall marginally in the future. However, the causes of population changes are imperfectly understood

(Section 10.6) and projections need to be treated with caution. In the Beveridge Report, HMSO (1942), Cmd 6404, for example, it was estimated that the proportion of the population over pension age would increase from 12 per cent in 1941 to 21 per cent in 1971 whereas the actual out-turn was 16 per cent.

The proportion of the population over pension age has an important influence on the size of the social security sector because, for a given level of benefits, it determines the magnitude of the major item of expenditure. This proportion is higher in the UK than in most other developed countries (OECD, 1976), and its increase over the post-war period has made a sizable contribution to the relative growth of social security.

Table 2.1

The UK population classified by age, labour force attachment, tax units and households, 1974

	Number, m	*Per cent or persons/unit*
Persons		
Over pension age[1]	9·4	16·8 per cent
Adults[2]	32·5	58·0 per cent
Children[3]	14·1	25·2 per cent
Working population[4]	25·6	45·7 per cent
Dependent population	30·4	54·3 per cent
Total population	56·0	100·0 per cent
Units		
Tax units[5]	28·4	2·0 persons/tax unit
Household units[6]	19·5	2·9 persons/household unit

[1] 60 years for women, 65 for men
[2] Over 16 years and under pension age
[3] Under 16 years
[4] June 1974 seasonally unadjusted

[5] For 1972–73

[6] Estimated

Source: HMSO (1975),
Annual Abstract of Statistics
Source: HMSO (1976)
Department of Employment Gazette, September
Source: HMSO (1975),
Social Trends, No. 6, 1975

Table 2·1 also shows that the working population, which includes the registered unemployed, accounts for less than half of the total population. About half of the dependent population is below school-leaving age and so has lower needs than the remaining half which is composed of students in higher or tertiary education, people over pension age and adults (mainly mothers not in the labour force). Adults not in the labour force include the sick and disabled while the unregistered unemployed fluctuate in importance with variations in the level of economic activity.

Most social security benefits are paid to individuals as groups of persons. The number of 'benefit units' is therefore of interest although the definition varies between programmes, as is shown in Section 2.6 below. But nuclear families, or groupings of individuals which have been referred to as 'tax units' in the literature (although they are no longer strictly tax units), provide proxies for the benefit unit. Tax units are defined as married couples or single people over the age of 15 years not in full-time education plus minors with investment income above the tax exemption limit (Ramprakash, 1975). A married couple with dependent children is in the great majority of cases defined as a single unit but if the child enters the labour market two tax units are formed: two or more unrelated individuals living together would also be considered as two or more tax units. Table 2.1 indicates that there are over 28 million tax units in the UK population so there is a roughly similar number of potential benefit units.

Households, which are defined as individuals living together at the same address having meals prepared together and with common housekeeping, can contain one or more benefit and tax units. There are about 19·5m households containing on average just under 3 people or almost one and a half tax units. As much of the analysis in this study is based on expenditure data, which are only available on a household basis, the household is the main unit adopted in later chapters. Some of the reasons for this approach are discussed in Section 3.5 below, while Table 6.1 shows the distribution of persons, tax units and households classified by household living standards.

2.3 The social security sector

In 1975 social security expenditure in the UK totalled £8918m (Table 2.2). Its relative size depends on the aggregate in terms of which it is measured and this in turn is determined by the context in which the sector is being considered. Social security expenditure amounted to 9·6 per cent of Gross Domestic Product at factor cost in 1975 and this ratio is of interest where the allocation of resources between private consumption, public consumption, the overseas sector and capital formation is being considered. But where the balance between private and public consumption and the financing of public expenditure is being examined national income is more relevant: in terms of this denominator social security amounted to 10·7 per cent in 1975.

Alternatively, social security benefits represented 14·1 per cent of consumers' expenditure. Since most benefits find their way into consumers' expenditure, which is the major component of total demand for goods and services, this third ratio is of interest where the focus is on the management of aggregate demand. Finally, social security amounted to one-fifth of total public expenditure, a figure which is important in deciding the balance within the public sector.

Table 2.2
Social security sector receipts and expenditure, 1975

Receipts	£m	Per cent
National Insurance contributions[1]	6286	71
Central government grant to NI Fund	1140	13
Interest on NI Fund balances	176	2
Less current surplus in NI Fund	855	− 10
From Consolidated Fund for Non-contributory Benefits	2171	24
Total	8918	100

Expenditure		
National Insurance Benefits	6435	72
Supplementary Benefits	1103	12
Family Allowances	499	6
War Pensions	249	3
Other Non-contributory Benefits	141	2
Goods and services—NI Fund	312	4
Goods and services—Consolidated Fund	179	2
Total	8918	100

Source: HMSO (1976), *National Income and Expenditure 1965–75*
[1] Excludes National Health and Redundancy Fund contributions

A social security sector balance sheet is shown in Table 2.2. The main source of receipts is from NI contributions paid by employees and employers and collected in the main by the Inland Revenue with income tax. A grant is also paid into the NI Fund by the central government amounting to about 15 per cent of contributions and this will increase to around 18 per cent in future years. Central government payments from the Consolidated Fund to cover the cost of non-contributory benefits account for about a quarter of sector receipts. Thus general revenue sources provide about one-third of sector receipts with the remainder coming from NI contributions.

On the expenditure side NI benefits are the main item with non-contributory Supplementary Benefits (SB) next in importance.

In addition to social security benefits many related public expenditure measures have an effect on the volume of goods and services which a weekly benefit payment will purchase. Expenditure on housing, food and nationalized industry subsidies is shown in Table 2.3. With the exception of compensation for price restraint, of which about half is allocated to consumers' expenditure, these subsidies mainly result in a direct reduction in retail prices. Rent rebates and school meals are also included in Table 2.3 because they have a similar effect, but agricultural subsidies have been excluded because their influence on retail prices is indirect although they are allocated as subsidies to consumers' expenditure in the national accounts.

Table 2.3

Social security benefit expenditure and some related subsidy measures, 1975

Programme	£m
Social Security Benefits	8427
Housing subsidies	1051
Rent rebates and allowances	261
Food subsidies	652
School meals and milk	385
Nationalized industries—transport	468
Nationalized industries—price restraint	285

Source: HMSO (1976), *National Income and Expenditure 1965–75*

Rate Rebates account for about two-thirds of the cost of Rent Rebates and Allowances, but are not shown in Table 2.3, being classified as an indirect tax remission rather than a subsidy although they affect the price of housing services just as directly as housing subsidies. Other 'tax expenditures', or what Titmuss (1963) has termed 'fiscal welfare benefits', are also excluded from Table 2.3 although personal tax allowances and child tax allowances do have as direct an effect on living standards as social security benefits. Ultimately all government activity influences the personal sector and the line is drawn at the items shown in Table 2.3 on the basis of existing conventions rather than any more fundamental reasoning about the immediate impact of measures on the living standards of social security beneficiaries.

Social security benefits are at present administered centrally in Great Britain (GB) by the Department of Health and Social Security

(DHSS). The main exception to this arrangement is Unemployment Benefit which is administered on behalf of DHSS by the Department of Employment through its network of employment exchanges and job centres. In 1975 DHSS had a central administrative staff dealing with social security numbering 2400 people, two central administrative offices involving 12,100 and 2500 people respectively and a large regional organization employing 64,900 people in a network of regional and local offices (HMSO, 1976, Cmnd 6565). Administrative costs are very much higher for non-contributory benefits due to the labour-intensive nature of the SB scheme where administration absorbed 13 per cent of total expenditure (HMSO, 1976, Cmnd 6615), compared with 5 per cent for other benefits. Although administered separately, social security benefits in Northern Ireland follow the same pattern. Thus benefit levels, rules and regulations are uniform throughout the UK.

The social security sector accounts for one-tenth of national income or one-fifth of the public sector in the UK. As such it may appear large. But recall that people over pension age, who are mainly dependent on social security, represent 16·8 per cent of the population. In addition, a further 5–10 per cent of the population also derives its main source of income from benefits, so that in total roughly a quarter of the population is dependent on social security. Viewed in this perspective the relative size of the sector is not large.

2.4 National Insurance contributions

National Insurance contributions constitute the main source of revenue for the social security sector and NI benefits account for three-quarters of expenditure. Contributions are divided into four categories—employees (Class 1), self-employed flat-rate (Class 2) and profits-related (Class 4) payments and voluntary (Class 3) contributions by the non-employed. Class 1 contributions are earnings-related and levied on employer and employee: in 1977–78 the employer contribution was 8·75 per cent while employees paid 5·75 per cent of all earnings up to £105 per week provided that earnings were at least £15. They entitle the insured to the full range of NI benefits where the individual contribution conditions are fulfilled. A reduced rate of Class 1 employee contributions of 2 per cent can be paid by some married women and recipients of Widows' Benefits but they are excluded from NI benefits on their own insurance. Class 2 contributions were £2·66 and £2·55 per week for men and women respectively: in addition they pay Class 4 contributions at a rate of

8 per cent of profits in the range £1750–£5500 subject to a small earnings exemption of £875 per annum. This group is entitled to most NI benefits except Unemployment and Industrial Injury Benefits. Voluntary Class 3 contributions are paid by the non-employed like the full-rate Class 1 or Class 2 contributors repairing a broken contribution record or by occupational pensioners below the NI Retirement Pension age maintaining an intact record. Class 3 contributions were £2·45 per week in 1977–78. Retirement Pensions and Widows' Benefits are the main benefits to which entitlement is given by Class 3 contributions. Where an insured person is in receipt of most benefits other than Retirement Pension, contributions are credited in order to maintain contribution records intact. On entering the NI scheme credits are also given which help to qualify the insured person for certain benefits.

Contribution rates, floors and ceilings are usually adjusted annually in the light of revenue requirements which are determined by benefit levels—the benefit uprating procedure is described in Section 2.6 below. The introduction in 1978 of the new pensions' legislation embodied in the Social Security Pensions Act 1975, and its maturation over a 20-year period, will involve an increase in contribution rates for those in the earnings-related state scheme. As the earnings floor and ceiling for contribution purposes are related to the flat-rate Retirement Pension, which in turn is linked to average earnings, in effect the floor and ceiling are set at about 21·5 and 150 per cent of average earnings. With the introduction of the new pensions' arrangements Class 1 contributors belonging to approved occupational pension schemes will pay contributions at a reduced rate (HMSO, 1974, Cmnd 5713).

2.5 Benefits

On the expenditure side social security is composed of a complex, interlocking and partly overlapping set of programmes which are operated according to different eligibility criteria, benefit levels, benefit units, rules and regulations. Benefits can be classified into NI and non-contributory categories as in Table 2.2 Although both groups had earlier origins they mainly date from the Beveridge Report (HMSO, 1942, Cmd 6404) and the post-war implementation of its main proposals. The more important of these recommendations included the provision of flat-rate NI benefits covering contingencies like retirement, sickness and unemployment for flat-rate contributions; Family Allowances helping to lift the larger families of the working poor out of poverty; and means-tested National Assistance (replaced in 1966 by Supplementary Benefit) providing a safety net for those not caught by the other arrangements. But in practice the relationship between NI benefits and non-contributory SB has been such that substantial numbers of NI beneficiaries have also been on SB.

Subsequent developments have involved the introduction of new contributory schemes such as Invalidity Benefit to deal with contingencies like continuing incapacity through illness. There have also been several new non-contributory benefits like Old Person's Pension, Attendance Allowance, Invalid Care Allowance and Non-contributory Invalidity Pension. In the main these covered contingencies which could not be dealt with within the framework of the NI scheme because those concerned were not, or had not been, in the labour market and so contributions were not feasible. In contrast, Family Income Supplement provided an earnings-related benefit for the low-paid and Child Benefit extended a cash benefit to the first or only child. But perhaps the largest change from the original proposals has been the move towards earnings-related contributions and benefits, a development which is central to the new pensions proposals (HMSO, 1974, Cmnd 5713) which are described in more detail below.

A breakdown of expenditure on the main NI and non-contributory benefits is given in Table 2.4 which also shows the number of beneficiaries involved. The numbers are not additive because there is considerable overlap between the various NI benefits and SB, and between all other benefits and Family Allowances. Retirement Pensions are by far the most important in terms of both expenditure and numbers of beneficiaries reflecting the age structure of the population. SB is next in importance in terms of expenditure, followed by Sickness and Injury Benefit, Unemployment Benefit, Widows' Benefits and Family Allowances.

In looking at the main benefits in more detail it is helpful to distinguish two broad categories which cut across the NI and non-contributory classification. Long-term benefits, which generally go to people dependent on social security for long periods as with retirement or disablement, are at a higher level than short-term benefits which are mostly paid to short-term beneficiaries like the sick or unemployed. The levels of benefits will be discussed more fully in Section 2.6 below.

Retirement Pensions (RP) are paid where the retirement ages of 60 for women and 65 for men have been reached, the contribution conditions are satisfied and a retirement condition is met. The contribu-

Table 2.4
Expenditure and number of beneficiaries on the main social security benefits, 1975

Benefit	Expenditure		Number of Beneficiaries, m
	£m	Per cent	
NI Benefits			
Retirement Pensions	4479	53	8·070[1]
Widows' Benefits and Guardians' Allowances	389	5	0·514
Industrial Death Benefits	21	0	0·031
Death Grant	15	0	0·520
Unemployment Benefit	399	5	0·605
Sickness and Injury Benefit	480[2]	6	0·550
Invalidity Benefit	409[2]	5	0·480
Industrial Disablement Benefit	142	2	0·200
Maternity Benefits	53	1	—
Grants Abroad	48	1	—
Total NI Benefits	6435	76	—
Non-contributory Benefits			
Supplementary Benefits	1103	13	2·930
War Pensions	234	3	0·405
Other Non-contributory Benefits	141	2	—
Family Allowances	499	6	7·170[3]
Grants Abroad	15	0	—
Total Non-contributory Benefits	1992	24	—
Total Social Security Benefits	8427	100	—

Sources: HMSO (1976), *National Income and Expenditure 1965–75*
HMSO (1976), *Parliamentary Debates (Hansard)*, Vol. 912
HMSO (1976), *Annual Report of the Department of Health and Social Security 1975*, Cmnd 6565

[1] Number of adult pensioners
[2] Estimated
[3] Number of qualifying children

tions requirements differ for married women: men and single women must have at least 156 flat-rate contributions and made on average at least 43 contributions in each year between 1948 and retirement, while married women must have contributed in half the period between marriage and age 60 although this 'half-test' is to be relaxed under the new pensions legislation. Failure to meet the contributions conditions results in reduced benefits, although some RP may be paid if average contributions exceed 11 per year. The retirement condition applies for the 5 years after minimum pension age is reached. Earnings, if any, must not exceed the earnings limit of £40 per week and if they do the pension is reduced by 50 per cent of the excess up to earnings of £44 and withdrawn at 100 per cent thereafter so that each £1 increase in earnings over £44 results in a £1 fall in pension.

If the contribution conditions are met a married woman can claim on her own insurance at the single-person rate. Otherwise when her husband reaches pensionable age he can claim at the married-couple rate: in the event of his death the single-person rate becomes payable to his widow and entitlement remains if she remarries or lives with another man as his wife. Increases are also paid for dependent children: all RP payments are at the long-term benefit rates. Increments are payable for deferred retirement and graduated pensions are currently paid to pensioners who have made graduated contributions.

Under the Social Security Pensions Act 1975 provision is made for an additional earnings-related component. This will amount to 25 per cent of earnings between the basic pension, which for a single person is about 21·5 per cent of average gross earnings, and up to seven times that level, which is about 150 per cent of average earnings. In terms of the November 1977 single pension of £17·50 per week this means that someone with the following average earnings over the best 20 years of employment would get:

Average earnings	Flat-rate pension	Earnings-related pension	Total pension	Earnings replacement ratio
£17·50	£17·50	—	£17·50	1·00
£35·00	£17·50	£4·38	£21·88	0·63
£105·00	£17·50	£21·88	£39·38	0·38

The earnings-related component, which will be introduced in 1978, will only be paid in full when the scheme has matured in 1998—in the interim it will be calculated at 1·25 per cent for each year in the scheme. Widows or widowers on RP will inherit the earnings-related pension component of their deceased spouse in place of their own entitlement if that is more advantageous. Participants in occupational pension schemes meeting specified requirements can be contracted out of the earnings-related state scheme and pay NI contributions at a reduced rate.

Widows' Benefits are paid where the deceased husband has satisfied the contribution conditions which are similar to those for RP up to the time of death: if the contribution conditions are partly met reduced benefits are paid. Unlike RP, they are not subject to an earnings rule but in the event of her marriage, or living with a man as his wife, entitlement ceases. *Widows' Allowance* is a benefit at a preferential rate above long-term benefits for the first 26 weeks provided that either the widow is below pension age or her husband was not entitled to RP. *Widowed Mothers' Allowance*, which is at the long-term benefit rate, is paid thereafter provided a child under 19 years is living with or dependent on the mother. *Widows' Pension* succeeds either of the previous two benefits if the widow is over 40 when they cease: it is paid at 30 per cent of the long-term benefit rate if it commences at age 40, increasing by 7 per cent for each year thereafter, being at the full rate if it begins at age 50 or later. Payments for dependent children are at the long-term rate for all Widows' Benefits and the personal element for the widow will become earnings-related under the new pensions' legislation.

Industrial Death Benefits are provided where the husbands' death is caused by industrial accident or disease. They are similar to Widows' Benefits except that the pension incorporates a small premium over the long-term rate.

Death Grant is a lump sum paid on the death of an insured person or dependant: it varies by age at death.

Unemployment Benefit is available to Class 1 (employed) contributors who have paid at least 26 contributions or contributions on earnings of at least 25 times the contributions floor if the NI scheme was entered since April 1975. To obtain the full benefit the insured person must also have paid, or been credited with, 50 contributions in a previous contribution year. It is paid at a reduced rate where contribution records are deficient but at least 26 contributions or the equivalent have been paid, but cannot be claimed by married women who exercise the lower contribution option, and is paid at a lower rate to fully insured wives although this is to be phased out under the new pensions' legislation. This reduced rate is also applicable where the applicant is under 18 and has no dependent children. Unemployment Benefit can be delayed if pay has been given in lieu of notice; it can be withheld for up to 6 weeks if unemployment is voluntary, is due to misconduct or if suitable employment is refused without good cause. Flat-rate Unemployment Benefit is paid at the short-term rate. It becomes available after 3 days for up to 312 days: thereafter no benefit is payable until the insured person has requalified. In addition to flat-rate benefit people over 18 and under pension age can qualify for an *Earnings Related Supplement* after 12 days for up to 156 days. This is calculated on the basis of earnings in an earlier tax year but the total benefit may not exceed 85 per cent of the claimant's average weekly earnings although this limit cannot be used to reduce the flat-rate component. Additions for dependants are also paid at the short-term rate, provided, in the case of a wife, that her earnings do not exceed the benefit addition for a spouse. *Sickness Benefit* is paid to both employed (Class 1) and self-employed (Class 2) contributors under similar qualifying conditions to Unemployment Benefit. It applies where the claimant is unable to work because of illness or disablement and this is normally established by a doctor's statement. Sickness Benefit becomes available after 3 days for up to 168 days, when it is usually replaced by Invalidity Benefit. Rates of benefit are the same as for Unemployment Benefit and Earnings Related Supplement is payable on a similar basis.

Injury Benefit is similar to Sickness Benefit except that incapacity arises from industrial injury or a prescribed disease. Although benefits do not depend on contribution conditions they are restricted to employees, i.e. Class 1 contributors. The personal benefit is at the long-term rate plus a premium and Earnings-Related Supplement is paid on the same basis as for Unemployment Benefit: increases for dependants are at the short-term benefit rates.

Invalidity Benefit, which is available to Class 1 and Class 2 contributors who have paid at least 156 weekly contributions or the equivalent, generally replaces Sickness Benefit after 168 days. *Invalidity Pension* and increases for dependants are paid at the long-term benefit rate: an earnings-related element will be added with the introduction of the new pensions' legislation. In addition, *Invalidity Allowance* is payable at three rates which decline where incapacity commences in older age ranges.

Industrial Disablement Benefit follows Injury Benefit, the *Industrial Disablement Pension* rate being determined by a medical assessment of the percentage degree of disablement. Other main NI benefits and their increases for dependants can be claimed in addition except where disablement is permanent. In this event *Unemployability Supplement*, which is at the long-term benefit rate, is paid together with the long-term benefit rates for dependants. *Hospital Treatment Allowance* brings the pension rate up to the 100 per cent level during hospital treatment for the industrial injury or disease and where regular attention is required additional allowances are paid. In certain circumstances, a *Special Hardship Allowance* can be paid to claimants who, because of industrial injury or disease, have to pursue a less well-paid occupation: it amounts to the difference in earnings between the two occupations up to a specified maximum.

Maternity Benefit is made up of two elements. *Maternity Grant* is a lump sum payment of £25 for which the contribution conditions, which are similar to those for Unemployment Benefit, can be satisfied by either parent. *Maternity Allowance* is payable for 18 weeks, normally commencing 11 weeks before the baby is due, to a mother who has been working and contributing at the full Class 1 or the Class 2 rate. It is normally paid at the short-term benefit rate for a single person but increases are also included for adults and children where they are solely dependent on the mother.

Supplementary Benefit is available as of right to any individual over the age of 16 who is not in full-time work or secondary education, if resources are less than requirements. Requirements less resources determine SB entitlement (HMSO, 1977, *Supplementary Benefits Handbook*). A man is liable to maintain his wife and children while a woman is liable to maintain her husband and children: a maintenance order can be applied for against a husband whose wife and children are drawing SB or an affiliation order can be applied for against the alleged father of an illegitimate child. Married couples and those living together as man and wife are treated as a single unit both for the award of SB and for the determination of entitlement which is vested in the man. SB is not paid for a person involved in a trade dispute although it is usually paid to dependants in such circumstances.

The resources, or income, of the SB unit are calculated according to the following rules. The main NI benefits, Child Benefit, Family Income Supplement and maintenance payments are counted in full. Reasonable expenses can be deducted from net earnings and a specified amount of the remainder, which varies by category of beneficiary, is disregarded. Sick pay, superannuation, annuities and payments from charities are also subject to a disregard as are benefits like War Widow's Pension or Industrial Death Pension which provide compensation. The capital value of an owner-occupied house is ignored but other capital assets and buildings with a value exceeding a specified amount are treated as producing income according to a prescribed tariff.

The requirements of the SB unit are defined as the scale rates appropriate to the claimant and dependants plus certain other allowances. The scale rates, which are set out in Section 2.6 below, are intended to cover all normal expenses other than housing: they vary according to whether the claimant is a householder or not, a single person, a married couple or man and woman living together as such, and vary with the ages of dependent children. Rent and Rate Rebates and Rent Allowances cannot normally be claimed while on SB and due to the differences in computing entitlement some people may be better off on housing benefits than on SB (HMSO, 1976, Cmnd 6615). Rent and rates, net of any proceeds from subletting, are added to the scale rate for a householder: in the case of an owner-occupier mortgage interest payments plus an allowance for maintenance and repairs are included with rates. An *Exceptional Circumstance Addition* can be added to requirements for items like extra heating, central heating, special diets or domestic assistance. In addition, a lump sum *Exceptional Needs Payment* can be made to beneficiaries to cover abnormal expenditure on necessary items like clothing, bedding or furniture.

Supplementary Pension is paid to a claimant over pension age and in calculating requirements the higher long-term SB scale rates are used. *Supplementary Allowances* are paid to beneficiaries below pension age. Those who are not unemployed and have been on SB for 2 consecutive years have their requirements calculated using the long-term scale rates. For beneficiaries of less than 2 years' duration, and for all unemployed claimants of whatever duration, the lower ordinary scale rates are used in calculating requirements. If the claimant is able to work Supplementary Allowance will normally be paid on condition that he registers for work at an employment exchange.

The SB scheme provides a minimum standard of living below which no one need fall and acts as a 'passport' providing exemption from prescription and certain other health service charges, free milk and free school meals. Due to reduced NI benefit entitlement, housing costs, or Exceptional Circumstance Additions many NI beneficiaries and people on other non-contributory benefits are also eligible for SB. Table 2.5 shows the SB caseload towards the end of 1975 broken down by the main NI benefits and the average SB entitlement in each category although the numbers are sensitive to the level of unemployment.

War Pensions are awarded for disablement or death in the armed services. *War Disablement Pension* varies according to percentage disability assessed by a medical board and varied by rank: the rate for officers is more generous than Industrial Disablement Pension but for other ranks it is the same. *Unemployability Supplement* is awarded where the disability precludes employment: it is higher than for Industrial Disablement Benefit and additions are paid for dependants at the long-term benefit rates. *Treatment, Constant Attendance, Severe Disablement* and *Lowered Standard of Occupation Allowances* are also paid as for Industrial Disablement Benefit but generally at a higher rate. *Age Allowance* is paid to a pensioner over 65 with a disability of 40 per cent or more, a *Clothing Allowance* is available if the disability causes exceptional wear and tear, and a *Comforts Allowance* can be used to provide comforts for the severely disabled.

Table 2.5

Numbers of Supplementary Benefit recipients and average payments classified by receipt of NI benefits, 1975, Great Britain

	Supplementary pensions			Supplementary allowances								Total
				Unemployed		Sick and disabled		NI widows	One-parent family not included elsewhere	Others	Total	
	NI benefits	Other	Total	NI benefits	Other	NI benefits	Other					
Number of recipients (Thousands)	1586	94	1679	135	406	77	165	30	276	24	1113	2793
Per cent of recipients	57	3	60	5	15	3	6	1	10	1	40	100
Average entitlement (£/week)	4·93	15·50	5·52	6·98	16·69	5·69	12·05	6·01	21·05	17·61	14·87	9·24

Source: HMSO (1977) Social Security Statistics 1975, Tables 34.34 and 34.38

War Widows' Pension varies with rank and age: it is considerably higher than the long-term benefit rate and the rates for dependent children are also somewhat higher. Where a pensioner was eligible for Unemployability Supplement or Constant Attendance Allowance for the first 26 weeks the widow is paid the husband's pension less the wife's allowance. *Rent Allowance* and *Age Allowances* are paid to War Widows and a *War Widowers' Pension* is also available.

Old Persons' Pension is paid to pensioners over the age of 80 who are resident in the UK and either fail to qualify for RP or qualify at a level below the non-contributory benefit rate, which is lower than both the long- and short-term benefit rates.

Non-Contributory Invalidity Pension is paid at the non-contributory benefit rate to men and women of working age who live in the UK and have been incapable of work for 28 weeks but are ineligible for Invalidity Pension and other NI benefits or are receiving them at a lower rate.

Invalid Care Allowance is paid at the non-contributory benefit rate to men and single women of working age who would be in paid employment but for the need to care for severely disabled relatives in receipt of Attendance Allowance.

Mobility Allowance is available to persons aged 5 and over but below pension age who, due to physical disability, are unable to walk. It will be increased from £7 to £10 per week in April 1978 and will be uprated in line with prices thereafter.

Attendance Allowance is a non-contributory benefit paid to a severely disabled person requiring frequent attention who meets a residence test. The higher rate is applicable where day and night attention is necessary and the lower rate applies where either day or night attention is required. The higher rate is somewhat lower than the short-term benefit rate for a single person and the lower rate is two-thirds of the higher rate.

Family Income Supplement (FIS) differs from most of the benefits considered so far in that it is paid to families of which the head is in full-time work. The amount of benefit payable is half the amount by which the family's total gross weekly income falls short of a qualifying level. This 'prescribed amount' is £43·80 per week for a family with one child, increasing by £4 for each additional child. The maximum FIS payment is £9·50 for a family with one child, increasing by £1 for each additional child. Awards are based on earnings averaged over the 5 weeks preceding the claim and run for 12 months regardless of any change in circumstances. Like SB, FIS is a 'passport' to other means-tested benefits.

Child Benefit replaced Family Allowances in April 1977. It is normally payable for all children at a rate of £1 per week for the first child and £1·50 for each subsequent child while *Child Benefit Increase* of £0·50 per week is paid for the first child in certain one-parent families. Child Benefit is tax-free and will gradually replace Child Tax Allowances which are being phased out: as part of this process the latter will be reduced in April 1978 and Child Benefit will be increased to £2·30 for all children, while Child Benefit Increase will be doubled to £1 per week. The change from Family Allowances and Child Tax Allowances to Child Benefit extended a cash benefit to first or only children who were previously excluded from Family Allowances. It also goes to families below the tax threshold who did not benefit from Child Tax Allowances and, unlike the latter, normally goes to the mother.

Grants Abroad in Table 2.4 are mainly payments of Retirement and War Pensions. Most other NI and non-contributory benefits cannot be paid to people living overseas.

In summary, the social security system is composed of a large number of benefits of which Retirement Pensions and Supplementary Benefit are the most important. National Insurance benefits are contingency-based and therefore only one can be obtained at a time except in the case of Industrial Disablement Pension. This contingency approach has been extended to non-contributory benefits covering invalidity, the need for continuous attendance, care of a severely disabled person and so on: the insurance principle has been maintained by setting benefits at levels below those prevailing for either long-or short-term NI benefits. An alternative approach was embodied in the SB scheme which was not contingency-based nor did it involve benefits at lower levels. But it did require a detailed means test which could be avoided in the contingency-based non-contributory benefits.

2.6 Benefit levels and relativities

A distinction was made between long- and short-term rates in describing social security benefits. Prior to October 1973 all NI benefits were at the same rates but subsequently long-term NI and non-contributory benefits have been uprated in line with the increase in gross earnings, whereas short-term benefits (Unemployment and Sickness Benefits, Maternity Allowance and the ordinary SB scale rates) have increased in line with increases in retail prices. This uprating procedure was given statutory effect in the Social Security Act 1975: long-term benefits would be increased in line with earnings, or by prices if that was more advantageous, while short-term benefits would be related to prices. Due to movements in prices and earnings in the period following 1972 a considerable gap had developed between short- and long-term benefits by November 1977.

The main benefit levels introduced in November 1977 are shown in Table 2.6 together with relativities for different household types. Although benefits are uprated annually they bear a fairly constant relationship to average earnings, the amount for a married couple representing about 30 and 25 per cent of earnings for long-and short-term benefits respectively. Short-term benefit rates for the single person and married couple are about 16 per cent below long-term NI benefit rates and non-contributory contingency benefits are 29 per cent below the short-term benefit rates or 40 per cent below the long-term rates. The ordinary SB scale rates are marginally below the short-term benefit rates whereas the long-term SB scale rates are higher than the corresponding NI levels. This comparison between NI and SB is not strictly appropriate because housing costs are added to the SB householder scale rates in determining requirements. Adding a typical housing cost of £5 makes the SB rate considerably higher than the corresponding NI benefits although in this event the insured person may be eligible for SB so that it is not entirely accurate to describe SB rates as more generous.

The levels of the main social security benefits have their origins in the subsistence budgets of the Beveridge Report (HMSO, 1942, Cmd 6406), adjusted for changes in prices or earnings and modified in some cases to take account of other factors. The relativities between benefits can therefore, in the main, be traced back to the Beveridge subsistence budgets (*see* Table 5.9). The single-person benefit is generally 62 per cent of the married-couple rate—although for FIS and tax purposes a lone parent is treated in the same way as a married couple. Children on short-term benefits get 19 per cent of the married-couple rate whereas on long-term NI benefits the relativity is 30 per cent. As the children of long-term non-contributory beneficiaries get the same cash allowance as their NI counterparts, whereas the adults do not, the relativity for a child amounts to 50 per cent of the married-couple rate.

SB scale rates for children are age-related but the same cash amounts are given for the children of both ordinary and long-term rate recipients. Thus the relativities for children are lower in each of the five age ranges for a long-term beneficiary compared with an ordinary rate recipient. Some empirical evidence which has a bearing on these benefit relativities is presented in Chapter 5.

The weekly social security payment for the individual benefit unit

Table 2.6

Main social security benefit levels (£) per week and relativities (R), November 1977

| Category of Beneficiary | Supplementary Benefits[1] | | | | NI short-term Benefits | | NI long-term Benefits | | | | Non-Contributory Invalidity Pension, Invalid Care Allowance, Old Persons Pension | |
| | Ordinary rate | | Long-term rate | | Unemployment & Sickness Benefits, Maternity Allowance | | Invalidity, Retirement & Widow's Pensions, Widowed Mother's Allowance, Industrial Disablement Benefit, Unemployability Supplement | | Widow's Allowance & Industrial Death Benefit, Widow's Allowance | | | |
	£	R	£	R	£	R	£	R	£	R	£	R
Married couple	23·55	1·00	28·35	1·00	23·80	1·00	28·00	1·00			16·80	1·00
Single person	14·50[3]	0·62	17·90[3]	0·63	14·70	0·62	17·50	0·63	24·50	0·88[4]	10·50	0·63
Child 16–17 years[2]	8·90	0·38	8·90	0·31								
Child 13–15 years[2]	7·40	0·31	7·40	0·26								
Child 11–12 years[2]	6·10	0·26	6·10	0·22	4·50	0·19	8·40	0·30	8·40	0·30[4]	8·40	0·50
Child 5–10 years[2]	4·95	0·21	4·95	0·17								
Child 0–4 years[2]	4·10	0·17	4·10	0·14								

[1] Reasonable housing costs are included in addition in determining requirements

[2] Including Child Benefit

[3] The non-householder scale rates are £11·60 and £14·35 plus a rent allowance of £1·45

[4] Based on the long-term rate for a married couple

is determined in the first instance by the composition of the unit. For example, a single pensioner who meets the various eligibility requirements is entitled to a flat-rate pension of £17·50, a married couple on the husband's insurance gets £28 and together with Child Benefit a further £8·40 would be paid for each dependent child. Any graduated or earnings-related pension entitlement, or increments for deferred retirement, are added to the flat-rate component.

This raises the question of what constitutes the benefit unit. The individual earner forms the unit for NI contribution purposes and the benefit unit depends on contributions: provided the contribution conditions are fulfilled a single person is usually treated as a benefit unit. But a married couple can constitute one or two benefit units depending on whether one or both satisfy the contribution conditions. Where there is only one insured spouse the other spouse and dependent children are part of the same benefit unit except that a married woman on short-term benefits cannot normally claim her husband and children as dependants. A widow dependent on her husband's insurance who remarries or lives with a man as his wife retains entitlement to Retirement Pension but not to Widows' Benefits. For non-contributory benefits a single person, a couple either legally married or living together as husband and wife, and dependent children constitute the benefit unit. But the definition of a dependent child varies somewhat. For Widowed Mother's Allowance the child can have an income yet provided it is below the age of 19 it is classified as dependent, whereas for SB purposes a dependent child in tertiary education is generally treated as a separate unit. The lower non-householder SB scale rates and the rent-sharing arrangements for non-dependants, while they recognize a separate SB unit, also take account of a wider household grouping which is not generally recognized throughout the rest of the social security system.

Thus the groupings of individuals to which benefits are paid vary between and within programmes: some theoretical aspects of this question are considered in Section 3.5 below. The level of benefits also differs with SB rates being highest, long-term NI benefits second, short-term NI benefits third and non-contributory benefits lowest in value. But in addition to these flat-rate benefits some beneficiaries are entitled to graduated pensions or earnings-related supplements so this ranking can only be regarded as a very broad generalization.

2.7 Behavioural influences

Social security contributions and benefits, and the rules and regulations surrounding them, may condition human behaviour in a number of ways.

(1) *Work–Leisure*. The provision of benefits may induce withdrawal from the labour market, the additional return from working being insufficient to justify the effort involved. The social security system can also influence the choice between work and leisure in a number of other ways. In the case of NI contributions a marginal increase in gross earnings to £15 results in Class 1 employee contributions of £0·86 (and employer contributions of £1·31), creating a notch on the marginal tax rate schedule. Thereafter up to earnings of £105 each additional £1 of gross earnings involves a 5·75 per cent employee contribution although, as Section 4.4 shows, this nominal incidence of contributions will differ from the effective incidence.

In the case of a married couple with two young children, if the head is working at least 30 hours per week the family may be eligible for FIS. The maximum FIS payment of £10·50 would be payable up to a gross income of £26·90, after which FIS would be reduced by half of any extra income; NI employee contributions and FIS combine to yield a cumulative marginal tax rate of 55·75 per cent. If the family consists of a single earner and is entitled to personal tax allowances only, it would become liable for income tax at the standard rate of 34 per cent when gross earnings reach £35·02. Thus the cumulative marginal tax rate would amount to 89·75 per cent for earnings in the range £31·94 up to £47·80 when the FIS-prescribed amount is reached. Thereafter it falls to 39·75 per cent until the contribution ceiling of £105 is reached, when it declines to the standard tax rate of 34 per cent.

In addition to FIS the family may be eligible for other means-tested benefits like Rent and Rate Rebates and Rent Allowances. These are also withdrawn as income rises and the cumulative marginal tax rates can exceed 100 per cent. There will also be notches at the points where benefits-in-kind like Free School Meals are withdrawn. Thus the combined effect of taxes and benefits can result in high cumulative marginal tax rates—the poverty trap.

In practice, however, the combination of the 12-month award period for FIS and the annual uprating cycle means that the prescribed amounts will have increased at least once during the currency of every award. Thus given normal increases in earnings no loss in FIS would occur: only families experiencing a permanent and above average increase in earnings are affected. As a relatively small number of families benefit from FIS (under 100,000) its contribution to the poverty trap is of limited quantitative importance. The income limits for most other means-tested benefits are also uprated at regular intervals and they are not always adjusted immediately with a change in earnings: both these factors help to mitigate the poverty trap.

A more serious work disincentive effect may arise from the 100 per cent marginal tax rates implicit in the SB scheme. After earnings exceed a certain amount (which varies from £2 to £6 per week for different groups of SB recipients) each £1 increase in earnings involves a £1 reduction in benefit.

(2) *Work—Retirement.* The provision of Retirement Pensions will influence the retirement decision. If pensions were paid in full on reaching retirement age the recipients would enjoy a higher standard of living if they continued to work as before. They might therefore decide to work less and earn a lower income or to retire entirely from the labour market. Thus the introduction of, or increases in, pensions may result in some reduction in labour supply.

If a retirement condition is also imposed in the form of an earnings rule the influence on work behaviour will be more complex. Consider a single man subject to the earnings rule and entitled to personal tax allowances alone. His flat-rate RP is £17·50 so in addition he can earn £6·54 before reaching the higher tax threshold of £24·04 provided by the age allowance. On earnings thereafter the standard tax rate of 34 per cent is paid until the earnings rule commences at £40. Each £1 increase in earnings between £40 and £44 leads to a £0·50 reduction in RP: tax liability is also increased but by only 17 per cent due to the withdrawal of pension. The cumulative marginal tax rate is therefore 67 per cent and increases to 100 per cent on earnings of £44 to £59·50 when RP entitlement is extinguished. Thus the reward for an additional hour of work is low on earnings of £40 to £44 and zero thereafter up to earnings of £59·50. Clearly this may affect work and retirement behaviour.

(3) *Work—Education.* The work—education choice may be conditioned by the provision of Child Benefit and benefits for dependent children, as these payments generally cease when education ends and employment is taken up. However, the benefits are small relative to the potential earnings of a dependent child and it is unlikely that they have a very marked effect. Grants for tertiary education are larger and may be a more important influence on the work—education decision.

(4) *Consumption—Savings.* National Insurance, by making provision for contingencies like sickness, unemployment, widowhood

and retirement, may reduce the amount of private insurance for these liabilities. The NI scheme is operated on a 'pay as you go' basis, current expenditure being financed from current revenue, whereas private schemes are funded. The analysis in Section 4.3 shows that the NI scheme *may* reduce the level of savings which would otherwise prevail in its absence and encourage current consumption by future beneficiaries. This behavioural influence was advanced as one reason for flat-rate contributions and benefits in the Beveridge Report (HMSO, 1942, Cmd 6404): it was also an argument for retaining an occupational pensions sector within the new pensions legislation (HMSO, 1974, Cmnd 5713). The possible impact of the system on savings and hence consumption is part of the much wider question of the consumption behaviour of beneficiaries. Many would have much lower incomes in the absence of benefit payments, reducing the consumption of market goods and service; and within that aggregate, the balance between commodities would differ.

(5) *Household formation.* The rules and regulations surrounding the definition of the benefit unit, which were discussed in the previous section, may induce changes in household and family formation. Treating wives and children as dependants could provide an incentive for them to remain within the family grouping. On the other hand making every individual a potential benefit recipient may encourage household formation. Different schemes embody a variety of benefit unit definitions so that the impact of the social security sector on the grouping of individuals within the population may depend to some extent on the policy measure in question.

(6) *Fertility.* Social security provisions may also affect fertility behaviour. Family Allowances or Child Benefit, Maternity Grant, Maternity Allowance and dependency payments for children reduce the cost of recipients of having a child. The provision of free health care and education may have a similar influence.

(7) *Benefit take-up and switching.* Finally the rules and regulations deployed in the administration of benefits, and the very nature of the scheme themselves, may determine whether those entitled to benefits actually claim them. Moreover these factors may condition whether an individual or group of individuals elects to claim one benefit and not another where entitled to both, or switches between benefits in similar circumstances. For SB and FIS take-up is about three-quarters (HMSO, 1976, Cmnd 6615), compared with 80 per cent for Rent Rebates and 35 per cent for Rent Allowances in unfurnished tenancies (HMSO, 1977, Cmnd 6851). The take-up of contingency benefits is generally complete but in the case of Non-Contributory Invalidity Pension it is estimated that take-up is two-thirds,

mainly because people on SB who are entitled to the new benefit decide not to claim as many would be no better off. Some SB recipients with small entitlements can be better off claiming Rent and Rate Rebates and Rent Allowances because the levels of the two forms of support are calculated in different ways. These two illustrations suggest that it would be better to define take-up in terms of the proportion who would be better off on benefit rather than eligibility.

The seven potential areas of behavioural response considered above by no means exhaust the ways in which the system may condition human action. But they are illustrative of how benefits combine and interact with one another and with other parts of the economy to influence human choice both directly and indirectly. Much of the analytical basis required for a fuller understanding of these behavioural issues is developed in Chapters 4 and 5. The importance which is attached to this aspect of social security will depend on a number of factors. But the pre-eminent question is the magnitude of the response and this represents an area where the myth and dogma discussed in Section 1.2 are widespread. The quantification of these phenomena represents one of the most important contributions which economics has to make to the social security sector and the available empirical evidence is reviewed in Chapter 10.

2.8 Objectives

The description of the social security system in Britain has shown that it constitutes an important part of the economy which annually transfers about one-tenth of the national income. The sector consists of a wide range of policy measures which are intricately related to one another and to other parts of the economy. Something of this size, complexity and diversity cannot be readily summarized but a synopsis of the major objectives of social security provides a guide to the principles embodied in the various measures, and pulls together the main threads of the earlier discussion.

From the description of the main benefits in Section 2.5 three primary objectives can be identified: maintaining a minimum standard of living for the population; replacing earnings; and providing compensation. These objectives are evident to a greater or lesser degree in most social security measures and are pursued within the wider purpose of the national economy which seeks to maximize national income as well as distributing it more equitably. However, it is sometimes argued that the purpose of the NI scheme is the provision of insurance and that income redistribution represents a primary objective of social security. These two arguments need to be considered before going on to look at the three objectives in more detail.

The Beveridge Report, on which the British social security system is largely based, laid great stress on the insurance principle. But the concept of insurance involves the payment of premiums into a fund in which assets are sufficient to meet future liabilities: in return the insured person obtains actuarially determined indemnity in the event of well-defined contingencies. National Insurance contributions are the counterpart of insurance premiums but they are related to earnings while in some circumstances contributions are credited. Being operated on a 'pay as you go' basis NI is not funded. Nor are benefits actuarially determined in three respects: the likelihood of contingencies is not taken into account in determining benefits; benefits are not financed out of accumulated assets; and the relationship between contributions and benefits is weak. This last point is perhaps the most important. We saw in Section 2.5 that earnings replacement ratios decline sharply with increasing average earnings. Moreover Section 2.6 showed that the return for a married man could be up to 60 per cent higher than for a single man making the same contributions and the return for a family could be even greater, whereas married women who exercise the reduced rate Class 1 option do not obtain any benefits in return for their contributions. We have also seen that the level of non-contributory SB is generally higher than contributory NI benefits so that those who do not pay premiums can obtain an indemnity as high as or higher than those who do contribute.

NI may therefore appear similar to private insurance in that contributions are involved and some well-defined contingencies like unemployment, sickness and retirement are covered. Unlike private insurance NI benefits are unfunded, there is no relationship between benefit levels and the risk involved, benefits are not paid out of accumulated assets, and the return on premiums varies enormously. On the basis of these considerations Peacock (1952) and Crosland (1957) argue that the insurance analogy is groundless while Diamond (1975) regards social security contributions as a relatively acceptable form of earmarked tax rather than insurance premiums. In the light of the evidence it seems that the provision of insurance, as that term is normally used, is not an objective of the NI part of the social security system.

In evaluating income security policy in the US Palmer and Minarik (1976) consider a fourth objective in addition to the three mentioned earlier—income redistribution. Maintaining a minimum standard of living and providing compensation may contribute to this end. And if one looks at non-contributory benefits in the UK, which are financed to some extent out of income tax which is progressive (i.e. becomes proportionately higher with increasing incomes), then clearly they do redistribute income. Similarly, for NI benefits the falling earnings replacement ratios with increasing earnings are evidence of a redistributional effect. Looking at the social security sector as a whole, with three-fifths of finance coming from contributions, income redistribution is less evident. It is true that people with earnings below the floor do not contribute, but thereafter contributions are proportional up to the ceiling and decline after approximately 150 per cent of average earnings. Thus contributions are regressive (i.e. become proportionately smaller with increasing incomes) for contributors as a whole. Indirect taxes, which account for over one-third of general tax revenue which in turn finances the remaining two-fifths of social security expenditure, also tend to be regressive in their initial impact. Looking at the social security system as an entity it does not seem that income redistribution *per se* is a primary objective.

(1) *Minimum standard of living.* The provision of a minimum standard of living is apparent in all the main social security benefits which, in the words of the Beveridge Report, 'should aim at guaranteeing the minimum income needed for subsistence'. The objective is clearest in the case of SB where the scale rates plus housing costs provide a minimum level of income below which people in general need not fall. The SB scheme also allows for exceptional needs so that the minimum income can, where necessary, be closely tailored to the requirements of the individual or family. In providing a minimum standard of living most benefits incorporate increases for a dependent wife or children—horizontal equity requires differentiation of benefits by family circumstances. From Table 2.6 it can be seen that the greatest emphasis on horizontal equity is in the SB scheme where scale rates are varied by the ages of children.

(2) *Earnings replacement.* In the Beveridge plan benefits were at a flat-rate in return for flat-rate contributions and this form of falling replacement with increasing earnings was consistent with the provision of a minimum standard of living. Subsequently there has been a move towards earnings-related benefits with the introduction of Earnings Related Supplements for short-term benefits and an extension to long-term NI benefits under the new pensions' legislation. The introduction of an earnings-related element was justified in the case of Unemployment Benefit in terms of promoting labour market

mobility, and as a means of cushioning the drop in earnings experienced with sickness or injury for the other short-term benefits. Earnings-related pensions reflect the fact that pensions are deferred pay (HMSO, 1974, Cmnd 5713). At present the earnings-related component of social security expenditure is small, and although it will grow considerably with the maturation of the new pensions scheme, under present legislation it will remain a minor part of the total. (3) *Compensation.* This objective of the social security system is evident in 'compensation' benefits like War Pensions, Industrial Death Benefit, Widows' Allowance or Injury Benefit which incorporate a premium over comparable NI benefits. The compensation embodied in Invalidity Allowance increases where invalidity begins at an earlier age while in Industrial Disability Pension and War Disablement Pension it is determined by the assessed percentage disability. In other cases compensation is related in a broad way to the need imposed by the disability: eligibility for Attendance Allowance at higher and lower rates is determined by continuous and partial attendance requirements respectively. In total these compensation premiums and payments are a small part of overall social security spending.

These three objectives of the social security system are to some extent in conflict and this can be appreciated by thinking in terms of a fixed social security budget—say one-tenth of national income. The minimum standard of living objective would be achieved by devoting the entire budget to flat-rate benefits, differentiated by family or other circumstances, and payable to everyone with an income below the specified level along the lines of the SB scheme. The pursuit of earnings replacement would involve paying benefits proportional to earnings: high benefits to people at the top of the earnings distribution on retirement, sickness or unemployment and no benefits to those not in the labour market. Under a compensation philosophy benefits for the specified contingencies would reflect the loss of earnings or diminished earnings potential with possibly an additional element to compensate for suffering.

In practice none of the three objectives is pursued exclusively. The social security system simultaneously strives to attain all three and in so doing has to reconcile each one with the others. These trade-offs are evident to a different extent in the various measures. Providing a minimum standard of living is predominant in the SB scheme, earnings replacement, if small, is of growing importance among contributory benefits: while compensation is more evident in the Industrial Disability and War Pensions' schemes.

In summary, the primary objectives of the social security system in Britain are the provision of a minimum standard of living, earnings replacement and compensation. The first of these predominates and is a manifestation of what Pinker (1974) has termed the welfare ethic, need being the main criterion of entitlement. But these ends are pursued within the wider context of national economic objectives where economic efficiency also has to be taken into account. The contingency basis of the NI scheme and the rules and regulations surrounding the payment of Unemployment Benefit and SB to potential workers are evidence of efficiency considerations.

3. Equity and the Measurement of Living Standards

3.1 Introduction

The description of social security indicated that the provision of a minimum standard of living for the population is a primary objective of the sector. Moreover equal treatment of different family types, or horizontal equity, is a very important feature of the system. This raises two basic questions which form the subject of this chapter. What do we mean by standards of living? And how do we measure living standards? In answering these questions it is helpful to deal initially in Section 3.2. with a homogeneous unit—a married couple without children, for example. This simplifying assumption can be relaxed subsequently with differences in household type being introduced into the analysis. These considerations lead to a number of related issues such as whether living standards are absolute or relative, the definition of the 'household' unit, and the appropriate accounting time period.

* 3.2 Standards of living—homogeneous households

Before considering how living standards can be measured it is useful to clarify the meaning of the term. Living standards describe the material well-being of the household or family unit as perceived by it and by society as a whole rather than personal happiness *per se* (Brandt, 1966). It could be argued that the concept is too vague to be of any practical use: more tangible notions like money income are of greater operational value. This section will indeed show that in the case of a homogeneous household money income is a good indicator of economic welfare where market prices are constant. But

* The general reader may wish to proceed to Section 3.4.

it is not a satisfactory measure where prices vary or household circumstances differ. Moreover, the work of Kilpatrick (1973) and Rainwater (1974) indicates that people in general appreciate the inadequacy of money income for calibrating living standards. They have quite definite ideas that varying levels of income are required to obtain the same standard of living in households of different size and composition or with changing relative prices and increasing affluence. Similar, but more concrete notions are to be found embodied in social security and tax systems which accord varying treatment on the basis of selected household circumstances.

The focus here will be on measuring the living standards of a homogeneous household type in terms of the quantities of goods and services consumed (it is recognized in Section 4.2 that leisure may influence living standards). This provides the conceptual basis for measurement in the case of the heterogeneous household which is considered in Section 3.3. In both the homogeneous and heterogeneous categories we will also show how living standards are linked to the more tangible concept of money income.

The usual economic model postulates that living standards (or utility) are determined by the *quantities* of goods and services consumed. The commodity bundle embraces both market and non-market goods and services. The first category is purchased out of money income and covers items like fuel, food and services. Non-market commodities such as free school meals, housing benefits, health or education are allocated to consumers by the state using non-market mechanisms, and also contribute to living standards. This study is primarily concerned with income transfers and hence with market goods and services purchased out of money income, so it will be assumed in this and subsequent chapters that market goods alone influence living standards. The effect of non-market goods and services on economic well-being will be introduced in Chapter 9.

A second simplifying assumption will also be made throughout this section. We will suppose that households are the same in all respects. They are composed of the same number of identical individuals (e.g. a married couple) with similar tastes or preferences, corresponding educational and consumption experience. Third, it will also be assumed that households pay the same market prices for commodities of similar quantity and quality. The sole difference between them is in their money incomes and hence in the quantities of goods and services which they consume.

Fourth, for presentational simplicity it will be assumed that households consume only two commodities—in what follows these will be labelled as food and housing services although they could equally be designated luxuries and necessities or any other commodities. The results obtained in this simple two-commodity world hold in the more complex multiple commodity case. All commodities are purchased and consumed in a single time period, e.g. a week or month: there is no saving or dissaving in this simple model.

These assumptions are highly restrictive and the reader may consider that they are totally unrealistic for the purpose in hand. But the object at this stage is not to be realistic: we ignore all but the essential features required to explain the measurement of living standards.

Consider a married-couple household consuming food and housing services. Both commodities are calibrated in physical units like floor area (square metres) and weight (kilos). The household can obtain a given level of utility or standard of living by consuming various combinations of food and housing services. It may be indifferent between 100 kilos of food and 25 units of housing services, or 50 kilos of food and 50 units of housing services, or 25 kilos of food and 100 units of housing services. These and other combinations of food and housing services giving the same standard of living (or number of 'utils') yield a continuous indifference curve (Figure 3.1).

A series of indifference curves representing different standards of living can be obtained in similar fashion. Note that these indifference curves are convex to the origin, indicating that to maintain a given standard of living each successive kilo of food forgone is replaced by an increasing volume of housing services and vice versa.

Suppose that the household has a given weekly income and faces fixed market prices. It can devote all its income to food and purchase OF kilos as shown on the vertical axis of Figure 3.2. Alternatively it can buy only housing and obtain OH units as shown on the horizontal axis. Various combinations of food and housing services can also be purchased with a given income and are shown by the solid budget line in Figure 3.2.

A change in the price of commodities will alter the slope of the budget line. For example, if the price of food doubles then only half the previous amount, OF' kilos, can be purchased with the same income. The various combinations of food and housing services which can be bought under this new market price regime are shown by the broken budget line in Figure 3.2. The slope of the budget line is determined by the price of housing relative to the price of food with the slope of the broken budget line being half the slope of the solid budget line. If both prices change in the same proportion then the new budget line will shift in parallel with the old one—towards the origin for a general price increase and away from the origin if prices fall. An increase (or decrease) in household income will lead to a similar, parallel, outward (or inward) shift in the budget line. The budget lines for households with different incomes at the

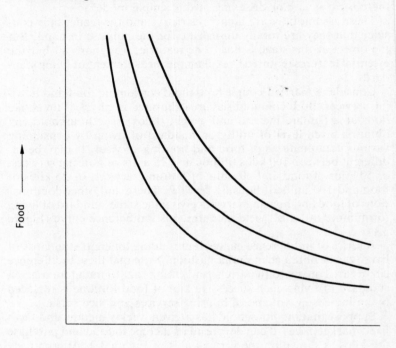

FIGURE 3.1   *At a given standard of living households are indifferent between various combinations of food and housing services*

same market prices will also be parallel to the budget lines depicted in Figure 3.2. Thus a rise or fall in the general price level is similar to a decrease or increase in income respectively: it is also analogous to comparing two identical households with different incomes.

Fifth, we assume that the household seeks to maximize utility or its standard of living. This assumption involves a judgement of the second type discussed in Section 1.3 and while it cannot be directly verified expenditure behaviour provides a lot of supporting evidence of an indirect nature. It is also a behavioural assumption which commands a wide measure of professional agreement. If a household maximizes its standard of living with a given income what combination of commodities will it choose to consume? Bringing together the household indifference curves and budget line (Figure 3.3), the

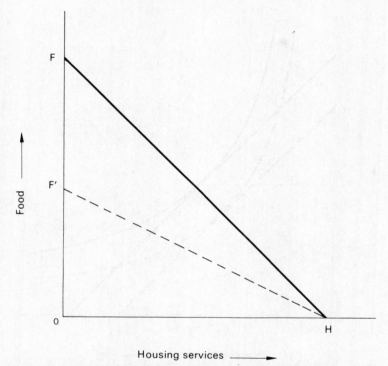

FIGURE 3.2   *The household budget line shows the various combinations of commodities which can be purchased with a given income and fixed commodity prices*

optimum is obtained when the budget line is tangential to the highest indifference curve. The household consumes OF_1 kilos of food and OH_1 units of housing. And with unchanged market prices the same household with a lower income, or another household with similar preferences and a lower income, will consume OF_2 kilos of food and OH_2 units of housing as indicated by the broken indifference curve and budget line in Figure 3.3.

Next, suppose the price of food doubles. From Figure 3.2 we know that the household with a fixed money income will face a new budget line. It will no longer be able to obtain the standard of living which it could achieve under the old price regime. A lower indifference curve is tangential to the new budget line and in Figure 3.4 this indicates that the optimizing household would consume OF_3 kilos of

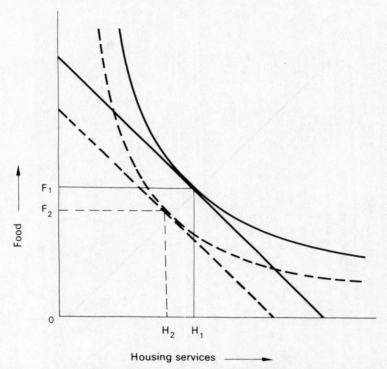

FIGURE 3.3   *Household utility is maximized when the budget line is tangential to the highest indifference curve*

food and OH_3 units of housing. It consumes less food and less housing than before because, in effect, it is worse off. And the share of food in the household budget increases because, although it consumes less, the price per kilo is doubled and consumption falls by less than half. Conversely, the budget share of housing falls. Thus an increase in the price of a commodity may lead to an increase or decline in its budget share depending on the structure of household preferences as reflected by the shape of its indifference curves.

This effect of a price change can be decomposed into a price substitution and income effect. The influence of the change in *relative prices alone* occasioned by an increase in the price of food is shown by a budget line parallel to the new (broken) budget line and tangential to the original (solid) indifference curve. This is represented by

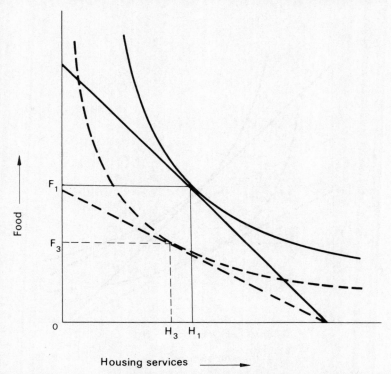

FIGURE 3.4 *An increase in the price of food reduces the slope of the household's budget line and leads to a new combination of commodity consumption at a lower standard of living*

the chained budget line in Figure 3.5. If relative prices change and income is increased to allow the household to obtain its original standard of living then it would do so at minimum cost by substituting housing services for food: it would reduce food consumption from OF_1 to OF_3' kilos and increase housing from OH_1 to OH_3' units. This is the price substitution effect.

The income effect is denoted by the parallel shift from the chained to the broken budget line. As a consequence of being poorer food consumption falls from OF_3' kilos to OF_3 kilos while housing declines from OH_3' to OH_3 units. The income effect shows the extent to which income would need to be increased to compensate for the increase in the price of food after the household had adjusted its consumption to the new relative prices. Due to the substitution of

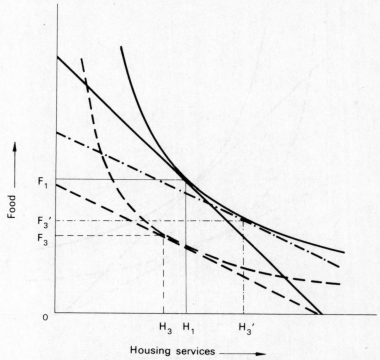

FIGURE 3.5   *An increase in the price of food can be decomposed into a price substitution effect holding living standards constant, and an income effect which reduces living standards*

housing for food the income effect is less than the income increase which would be necessary to purchase the old commodity bundle of OF_1 kilos of food and OH_1 units of housing at the new prices.

For a homogeneous household type facing constant market prices living standards can be measured in terms of the quantities of goods and services consumed. Alternatively, income alone provides an indicator of standards of living in this situation. But if relative prices change, or if there is a movement in the general price level, income is no longer a satisfactory measure: price substitution and income effects need to be taken into account. Thus living standards can only be quantified by going beyond simple measures like income and commodity expenditure. Variation in relative prices and incomes, and hence in expenditure patterns, provides evidence from which the price substitution and income effects depicted in Figure 3.5 can be estimated. In the case of a change in the general price level only the income effect is required to show the adjustment in expenditure on each commodity, and hence income, needed to obtain the previous standard of living. With a change in prices both substitution and income effects have to be taken into account.

The difficulties which arise in measuring the living standards of homogeneous households with changing relative prices or movements in the general price level are very similar to the problems which arise with heterogeneous households. The heterogeneous household case will be considered in Section 3.3 below but first a digression is made to consider two issues which arise out of this section. A lot of attention has been given in the economic literature to whether living standards can be cardinally measured and whether interpersonal (strictly speaking, inter-household) comparisons of utility are feasible or desirable.

Cardinal measurement of living standards involves placing households on a numerical scale whereby the position of one can be quantified relative to another. In terms of Figure 3.3 and the related discussion a household with an income of £50 is, say, 25 per cent better off than an identical household with an income of £40 per week. In contrast, ordinal measurement requires only that households be ranked. Thus cardinality involves a value judgement about how living standards vary with income or commodity consumption: we assume that a 25 per cent increase in income leads to a 25 per cent increase in living standards whereas they may have increased by 50 per cent or by only 10 per cent. Cardinal measurement allows more comparisons, and more exact comparisons, to be made between households. It is desirable that the judgements involved—which are of the second type distinguished in Section 1.3 and correspond to the distributional weights in Section 4.5—should be made explicit. Doing so engenders an awareness that judgements are being made, encourages the use of alternative judgements, and promotes consistency with similar judgements made in different areas.

Another tradition goes even further than rejecting cardinal measurement of utility. It is argued that, like cardinal measurement, ordinality involves interpersonal comparisons of utility which in turn requires value judgements on the part of the economist making the comparison. Many important results could be obtained by ruling out inter-household comparisons of living standards although the ranking of utility within households by the individual households themselves is still required. A Pareto improvement occurs when one household can be made better off without making another worse off: when no household can be made better off without making at least one other household worse off a Pareto optimum is achieved. Thus individual evaluation is substituted for inter-household utility comparisons and many useful theoretical results are possible within this framework. Most of the problems addressed in this study cannot be answered if cardinal measurement and inter-household comparisons are ruled out (Churchman 1966; Brandt 1966; and Ward 1972), and for this reason they are accepted as both desirable and feasible.

* 3.3 Heterogeneous households

To extend the analysis of Section 3.2 to heterogeneous households the second assumption that households are identical in all respects needs to be relaxed. We will therefore consider two households which differ only in composition, e.g. a married couple with and without a child. The exposition which is given below is based on Barten (1964) and is also developed in McClements (1977b).

It is assumed that the child consumes 50 per cent of the food eaten by a married couple alone but that no additional housing consumption is required to obtain the same standard of living as in the smaller household. This does not mean that the child consumes food but does not benefit from household expenditure on housing. Rather, it reflects the supposition that food consumption by individuals within the household is independent and additive whereas housing is jointly consumed. Thus the addition of a child involves extra food consumption if the previous standard of living is to be maintained but due to the complete sharing of housing services no further housing expenditure is required. Food can only be shared by reducing the amounts consumed, and hence the satisfaction derived, by the adults, whereas housing can be shared with the child without detriment to adult satisfaction from the exiting volume of services.

In reality it is unlikely that food consumption by individuals within the household is fully independent and additive. For example, wastage may decline as a proportion when the quantity cooked increases. And while a child may share kitchen, living and bathroom

* The general reader may wish to proceed to Section 3.4.

areas with adults an extra bedroom may be required to maintain their standard of living. Nevertheless it does not seem unreasonable to suppose that food consumption is near to the non-sharing end, while housing is closer to the fully shared end of the consumption spectrum. These polar cases will therefore be adopted as approximations to the real world in the exposition which follows. The question of joint consumption arises again in the context of the household unit in Section 3.5 and is discussed more fully in terms of economies of scale in Section 5.3.

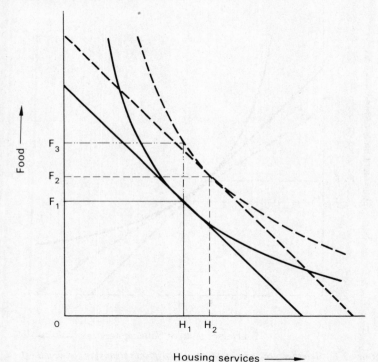

FIGURE 3.6   *Heterogeneous households consume different quantities of commodities and require different incomes to obtain the same standard of living*

The two households are depicted in Figure 3.6. The solid indifference curve represents the combination of food and housing service consumed by a married-couple household at a given standard of living. At each level of housing services the larger household including the child needs to consume 50 per cent more food to obtain the same standard of living. This is depicted by the broken indifference curve in Figure 3.6 which at each point on the horizontal axis lies 50 per cent above the solid indifference curve for the married couple. The vertical distance between the two budget lines indicates the direct effect of a child on consumption if living standards are to be maintained. Market prices are fixed and for the married couple the optimum is achieved with the income depicted by the solid budget line: the optimizing household will consume OF_1 kilos of food and OH_1 units of housing services.

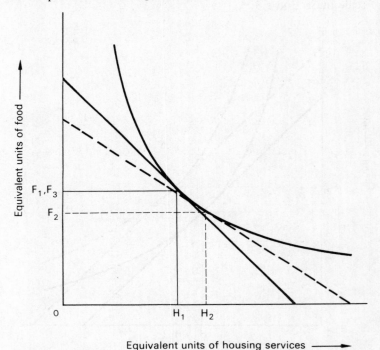

FIGURE 3.7   *Heterogeneous households on an equivalent commodity consumption basis face different apparent prices and budget lines leading to a quasi-price substitution effect*

Market prices are the same for the married couple and child, but if they consumed the same amount of housing OH_1 and 50 per cent more food OF_3 it would result in a sub-optimal point on the broken indifference curve. The same standard of living could be obtained by consuming OH_2 units of housing and OF_2 kilos of food involving a lower income as represented by the broken budget line. This result, is at first sight paradoxical. The child involves 50 per cent more food consumption and the same amount of housing in constructing the broken indifference curve yet the household actually consumes more food *and* more housing.

A different approach helps to explain the paradox. The physical quantities on the axes of Figure 3.6 are divided by scales reflecting household composition (Figure 3.7). These *equivalent commodity scales* represent the extent to which the various combinations of food and housing need to be increased to yield the same standard of living in the larger household. Taking a married couple as the reference household with scales of 1·00 for both commodities, the commodity scales for a married couple and child in our example are 1·50 for food and 1·00 for housing.

By definition the same number of equivalent food and housing units provide similar living standards for the heterogeneous households. Thus in Figure 3.7 the same standard of living for both households is denoted by the solid indifference curve—converting the 'utils' of Figure 3.6 into 'equivalent utils' in Figure 3.7 leads to a merging of the separate indifference curves. With the same money income as before the married-couple household will be able to purchase the same number of *equivalent* units of food and housing, or the various combinations indicated by the solid budget line. But each equivalent unit of food will cost the larger household 50 per cent more whereas the cost of housing will be unchanged. Thus for any money income the budget line facing the larger household in equivalent commodity terms will be less steeply sloped than that facing the married couple household. In the case of our simple example in Figure 3.7 the slope is two-thirds (1·00/1·50) of that for the smaller household. It is in response to this change in apparent relative prices that the larger household substitutes housing for food. Less food and more housing is consumed than the direct effect of a child on household consumption, as reflected by the equivalent commodity scales, would indicate.

To summarize, Figures 3.6 and 3.7 have shown that changes in, or differences in, household circumstances have a threefold influence:

(i) a direct effect as reflected by the equivalent commodity scales and the shift in the indifference curve in Figure 3.6;
(ii) a price substitution effect resulting from the apparent change in relative prices faced by the household (Figure 3.7);
(iii) an income effect as reflected by the shift in the budget line in Figure 3.6.

The income effect or *equivalent income scale* is measured after allowing for the direct and price substitution effects. First suppose there is only a direct effect with consumption of housing remaining at OH_1 in Figure 3.6 and food increasing by 50 per cent to OF_3 with the addition of a child. Given constant market prices the extra income required to obtain the same standard of living is given by the commodity scale for food $OF_3 - OF_1$ times its budget share $OF_3/(OH_1 + OF_3)$ plus the commodity scale for housing $OH_1 - OH_1$ times its budget share $OH_1/(OH_1 + OF_3)$. Second, the 'gross' income effect obtained in the first stage has to be adjusted for the price substitution effects to arrive at the overall income effect. Alternatively, the overall income effect can be arrived at by working in terms of the direct effect net of the price substitution effect in a composite commodity scale composed of the direct commodity scale adjusted for the price substitution effect. In terms of Figure 3.6 these composite commodity scales are given by $OF_2 - OF_1$ for food and $OH_2 - OH_1$ for housing. Thus the equivalent income scale can also be obtained from these composite scales weighted by their budget shares—$OF_2/(OF_2 + OH_2)$ and $OH_2/(OF_2 + OH_2)$ for food and housing respectively. Note that although the commodity scale for housing is zero for a child, due to the positive price substitution effect the composite commodity scale for housing is positive.

In principle it should be possible to estimate the direct, price substitution and income effects of variations in household circumstances from consumption data and incomes for a sample of heterogeneous households. The estimation process is very involved in practice and the method used in Chapter 5 provides composite commodity scales which combine the direct and price substitution effects. Where market prices are constant and interest centres on the equivalent income scale these composite commodity scale estimates are perfectly satisfactory. But if we are concerned about the impact of changing relative market prices on the living standards of households in different circumstances then the two effects need to be known.

In extending the measurement of living standards to heterogeneous households cardinal measurement and interpersonal comparisons are inevitable. Interpersonal comparisons can be avoided if the problem is restricted to a single household undergoing a change in circumstances but this situation is of very limited practical interest. And cardinal measurement would be unnecessary if the precise income changes required to obtain a given standard of living were not required. But the equivalent income scales are in many ways the object of the analysis and therefore it seems that cardinality cannot be avoided.

3.4 Absolute or relative?

The previous two sections showed that household living standards could be measured in terms of the quantities of goods and services consumed. In the case of a homogeneous household type (like a married couple with similar preferences facing constant market prices) income alone provides an index of living standards. But where market prices change income is no longer a suitable measure because, for example, the price of necessities to which the poor devote a larger part of their budgets may increase proportionately more than the price of luxuries. Problems of a similar nature arise when differences in household circumstances are introduced.

The addition of a child may lead to a considerable increase in food consumption if living standards are to be maintained, but due to sharing there may be little increase in housing expenditure. These direct effects of a change in household circumstances, or equivalent commodity scales, are similar in their consequences to a change in relative market prices. The household will tend to substitute housing for food consumption, yielding composite commodity scales composed of the direct and price substitution effects. These composite commodity scales weighted by their budget shares yield the income effect of a change in household circumstances. For example, if the composite commodity scales for food and housing for a child are 140 and 120 per cent respectively of the married-couple scales and each commodity accounts for half the budget then the equivalent income scale for a child would be 30 per cent of the married-couple scale.

Observed variations in household expenditure patterns provide a rich source of information from which the equivalent commodity and income scales can be estimated. Within each household type in the population there is a wide range of living standards and considerable variation in expenditure patterns. The rich spend more on luxuries and the poor more on necessities. And between household types at the same standard of living systematic variations in consumption behaviour are also evident. Small households allocate a larger share of their budgets to housing while larger households devote more to food. These variations in household expenditure patterns can be used to provide estimates of the equivalent commodity and income scales. Some results of applying these methods are presented in Chapter 5.

Thus we can measure the incomes required by households in different circumstances to obtain similar standards of living on the basis of observed expenditure patterns. A single adult may need an income of £30 per week to obtain the same equivalent income as a married couple with an income of £50: taking a married couple as the reference group with a scale of 1·0 the equivalent income scale is 0·6 for a single adult. In applying these concepts use is made of some additional terminology and it is helpful to deal with it at this stage before going on to contrast the various methods which have been used to measure living standards. This in turn raises the question of whether poverty, and more generally, the standard of living, is a relative or an absolute notion.

The term *horizontal* is used throughout this study to distinguish factors associated with differences in household circumstances. Thus horizontal variations in incomes describe the fact that money incomes vary with household size: larger households have, on average, larger incomes. *Horizontal equity* has a more specific meaning. It describes the situation where equivalent incomes are the same for households in different circumstances, i.e. the same standard of living prevails. In the earlier example there would be horizontal equity when the one- and two-adult households had money incomes of £30 and £50 respectively or both had an equivalent income of £50.

The concept of horizontal equity is useful because it is a very important feature of the social security system (Section 2.6), and fundamental to the objective of providing a minimum standard of living. But it is also valuable in more general studies of income distribution. Variations in money incomes which can be justified by differences in household circumstances can be removed by considering the equivalent income distribution—*see* Table 6.1 below. The remaining income variations can be discussed in terms of *vertical equity*: thus vertical inequality denotes heterogeneous households with different levels of equivalent income—or homogeneous households with different money incomes. Note that horizontal equity can apply to households at various points on the vertical distribution, e.g. assuming an equivalence scale of 0·6 at all income levels for one- and two-adult households, money incomes of £30 and £50 or £60 and £100 would yield horizontal equity. But horizontal *and* vertical equity would only prevail at one point on the equivalent income distribution—when all households had the same equivalent income.

Many alternative approaches to the one described in the previous section have been adopted in the literature. The use of these other procedures in determining the poverty line is reviewed by Stanton (1973) and we will contrast the method developed in the previous section with three broad approaches which have been used in other studies.

(1) *Budget studies.* Household budget studies have been extensively

applied in calculating the level at which benefits should be set and the relativities required for horizontal equity. The Beveridge Report (HMSO, 1942, Cmd 6404) provides a good illustration of this approach. On the basis of a survey of working-class family expenditure, budgets were calculated showing expenditure on necessities which were defined as housing, food, fuel and clothing with a margin for wastage and purchases of other goods.

(2) *Budget shares.* Another tradition has stemmed from Engel's observation that the share of income devoted to food is a useful indicator of poverty. Orshansky (1965) takes a low-cost food plan which provides a nutritionally adequate diet, and an economy food budget costing 75–80 per cent of the low-cost plan, then defines the poverty line as three times the food budget. Seneca and Taussig (1971) adopt a wider range of necessities (food, housing, clothing and transport) in calculating equivalent incomes and show that the measures are sensitive to the commodity bundle defined as necessities.

(3) *Deprivation indices.* A third approach is pursued by Titmuss (1962), Rein (1970) and Townsend (1974). They view poverty not as an absolute but as a relative concept. In the words of Mencher (1967), 'luxuries become comforts, comforts become necessities' and the cost of living is 'not the cost of buying some fixed set of goods and services . . . [but] the cost of participating in the social system' (Jencks *et al.*, 1972). A deprivation index is described by Townsend (1974) which is, in effect, a description of some aspects of living standards at the lower end of the income distribution. The income thresholds at which certain types of goods begin to be purchased, or where there appears to be a 'kink' in the Engel curve, have also been suggested as a means of identifying a poverty line.

These broad approaches differ from the method described in the previous section in several fundamental ways:

(i) certain commodities are identified as necessities;
(ii) some aspects of expenditure behaviour on these commodities are taken as indicative of living standards;
(iii) the selected aspect of expenditure behaviour is linked to household living standards.

All three approaches identify certain commodities as necessities or as indicators of living standards, whereas the utility approach is based on consumption of all goods and services. First, the utility approach avoids the difficult judgement involved in selecting necessities or indicators of living standards and the variety of results which can arise from using these various commodity bundles. Second, selecting commodities as necessities (or indicators) raises problems of horizontal equity as the equivalent income scale may differ from the scale or scales for the chosen commodities. For example, in the case of children the food scale exceeds the income scale, while the fuel or housing scales are generally smaller than the food scale. Selecting food expenditure as a measure of living standards, or using the budget share of food to define the poverty line, will favour large families at the expense of small households because at a given standard of living they tend to spend more on food. Conversely, fuel or housing will favour small households at the expense of large households. Thus the use of a single commodity or sub-group of the total can lead to horizontal inequities which will not arise with the method described in the previous section. Third, there is the problem of how to weight the components of the sub-group of necessities relative to total expenditure or income. In the budget approach the weights are determined implicitly by the relative amounts allowed for the various necessities and other commodities. The budget share procedure has adopted an arbitrary figure of one-third for food: different, but equally plausible, proportions would lead to different results. Indices of deprivation may appear to circumvent this problem but the threshold or kink will depend on the commodity selected. And if there is more than one commodity the problem of weighting arises. The utility-based approach of the previous section uses the actual budget shares of households in weighting the commodity scales.

Thus our approach is more objective than the other procedures to the extent that it avoids difficult judgements in these three important areas. It should therefore yield better estimates of horizontal equity and hence of the vertical distribution of living standards. But even if equivalence scales allow horizontal factors to be more accurately and objectively taken into account, and so provide a more exact measure of vertical inequality, there remains a fourth problem. How do we determine the point at which benefits are to be set or the poverty line is to be drawn? Budget studies and the budget share approach deal with this difficulty by defining a minimum expenditure on necessities or food. But this is almost entirely a matter of judgement. A given nutritional standard, for example, can be obtained at a very wide range of costs.

Budget studies and the budget share approach have usually been associated with an absolute view of living standards. Thus the budgets of the Beveridge Report (HMSO, 1942, Cmd 6404) were used to obtain 'the minimum income needed for subsistence'; while the US official poverty line based on the Orshansky (1965) method has been adjusted over time to allow for changes in prices alone reflecting an absolute view of poverty (Plotnick and Skidmore, 1975). But they could also be applied to determine various levels, or to evolve a relative standard over time by upgrading the amounts of necessary commodities, introducing new necessities into the budget or changing the budget share. Their use in this way would help to avoid the impression of accuracy which a single absolute measure tends to convey. However, the difficult judgements in the three areas discussed earlier would still remain and if anything they would become more vexing. There is no reason in principle, therefore, why budget studies and the budget share approach cannot embody a relative view of living standards. Their association with an absolute approach largely reflects the sort of questions which they have been used to answer and the way in which they have been applied.

Is poverty an absolute or relative concept? At one point in time the question is unimportant because an absolute point on the equivalent income distribution coincides with a relative point. It would only be a matter of determining the absolute or relative point at which the poverty line should be drawn. But over time the answer will depend on the interdependence of household utility. If households and society as a whole are generally concerned about living standards in other households, and consider deficient or excessive consumption compared with their own position or the national average undesirable, then a relative view will prevail. But if they are only concerned that their neighbours should have enough to stay alive then an absolute view of poverty will tend to predominate. Alternatively, the definition of basic requirements might improve over time, indicating that the notion is neither absolute nor relative. Thus there are three possible answers to the question: living standards may be viewed as absolute, relative, or somewhere between the two extremes.

The historical review by Lamale (1958) and the empirical work of Easterlin (1972), Kilpatrick (1973) and Rainwater (1974) suggest that living standards are not generally viewed in absolute terms. The practice in Britain of uprating long-term benefits, which account for the major part of social security spending, in line with average gross earnings (Section 2.6), also reflects a relative view. However, short-term benefits in Britain are only uprated in line with prices (although some beneficiaries get Earnings Related Supplements) and a similar procedure is followed in setting the poverty line in the US. This suggests an absolute view of poverty—but the practice would need to be followed in perpetuity to be entirely absolute. The evidence is that over long periods of time, and across countries, the minimum standards embodied in legislation bear a fairly constant relationship to average income. Living standards and poverty lines are generally regarded in relative terms although absolute views may apply for short periods: they are certainly more relative than absolute (OECD, 1976).

If we consider living standards as relative rather than absolute, and involving a continuum rather than a minimum level, how is the poverty line to be determined? And at what level should benefits be set? A relative view suggests that a single poverty line does not exist. If attention is to be focused on a single point of the equivalent income distribution then it might be defined as a percentile of the mean or the level below which a given quantile of households fall. Some examples of this approach are given in Section 6.3 and it has the advantage of avoiding the spurious impression of exactness which a single absolute measure might convey. A single absolute poverty line would be very useful in deciding the level at which benefits should be set. But we have seen that it is almost entirely a matter of judgement. In practice many considerations determine benefit levels: the revenue required to finance a given benefit level, the relationship between benefits and earnings, other calls on public expenditure and a host of other economic and political factors (Aaron, 1967). Even if a more objective poverty line could be established it would have a very limited influence on the level of social security benefits.

In conclusion, the general theoretical approach developed in earlier sections of this chapter lends no support to the absolute view of poverty and living standards. Certain types of utility function, like the form underlying the Linear Expenditure System of consumer demand equations, are nevertheless consistent with an absolute approach. But the empirical evidence points mainly to the relative end of the spectrum and a relative view of living standards will be adopted throughout most of this study.

3.5 The household unit

So far the household has been taken as the basic unit of analysis. The term 'household' is defined as a single person or group of people sharing the same tenure and with common cooking and eating arrangements (Section 5.3). Thus consumption of housing services and food by individuals together serves to identify the household unit. Yet the grouping of individuals adopted in social security measures varies considerably as Section 2.6 showed and it is not, in general, the household. Furthermore, Section 6.3 indicates that over one-fifth of household units contain more than one tax unit and from Table 2.1 it can be seen that on average there are 1·5 tax units per household. Thus at least one-fifth of households are composed of what would usually be more than one unit for benefit purposes. The distinction between the household and other groupings of individuals is therefore of some importance and merits more detailed consideration. The potential influence of the social security sector on household or benefit unit formation, which was mentioned in Section 2.7, is related to this issue and will also be explored below.

The definition of the unit of analysis involves two basic questions. First, it is necessary to decide the types of persons and combinations thereof which constitute a unit. And second, where the unit consists of more than one person the individual or individuals to receive the income or benefit payment has to be identified. Stated in terms of these two essential features the definition of the unit of analysis seems quite straightforward, even trivial. But they in turn involve some very complex and quite fundamental issues as a simple illustration will show.

Consider a one- and a two-adult household with equivalent income scales of 0·60 and 1·00 respectively. The single-adult household requires 60 per cent of the income needed by the two-adult household to obtain the same standard of living—for example, incomes of £30 and £50 per week. Since the two adults living separately would require aggregate incomes of £60 the example implies that joint or collective consumption within the two-adult household accounts for £10 of expenditure with the remaining £40 being allocated to items which can be attributed to the two adults individually. Horizontal equity between the one- and two-adult households could be achieved by giving income to the two-adult household in a number of different ways:

(i) as a lump sum of £50 to the household head;
(ii) allocating £30 to the head and £20 to the second adult;
(iii) dividing the total equally giving £25 to each adult.

These three possibilities uncover three related issues which arise out of how the unit is defined—involuntary income redistribution, voluntary income redistribution and the decision process itself. We will consider each in turn.

(1) *Involuntary income redistribution* is used to describe the involuntary sharing or pooling of income which arises out of joint or collective consumption. In the extreme case where the first adult has an income of £50 and the second adult has no income from any source,

the second adult will benefit to the extent that items of household expenditure are collectively consumed—by £10 in our example. Moreover, the second adult benefits without reducing the welfare of the first adult in any way.

(2) *Voluntary income redistribution* may also occur within the household. Continuing with the extreme case where one adult receives all £50, part of the £40 not devoted to collectively consumed goods might be divided with the second adult. This could take the form of either an income transfer or the transfer of commodities purchased out of income.

(3) *A decision-making process* is required for the voluntary allocation (or non-allocation) of income or consumption within the household, and where there is more than one income, to arrange the finance of collective consumption. The head may make decisions on behalf of the household or such powers may be invested in the head (Sen, 1966), which would be consistent with rule (i) in our earlier example. However, Samuelson's (1956) casual anthropology rejects the idea that the family behaves like a dictatorship or a unanimous committee. Rothenberg (1961) considers several decision modes which may operate within the family while the studies reviewed by Davis (1976) indicate that the process may vary by commodity. The decentralization of decision-making which Samuelson discerns might be captured by rule (ii) whereby the head is given an income of £30 and the second adult an income of £20. This would be appropriate where the head either charged the second adult for the additional expenditure imposed on the household or where each purchased individually consumed items. Approach (iii), which involves giving both adults an income of £25, would be suitable if they shared the cost of jointly consumed items on an equal basis. Different divisions of the total would be appropriate where collective expenditure is allocated according to some other arbitrary formula.

Our simple example illuminates the fact that the choice of an appropriate unit depends on the decision process and allocative mechanism within the household and its outcome in terms of the division of consumption and income. This is an issue about which little is known (Young, 1952); and to make matters worse the evidence cited by Sussman (1953) is indicative of an extended family decision and transfer process. There is little theoretical literature which deals with the household decision process and allocation mechanism. Lancaster (1975) has explored some of the relationships between individual and household behaviour assuming that each person has an income and acts independently or that the decision process is centralized. Becker (1974b) assumes that individuals within the household care about one another and goes on to show that intra-household redistribution will not affect individual or aggregate welfare. The problem of collective consumption has received growing attention at the macro level and much of the literature on public choice surveyed by Mueller (1976) is applicable to the household unit.

What does this discussion amount to in practical terms? The various payment rules adopted in the earlier example and the limited theoretical literature have one thing in common. All are based on judgements of the second kind in Section 1.3 which postulate how decisions might occur within the household. Payment to the head assumes that voluntary and involuntary income redistribution takes place within the household, whereas payment to each individual assumes the opposite. It is important to be aware of these judgements as some may be more appropriate in certain contexts than others (Suits, 1963). Moreover, Morgan *et al.* (1962) demonstrate the extent to which measured inequality varies with the definition of the unit. The smaller the unit the more limited the voluntary and involuntary income redistribution which is assumed and the greater the inequality.

Replacement of these judgements by empirical evidence will involve the difficult process of discovering how households actually make decisions and redistribute income. In lieu of this information it is only possible to suggest that the appropriate unit may well vary depending on the individuals in the household. Where it is composed of a married couple and young children the household unit might be most appropriate. But as the children grow older, become increasingly independent, eventually having incomes in their own right and forming new households with unrelated contemporaries, the household unit becomes increasingly unsuitable. It implies voluntary income redistribution to an extent which does not occur. On the other hand adopting the adult unit implies that there is no joint consumption and voluntary redistribution which may not be true either.

Some empirical evidence on joint consumption within the household is presented in Sections 5.4 to 5.7 below. Due to the extent of both joint consumption and income redistribution, expenditure data are only available on a household basis. For this reason the household is adopted as the unit of analysis throughout the present study, although it is recognized that it is not necessarily the appropriate unit in all circumstances.

From the description of the social security system in Section 2.6 it was evident that different benefit units were utilized both within and between programmes: the situation in the US is discussed in

Klein (1971) and Cox (1973). Children and wives are largely treated as dependants with benefits paid to the father or husband. But even in this case legal dependency is not the universal criterion. The payment of Child Benefit to the mother may reflect a judgement that income distribution within the household is not entirely equitable and the placement of some children in local authority care may mirror a similar concern. In the SB scheme persons over the age of 16 who have left school become separate units in their own right. However, unless responsible for housing expenditure they receive a lower non-householder rate of benefit which recognizes an element of collective consumption in the household. Where individual adults have satisfied the contribution conditions in the NI scheme they are given equal long-term benefits so that no account is taken of joint consumption or voluntary income redistribution.

This discussion of the appropriate unit of analysis throws some light on another issue. Section 2.7 indicated that social security measures may influence the formation of separate household or benefit units. Becker (1973; 1974a) assumes that marriage, or household formation, will occur where an increase in utility is expected. By the same token household splitting will arise if utility would be increased by living apart. Brady (1958) suggests that economies of scale (or joint consumption) encourage doubling up while rising incomes have facilitated household splitting, a point which is also made by Rivlin (1975). A good discussion of the relationship between social security measures and household formation in the US is given in Lerman (1973). The greater the extent of joint consumption, *ceteris paribus*, the more incentive there will be for doubling up and vice versa.

Assume for the moment that there is no interdependence between the utility derived by individuals either within or between households. Collective consumption therefore provides the only incentive for individuals to reside together. Continuing with the earlier example, in the case where the benefit unit is defined as the household two adults might receive £25 each if they lived together compared with £30 where they occupied separate households. In this situation the individuals would be equally well off in either one- or two-adult households and the benefit system would be neutral in the sense that it neither encouraged nor discouraged household formation. But if the single-adult household was paid more than £30 then the two adults would be better-off living apart and household formation would be encouraged while a benefit of less than £30 would discourage splitting. Thus benefit relativities may influence household formation.

The definition of the benefit unit may have a similar effect. Sections 2.5 and 2.6 showed that a cohabitation rule operates both for Widows' Benefits and for Supplementary Benefits. This means that the benefit unit consists of a single adult with or without children: doubling up will eliminate entitlement to Widows' Benefits and may reduce or eliminate entitlement to SB. These measures would appear to embody a disincentive to household doubling.

If the assumption of utility independence, and hence of no voluntary income redistribution, is relaxed the analysis becomes much more complex. Living together may increase the living standard of two individuals (Becker, 1973; 1974a); or it may reduce their welfare (Brady, 1958; Rivlin, 1975). Where voluntary income distribution within the household is unequal the provision of benefits like SB for one-parent families may encourage splitting and the higher the benefit the greater the incentive. In the present state of knowledge it is only possible to make these relatively simple statements of the potential influence which the social security system might have on household formation. To go further will require a better understanding of the household decision-making process which poses formidable conceptual and methodological problems.

3.6 The time period

The accounting period over which income and consumption are measured has not yet been considered. Is a weekly, monthly or yearly time period appropriate? Or possibly a decade, household or human life-cycle might be more suitable? The choice of an accounting period, like the selection of the basic unit of analysis, has implications which may not be immediately obvious.

It was assumed above that consumption is measured in terms of a flow of services. Opening or closing stocks are either non-existent or taken into account in calculating this flow. Stocks become more important the shorter the accounting period: in a very short time period like a week stocks of even non-durable commodities such as food may be important. For many more durable items like household furniture or kitchen equipment well-developed second-hand markets do not exist, making it difficult to evaluate opening and closing inventories. Moreover, rental markets may be rudimentary so that the alternative course of imputing a rental may be equally impractical.

The shorter the accounting period the more important will be search and information costs. It takes time to acquire and evaluate information and there are various adjustment costs which militate against instantaneous adjustment to new circumstances. Thus a household may take some time to adjust to a change in relative prices by substituting cheaper for dearer commodities in the way that Figures 3.5 and 3.7 suggest. The growing literature on the dynamics of demand is relevant in this context. Benus *et al.* (1976) show that the adjustment of food expenditure to changing circumstances is quite gradual. The adjustment process can be taken into account when measuring living standards (Pollak, 1975) but might raise some ethical problems. For example, the approach could imply that the rich should get more because they have developed more extravagant tastes in the past whereas the poor should get less due to their more limited historical consumption experience. But these difficulties are not arguments against investigating the dynamics of household behaviour: rather they caution against the uncritical acceptance of societal norms and may indicate the need for judgements of the first type discussed in Section 1.3.

In the case of durable goods consumption behaviour will also be influenced, and possibly dominated, by expectations about future developments and the consequences of past decisions. Future price increases lead to anticipatory purchasing while expectations about family sizes are reflected in house purchase. Historical family size decisions continue to exert a considerable influence on housing consumption in the later stages of a household's life. Dynamic household behaviour, and the opportunity to reduce expenditure without a corresponding fall in living standards by consuming durable assets, have a bearing on the differential between short- and long-term benefit rates discussed in Section 2.6. However, it is not clear *a priori* whether the short-term rate should exceed or be less than the long-term rate. Adjustment costs and the difficulty of altering consumption would argue for a higher short-term rate to cushion a fall in earnings whereas the ability to defer expenditure on durables leads to the opposite conclusion.

These various considerations suggest that a longer accounting period than a week or month may be desirable. Yet there are practical arguments which favour a short-time period. Information on expenditure and income is much easier to obtain for a large and representative sample of households if it relates to the last week or month rather than a continuous period of a year or years. The data are more likely to be accurate, and so on.

In a study of social security a short accounting period is also appropriate. Section 2.8 indicated that a primary objective of the sector is to provide a minimum standard of living, and this means a minimum at all times. So social security is largely organized to provide income maintenance on a weekly basis and SB payments are possible for an even shorter time period. Fundamental to the social security system is the conscious ethical judgement that an income deficiency, whatever its cause, should be corrected. It may be due to old age, bereavement, unemployment, sickness or disability. Or the income deficiency may arise because an individual is forgoing income to acquire education. On a lifetime income basis, or in terms of what Garfinkel and Haveman (1974) call earnings capacity, this individual might be judged to be relatively rich because the investment in human capital will be rewarded by higher earnings at a later stage. Yet if income at any point in the life-cycle falls below the minimum set in the social security system the deficiency is made good regardless of past experience or future prospects.

*3.7 Some further complications

Some further real-world complications need to be mentioned before leaving the highly stylized model developed in this chapter. One such complication has already been touched on: the household is usually viewed as consuming a commodity bundle of more than two goods. The concepts developed earlier can be readily extended to this more general case. Indeed the earlier exposition is based on the seminal paper by Barten (1964) which deals with the household consuming many commodities and composed of one or more types of individual or circumstance. Within this more general framework different qualities of goods or services can be accommodated by defining them as distinct commodities.

Some recent research by Muellbauer (1977) has questioned one aspect of the Barten model. Preliminary results suggests that the quasi-price substitution effect of a change in household circumstances depicted in Figure 3.7 may be smaller than those in Figure 3.5 which stem from changes in market prices. Separating out the direct, quasi-price and income effects identified in Section 3.3 is extremely involved and much further work needs to be done on this question.

It has been assumed so far that the market prices faced by the household are constant. But some prices vary with the quantity of goods and services consumed. Gas and electricity tariffs embody a fixed charge or its equivalent whereby average price per unit declines with increasing consumption. The budget line in Figure 3.2 becomes

* The general reader may wish to proceed to Section 3.8.

slightly modified as a result. If fuel consumption is on the horizontal axis then the origin shifts to the right by the extent of the fixed charge—even if no fuel is consumed the fixed charge has to be paid. Moreover, 'off-peak' consumers may face a lower marginal price per unit so that their budget line will be less steeply sloped for off-peak consumption. Standard rate and off-peak electricity could be treated as different commodities within the general model. Some distributional aspects of fuel consumption will be examined in Chapter 8 below.

The market prices faced by households may not be the true decision variables. Becker (1965) views the household as a production unit combining market commodities with the time of individuals in the household to produce final consumption commodities which yield utility. Thus market goods are intermediate rather than final inputs into the household consumption process and market price plus the implicit value of the time inputs, or 'full-price', becomes the relevant decision variable. Money income no longer provides the budget constraint because the household members can choose to devote time to work in the labour market, to household production which yields utility, or to leisure which also contributes to living standards. Instead 'full income', which would be obtained if the time devoted to market work, household production and leisure was entirely spent in the labour market, provides the budget constraint.

This model of household production has been extended to encompass fertility behaviour (Willis, 1973). Household utility is assumed to be a function of household production (based on the combination of market goods and time inputs), the number of children chosen by the family, and child quality. Child quality in turn is chosen by combining market goods and the time of household members to produce children. Thus children are assumed to generate utility *per se*, whereas it was assumed in Section 3.3 that only market goods and services contributed to living standards. In terms of the earlier model, if children generate utility then the consumption of other utility-producing commodities will be reduced in obtaining a given standard of living. The household will consume less food, fuel and so on than the composite equivalent commodity scales would indicate. However, in the special and highly unlikely case where children contributed to utility in the same ratio as they reduce utility by pre-empting resources, the equivalent commodity scales would pick up the net effect of the child. This improbable case prompts a number of difficult questions. Does the utility produced by children increase linearly with their number? Does it increase or decline with age? If it increases with age how does one rationalize the child's eventual departure from the parental home? The issues involved are similar to those discussed in Section 3.6 in the context of household formation and their resolution would seem to be equally intractable.

Clearly models of fertility behaviour need to be extended to encompass household formation both through the combination of individuals and the splitting of existing households. Much theoretical work remains to be done and new information will be required to test the hypotheses which result. And existing theories do not fully take account of phenomena like imperfect knowledge about the stream of utilities and disutilities which a child will impose before the irreversible conception decision is taken (Tobin, 1973). It may be that, as Ryder (1973) and Leibenstein (1974) have stressed, fertility is largely conditioned by social norms and social influence groups in which case the model of Section 3.3 would be appropriate. Some of the empirical evidence on fertility behaviour is reviewed in Section 10.6.

What do these various complications mean for the model formulated in Section 3.4? The idea that additional individuals in the household involve additional consumption certainly has a strong intuitive appeal. If two people eat in a restaurant or travel by public transport it costs twice as much as for one person and this provides the basic rationale for the Barten model. But the fertility model is also appealing in that it helps to explain movements in the birth rate, family size, the fact that richer households spend more on their children than poorer families, the increasing tendency for mothers with smaller families and older children to work, and so on. The temporal perspective of the two models is quite different. The Barten model is relatively short-term whereas the fertility models deal with lifetime income and consumption. But the fundamental difference lies in the judgement that children *per se* do not contribute to living standards on the one hand and that they make an important contribution on the other hand. If children do contribute to household utility then parents will be willing to consume fewer material goods and services—less housing, less food—to obtain a given standard of living. And if living with relatives involves disutility then other things being equal these households will tend to be more indulgent in material terms. While it would be satisfying to integrate the various approaches it may well be that they are designed to answer different questions and that such a reconciliation is not possible.

Even if parents do choose to have children because of the utility which they expect to obtain there are a number of circumstances when this would not matter for income maintenance. The child's contribution to living standards may be small, it may not transpire as expected, parents may have been too optimistic in assessing their future earnings, and so on. Thus ignoring any contribution which children may make to parental living standards may not be a serious error in the present context.

3.8 Summary

This chapter has been principally concerned with the measurement of living standards in households of different size and composition. If the consumption of market goods and services determine living standards then the effect of the addition of, say, a child can be captured by introducing equivalent commodity scales. These show the extent to which household expenditure on commodities at constant market prices would need to increase if living standards are to be maintained.

The overall influence of a change in household circumstances can be decomposed into three elements—direct, price substitution and income effects—which underlie the observed variations in the expenditure patterns of heterogeneous households. For example, the 1975 FES shows that a one-man and one-woman household with the head aged under 65 years spent £12·66 per week on food out of a total expenditure of £57·26, while one man and one woman with a child allocated £14·53 to food out of a total of £59·71. In contrast, housing expenditure by the two household types was very similar. These variations in expenditure patterns can be analysed to yield estimates of the equivalent commodity and income scales.

Comparisons of living standards involve many assumptions and difficulties. Inter-household utility comparisons are inevitable and cardinal measurement is required. Yet the method developed in this chapter has some advantages over alternative approaches which have been used in the literature. It involves fewer judgements about expenditure behaviour and makes maximum use of observed expenditure patterns. A relative view of living standards, rather than the absolute approach adopted in earlier studies, would also seem to be more consistent with the empirical evidence, in which case 'poverty' can never be abolished unless all households have an equal standard of living.

Although the household unit will be adopted throughout this study it involves assumptions about joint consumption, voluntary income redistribution, and the decision-making process within the household which may not be entirely realistic in some cases. As more empirical evidence becomes available on both these questions it should be possible to define the unit of analysis more satisfactorily. Adopting the week as the time period for the analysis is also open to objection on several grounds, but nevertheless a short accounting period seems consistent with the fundamental ethical judgement on which the social security system is based. Finally, if children generate utility there would seem to be good reasons for ignoring the fact in many social security measures.

4. Equity and Efficiency

4.1 Introduction

The previous chapter focused on questions of horizontal equity. While the provision of a minimum standard of living is a primary objective of the social security system, Section 2.8 argued that it is not the only purpose of the sector. The aims of social security are pursued within the wider objectives of the overall economy where efficiency considerations are also important. The level of national income has a direct influence on the social security sector. NI contributions account for about two-thirds of sector receipts and given their earnings-related nature the size of the national income partly determines the magnitude of this source of revenue. Direct and some indirect taxes also tend to increase with national income if tax legislation remains unchanged and are the main origin of the remaining one-third of sector revenue. Thus the level of national income may influence the size of the social security sector. Moreover, Section 2.7 showed that policy measures can influence behaviour and hence affect national income by varying the supply and productivity of labour and capital.

A theoretical basis for analysing some efficiency aspects of social security measures will therefore be developed in this chapter. It will deal with the choice between work and leisure, retirement, consumption and saving. As a consequence of these behavioural responses, instruments may have much wider effects than had been intended by their designers: the final effect will differ from the initial incidence. Moreover, a balance has to be struck between equity and efficiency. In the final analysis this trade-off is an ethical matter although economics has an important role to play in articulating distributional judgements, ensuring that they are consistent and minimizing the contribution of judgements of the third type discussed in Section 1.3 which are based on lack of information.

*4.2 Labour–leisure choice

It has been assumed so far that living standards are determined by the quantity of goods and services consumed (Section 3.2), or in the case of heterogeneous households by the quantities divided by the appropriate equivalent commodity scales (Section 3.3). This assumption is not unreasonable for households consisting of a single earner working a given number of hours per week. But for comparisons where hours of work vary the abstraction is less realistic. An income of £70 per week for one earner is hardly comparable with a similar income for two people in an otherwise identical household. Nor is an income of £70 for a 10-hour week quite the same as £70 for a 50-hour week. Most people would agree that in both examples the first household is better off than the second.

Thus work needs to be taken into account in measuring living standards, and this in turn involves the household's choice between work and leisure which in aggregate may influence the level of national income. For simplicity we will consider a typical household consisting of a single earner or potential worker. After eating, sleeping and performing other necessary functions a total of 80 hours per week may be available for work and leisure. Leisure yields utility at the expense of forgone earnings whereas work involves disutility but generates income. Given a constant wage W per hour the household may vary the number of hours worked H and therefore vary its income Y since $Y = WH$. But by working longer hours leisure time L is reduced because $L = T - H$, T being the total available time for work and leisure. Thus the household can choose between work and leisure: it can work longer hours, have a higher income and 'consume' less leisure or it can enjoy more leisure but have a lower income with reduced consumption of market goods and services. Living standards depend on leisure consumption in addition to consumption of market goods and services.

As in Chapter 3 we assume that the household behaves rationally as a decision-making entity and maximizes the utility derived from consuming market commodities (which is equal to income if saving is excluded) and leisure. The household has perfect knowledge, there are no information or adjustment costs and no work-related expenses. For any given wage rate the household is free to vary its hours of work: there is no involuntary unemployment and no non-competing groups of workers stemming from education, training or other screening devices (Stiglitz, 1975). The choice between income

* The general reader may wish to proceed to Section 4.4.

(or work) and leisure is depicted in Figure 4.1. The abscissa denotes leisure consumption L in hours. Provided the hourly wage is constant irrespective of the number of hours worked income is given by the product of hours worked and the wage rate as shown on the ordinate. If the household member worked the full 80 hours per week at wage rate W_1 income would be at a maximum OY_{t1} and no time

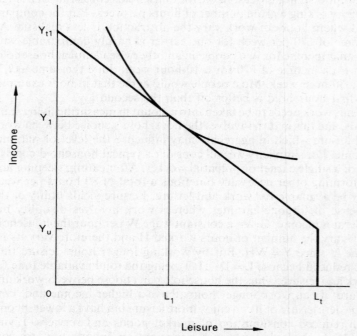

FIGURE 4.1   *The choice between work and leisure*

would be devoted to leisure. As leisure consumption increases income falls until at L_t all 80 hours are devoted to leisure, earned income is zero and household income amounts to OY_u representing unearned income made up from social security benefits like Retirement Pension or Child Benefit and investment income. Note that the slope of the budget line is given by the wage rate W_1.

The household will be indifferent between various combinations of income and leisure. For a very high income it would be prepared to forgo most of its leisure, while for each additional hour of leisure smaller increments of income would be sacrificed. These combinations of income and leisure yielding the same standard of living are shown by the indifference curve in Figure 4.1. The optimizing household chooses the labour–leisure combination yielding the highest standard of living. This arises where the budget line is tangential to the highest indifference curve giving OL_1 hours of leisure,

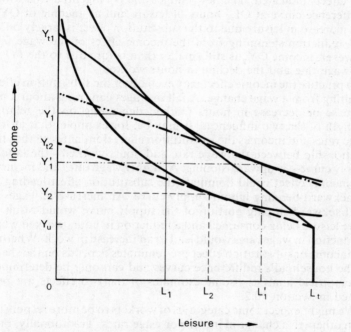

FIGURE 4.2 *Substitution and income effects of a reduction in the hourly wage rate*

involving $H = OL_t - OL_1$ hours of work, providing an earned income of $W_1H = OY_1 - OY_u$ per week and a total income of OY_1.

Consider a reduction in the standard wage rate to W_2 so that by working the full 80 hours the household can only earn an income of OY_{t2} (Figure 4.2). Will this change result in more or less work? On the one hand each hour of work which the household forgoes in favour of leisure has a lower opportunity cost since the earnings loss is smaller. But on the other hand achieving the previous level of income requires more hours of work. The first influence is a price substitution effect: holding living standards constant the reduction in the wage rate changes the slope of the budget line and the household substitutes leisure for the consumption of market goods and services. In consequence leisure time increases to OL_1' and income falls to OY_1'. But with the reduction in the wage rate living standards cannot be maintained. In an effort to achieve the highest standard of living the household works longer hours than the pure substitution effects indicated. The new budget line is tangential to a lower indifference curve at OL_2 hours of leisure and an income of OY_2. The increase in leisure due to the substitution effect is largely offset by a reduction stemming from the income effect of the wage fall. However, income OY_2 is still smaller than before due to the fall in the wage rate and the decline in hours worked.

In practice the income effect may even offset the substitution effect resulting from a wage change. A fall in wages can bring about a net increase or decrease in hours worked depending on the relative strength of the two influences. It may be, for example, that at low wage rates and incomes the substitution effect dominates so that the relationship between the wage rate and hours worked—the labour supply curve—is upward-sloping. At higher wage rates and incomes the income effect could dominate the substitution effect leading to a backward-bending labour supply curve. An increase in wages in the backward-sloping portion of the supply curve would result in more leisure being consumed and a reduction in hours worked while a reduction in wage rates would lead to an increase in work. Whether the income or substitution effect predominates depends on the shape of the household's indifference curves and can only be determined by empirical analysis—some estimates of the two effects are presented in Section 10.2.

We might expect some categories of workers to be more responsive than others to a change in income or wage rates. Traditionally, men in the 20- to 60-year age range have had a strong attachment to the labour force: there are strong social pressures to work and most alternatives are stigmatized. Housewives, on the other hand, have the opportunity of work within the home which, although unpaid, contributes to family well-being. Younger people can undertake training or tertiary education rather than engage in productive work while older workers can retire without the opprobrium attached to unemployment. Housewives, younger workers and the elderly may therefore be more responsive to economic stimuli than males aged 20 to 60 years. In terms of Figures 4.1 and 4.2 these three groups have different preferences as reflected by indifference curves which yield a larger substitution of work for leisure with changing wage rates or unearned incomes—where the term leisure embraces work in the home, education, retirement and all other forms of activity outside the labour market.

The analysis of choice between work and leisure is relevant to several aspects of social security provision. Higher benefits will bring about higher taxes and National Insurance contributions leading to a reduction in net earnings. Some benefits are earnings-related and, as Section 2.7 showed, can incorporate or contribute to high marginal tax rates which may influence the choice between work and leisure. Other benefits are conditional on a contingency like sickness, unemployment, retirement and disablement which involve withdrawal from the labour market. Finally Child Benefit depends on presence of children and is more in the nature of a lump sum payment: by increasing household incomes such measures may also influence the work decision through an income effect. To the extent that these social security measures influence the returns to work, or the opportunity cost of leisure, they will affect work behaviour. But the outcome will depend on whether the labour supply curve is upward-sloping or backward-sloping. If the labour supply curve is positively sloped higher contributions and taxes will, *ceteris paribus*, result in a reduction in labour supply, whereas the converse will hold if it is negatively sloped. These changes in labour supply are important because they will bring about a fall or increase in the level of national income.

The next section recognizes that NI contributions by employees may, to a limited extent, be perceived as an inter-temporal transfer by the household to itself. However, given the very loose relationship between contributions and benefits they are more in the nature of a tax and this is assumed in what follows. At the earnings floor Y_f contributions on the first £15 will lead to a downward shift in the budget line (Figure 4.3—which depicts the mirror image of the earlier indifference curve diagrams): thereafter, up to the ceiling Y_c, proportionate contributions will make the budget line less steeply sloped. It is assumed that the substitution effect dominates the income effect, as reflected by the upward-sloping labour supply curve SS in Figure 4.4. Below the earnings floor Y_f labour supply will be unchanged but at that point the net wage will be reduced by the extent of contributions. A higher gross wage rate will be necessary to bring forth the same supply of labour. We would therefore expect to observe a concentration of earnings just below the floor as employees would be better-off there than at the floor, or in the case of employers, just above it. Between the floor and ceiling the labour supply curve shifts upwards, reflecting the less steeply sloped budget

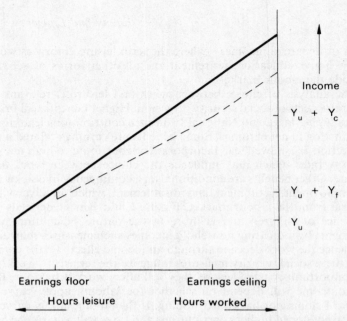

FIGURE 4.3 *The budget line with and without National Insurance contributions*

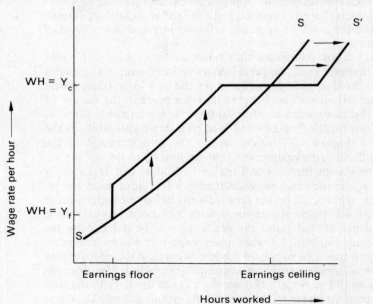

FIGURE 4.4 *The labour supply curve with National Insurance contributions*

line in Figure 4.3 and the dominance of the substitution effect over the income effect (MacRae and MacRae, 1976).

But at the earnings ceiling the budget line becomes parallel to the pre-contributions budget line since contributions are a fixed sum and no longer increase with earnings. This lump sum reduction in earnings will therefore involve no substitution effect. Only an income effect will arise which, provided the labour supply curve is upward-sloping, will bring about an increase in hours worked and a right-ward shift in the labour supply curve yielding the modified curve SS′. Again there will be a few earners exactly at the ceiling: due to the kink in the budget line all employers would be better off at points above the ceiling. Thus with an upward-sloping labour supply curve the introduction of National Insurance contributions would result in a reduction in hours worked between the floor and ceiling and an increase above the ceiling with a concentration of earners below the floor and above the ceiling. But if the labour supply curve is back-ward-bending above the ceiling then the income effect would be even larger, leading to a greater rightward shift in the backward-sloping section of the curve and a more marked increase in hours worked. A labour supply curve which is backward-sloping over the entire wage rate range would be shifted to the right between the earnings floor and ceiling.

The overall effect of National Insurance contributions on the supply of labour depends partly on the shape of the labour supply curve. If it is upward-sloping the increased labour supply of those above the ceiling will offset the reduction in hours worked by those between the floor and ceiling and the net effect may be positive or negative. But if the labour supply curve is backward-bending above the ceiling then an increase in labour supply is more likely and an unambiguous increase will occur where the labour supply curve is entirely backward-sloping. Whether there is an increase or reduction in aggregate labour supply will therefore depend on two factors. First, household preferences for work and leisure, as reflected by the shape of indifference curves and the associated labour supply curve, determine the strength of substitution and income effects. Second, the distribution of earners below the floor, between floor and ceiling and above the contributions ceiling will also have an important influence on the overall labour supply effects.

It was noted in Section 2.7 that SB is withdrawn at a 100 per cent rate with earnings above the disregard while some benefits like Family Income Supplement and the Retirement Pension earnings rule are earnings-related. Moreover their interaction with the tax system and other means-tested benefits can result in high cumulative marginal tax rates. The higher the marginal tax rate the lower the net wage obtained from working an extra hour and the lower the opportunity cost of leisure, i.e. the cost of an extra hour of leisure measured in terms of earnings forgone. As in Figure 4.3 the household budget line becomes less steeply sloped resulting, *ceteris paribus*, in a pure substitution effect and increased leisure consumption. But the income effect will offset and possibly outweight the substitution effect. While it may appear at first sight that high marginal tax rates will result in a reduction in labour supply there is no *a priori* reason why this should happen.

In the case where cumulative marginal tax rates are 100 per cent or higher there will be an unambiguous increase in leisure consumption. Over the range of hours where marginal tax rates are 100 per cent or more the budget line in Figure 4.1 will be horizontal (as in Figure 4.5) or positively sloped respectively and stepped upwards to the existing budget line where the high marginal tax rates cease. In this region of the budget line the household would be on a higher indifference curve working fewer hours, i.e. at the right-hand kink in the horizontal or upward-sloping segment. In consequence there will be a break in the labour supply curve over the range of hourly wage rates producing earnings which are subject to high marginal tax rates with a concentration of earners below and above the points where the high marginal tax rates prevail. There is no incentive to increase earnings by greater work effort—hence the term 'poverty trap'.

The majority of social security benefits are not earnings-related. Unemployment Benefit is conditional on no suitable employment being available, Sickness Benefit is paid in event of sickness and Industrial Disablement Benefit entitlement usually arises where an industrial disease or accident impairs the ability to work. To the extent that contingency benefits are paid to households where unemployment, sickness, disablement or retirement are involuntary the earlier analysis is not applicable. These beneficiaries are not potential labour market participants. But the screening devices used to identify these various contingencies are not perfect and the criteria themselves cannot always be exactly defined so that the categories may exclude some involuntary participants and include some voluntary participants.

Voluntary contingency benefit participation can be analysed within the earlier framework. Benefit payment $Y_b - Y_u$ is conditional on withdrawal from the labour market and is represented by the vertical and horizontal section of the budget line (Figure 4.5). Where benefit payment is well below the chosen level of earned income, as would be the case where preferences are indicated by the solid indifference curve, there would be no incentive for voluntary benefit participation. But if benefit entitlement approaches or exceeds earnings, as would happen for preferences depicted by the broken indifference curves, the household would be better off on benefit. It could achieve both a higher income and consume more leisure,

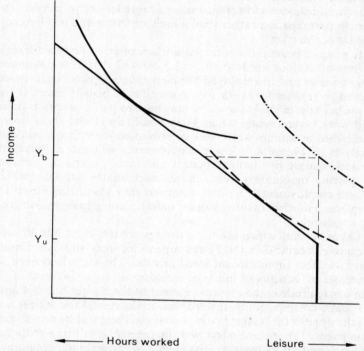

FIGURE 4.5 *The choice between work and voluntary benefit participation*

thereby obtaining a higher standard of living as reflected by the chained indifference curve. The importance of this phenomenon, and the consequent reduction in labour supply, will depend on three factors. First, it will be influenced by the efficiency of contingency benefit entitlement rules at screening out voluntary participants and on the level of benefits relative to earnings. Second, there may be a stigma attached to benefit participation so that the direct relationship between earnings and benefit entitlement is not the appropriate decision variable. Income from benefit payments may be perceived as generating less satisfaction than income from the labour market so that, in effect, the horizontal benefit segment of the budget line in Figure 4.5 is some proportion of the monetary amount (Albin and Stein, 1968). The downward displacement of the benefit segment would provide a monetary measure of this stigma factor. Third, the structure of household preferences for income and leisure will determine the number of workers with earnings at or above benefit levels who would choose a lower income and more leisure from voluntary benefit participation rather than a higher income and less leisure in the labour market.

In practice benefits for potential workers often embody work regulations of various kinds. Section 2.5 showed that Unemployment Beneficiaries and unemployed Supplementary Beneficiaries are required to register for work as a condition of benefit. Stein (1976) describes how in the US workers may have to participate in training and work programmes, while Albin and Stein (1968) show how a prescribed maximum work week or minimum wage rate modify the analysis of Figure 4.5. These requirements will act as screening devices against involuntary benefit participation and as a means of placing involuntary beneficiaries back in the labour market. Where employment is limited, however, they may bring about the displacement of an existing worker unless accompanied by job creation measures.

Other benefits which are not earnings-related like Child Benefit, Negative Income Tax (NIT) guaranteed incomes and Tax Credits have an effect similar to unearned income. The introduction of, or increases in, benefits of this type would result in an increase of the same magnitude in the vertical segment of the budget line in Figure 4.1 and a corresponding upward shift in the rest of the budget line. As the slope of the budget line is unchanged there will be no substitution effect. The income effect will, in general, result in a reduction in work and an increase in leisure with all households obtaining a higher standard of living. In the case of voluntary contingency benefit participants an increase in the share of income of this type will increase the incentive for labour force participation: in terms of Figure 4.5 it will lead to an upward shift in the solid budget line. Given that the number of voluntary benefit participants is small relative to the total labour force the overall effect will probably be a reduction in work.

This conclusion, like all the analyses in this section of the influence of the social security sector on the choice between labour and leisure, is only part of the story. We have focused on the labour supply effects of taxes, contributions and benefits in isolation although the sector balance sheet in Section 2.3 emphasizes that a change in the revenue side is associated with a corresponding adjustment on the expenditure side of the account and vice versa. Thus a more complete analysis would allow not only for the labour supply effects of a benefit increase but for the corresponding effects of an increase in National Insurance contributions and taxes. This in turn leads to the wider question of the initial and final incidence of measures which will be discussed in Section 4.4 below. But first we need to extend the highly simplified model adopted in this section to take account of the impact of social security measures on the choice between consumption and saving.

*4.3 Consumption and saving

Saving permits deferred consumption: households can choose to forgo part of current income in favour of future consumption. The motivation for sacrificing current for future consumption includes the possibility of unavoidable losses of future income due to unemployment, sickness or disablement; the desire for voluntary retirement from the labour market at some future date and a wish to leave bequests to heirs. By providing a minimum standard of living, and an element of earnings replacement, social security may influence the balance between current and future consumption. Moreover, Section 2.3 showed that social security is financed on a 'pay as you go' basis from current revenue. In contrast, although the actuarial component of private insurance involves current income transfers, the endowment part is financed out of accumulated premiums and the compounded return yielded by their investment. The replacement of funded private insurance by current social security transfers may therefore result in a reduction in personal saving. Moreover, by shifting the balance between current and future consumption and generating inter-household transfers indirect effects on consumption and saving may arise. Finally the earnings rule, increments for deferred retirement, the earnings-related element in benefits and similar features of social security will also affect future income and the accumulation of assets.

The static single-period model of household behaviour which has been employed so far is unsuitable for analysing the choice between consumption and saving. A longer temporal perspective, the household life-cycle, is required to understand the allocation of income

* The general reader may wish to proceed to Section 4.4.

between current and future consumption. The main elements of the problem can be captured by a highly simplified two-period construct in which the household life-cycle is divided into an earnings-consumption-saving era and a non-earning-consumption-dissaving period. The household works during the first period and is involuntarily withdrawn from the labour market in the second as with unemployment, sickness, disablement or compulsory retirement. To simplify the analysis it is assumed that the second period commences after a fixed time has elapsed.

Consider the choice between current consumption and saving in the absence of social security. Households know that in the event of various contingencies, including retirement, earned income will cease and the second period of consumption out of savings will commence. During the first period they therefore have to decide how to divide income between current and future consumption. By applying an appropriate discounting factor to future consumption the choice between consumption and saving can be depicted in Figure 4.6 (Feldstein, 1974a). The vertical axis denotes current consumption out of current income OY and the horizontal axis shows the present value of future consumption. Given household preferences, as reflected by the indifference curves in Figure 4.6, the level of current consumption and saving will be optimal at the point where the budget line is tangential to the highest indifference curve. Consumption amounts to OCC_1 in the first period, saving is $OY - OCC_1$, giving the present value of future consumption FC_1.

The introduction of social security or its substitution at the margin for private insurance will alter the budget line in two ways. Earned income is reduced from OY to OY_s by social security contributions and higher direct taxes, while future consumption is also changed by a parallel shift in the budget line—in Figure 4.6 an increase in future consumption is assumed. Provided there is no change in preferences with the introduction of social security the new equilibrium level of current consumption increases to CC_2 and future consumption also increases to FC_2, yielding a higher lifetime standard of living. Saving falls from $OY - OCC_1$ to $OY_s - OCC_2$ in Figure 4.6, but a fall in savings, or a large fall in savings, will not necessarily occur in all cases.

Consider a household at the bottom end of the earnings distribution. Little or no saving will occur in the absence of social security so contributions will be entirely financed out of current consumption. The higher earnings replacement ratio for the poor (Section 2.5) will result in a substantial rightward shift in the budget line and a corresponding increase in second period consumption. The overall effect would be a negligible reduction in saving, a reduction in current consumption by the extent of social security contributions or higher taxes and a marked increase in future consumption.

The case depicted in Figure 4.6 represents a household with savings in the bottom half of the distribution which receives a net transfer of lifetime income under social security. If this household saves at all then its savings will decline as it substitutes the social security

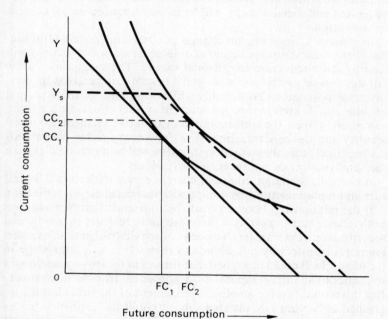

FIGURE 4.6   *The relationship between current and future consumption under private insurance and social security*

transfer in the second period for private insurance. The extent of any decline in savings will depend on the shape of household preferences: if high priority is attached to future consumption then the reduction in savings will be small with most of social security contributions being financed out of current consumption.

At the upper end of the earnings distribution savings will be relatively high compared with other households. Due to the ceiling social security contributions will constitute a small proportion of earnings although this will be offset to the extent that the sector is financed from progressive taxation. Earnings replacement is also considerably lower for better-off households in the second period. The household budget line will have a small horizontal segment with the remainder shifted to the left reflecting the net transfer away from the rich. In this case savings will probably decline. But the fall may be less than social security contributions and higher taxes would suggest because their future consumption will be lower. Thus if sufficient importance is attached to future consumption the fall in savings will be limited and social security will be mainly financed out of current consumption.

In summary, assuming no change in other dimensions of household behaviour the introduction of or increases in social security will lead to some reduction in personal saving. The magnitude of the fall will depend on the extent to which benefits are received by non-savers as opposed to households which save and on the structure of household preferences for current rather than future consumption. Given the substantial redistributive element in social security and the concentration of saving among richer households it seems likely that the reduction in saving will be much smaller than the total receipts of the social security sector.

As benefits are financed out of current revenue (Section 2.3) and earnings replacement ratios decline with increased earnings (Section 2.5) the relationship between contributions and returns is tenuous both *ex ante* and *ex post*. It is therefore more realistic to treat social security as current transfers between households rather than as inter-temporal transfers by households to themselves at a later stage in the life-cycle. It could be argued that the social security system ought to change to an inter-temporal intra-household transfer mechanism. But this would involve an ethical judgement of the first kind distinguished in Section 1.3: alternatively, it could be justified in terms of an increase in saving and economic efficiency. But this argument involves an implicit distributional judgement which should be made explicit, and there are other instruments which can be used to achieve the same end. Feldstein (1974b) employs a life-cycle savings model in which social security contributions and benefits are assumed to be inter-temporal transfers. Household contributions and taxes in the first period determine benefit payments in the second as though social security operated on a funded basis like private insurance. This model predicts that social security contributions will lead to an equivalent reduction in saving. In terms of Figure 4.6 it involves a straightforward substitution of contributions for saving, leaving current and future consumption unchanged. Similar assumptions in Feldstein (1976a) and Munnell (1976) lead to the prediction that social security will substantially reduce saving *ceteris paribus*. The earlier model, which suggests a much smaller reduction in saving, is more in keeping with the institutional features of social security in Britain.

The assumption of involuntary benefit participation at the commencement of the second period can be relaxed. The two-period life-cycle model can be elaborated to take account of work, and hence earnings in the second period. The budget line will shift to the right by the extent of the discounted value of second-period earnings. Earned income will have a similar effect to social security benefit payments in the second period: it will lead to some reduction in savings during the first period. For example, increments for deferred retirement will increase labour supply by potential beneficiaries although to a different extent compared with private insurance. The earnings rule on the other hand will discourage work above the earnings limit and so tend to induce retirement. Earnings-related benefits will encourage voluntary benefit participation and Section 4.2 showed that a high level of benefit payments will have a similar effect. This increase in voluntary benefit participation will lead to an *increase* in first-period saving to provide for earlier and longer retirement.

This analysis of the impact of social security provision on consumption and saving has indicated two offsetting influences. Assuming no change in household behaviour, other than in consumption and saving, social security will bring about a reduction in saving. However, the decline in saving will be very much smaller than total sector revenues due to the considerable redistributive element in social security transfers and the concentration of saving among richer households. On the other hand higher benefits and mechanisms like the earnings rule will induce voluntary benefit participation and earlier retirement. These behavioural responses will lead to an increase in saving which will partly offset, or possibly more than offset, the reduction caused by contributions. The magnitudes of these two offsetting influences are an empirical matter and the available evidence will be reviewed in Chapter 10. Other factors like changing demographic conditions will also influence the savings ratio. An ageing population will lead to increased dissaving, and Leff (1969) shows that an increasing child dependency ratio is associated with increased current consumption at the expense of saving.

4.4 Wider effects

Social security measures may influence labour supply and saving in a number of ways. NI contributions reduce wage rates and so may lead to a reduction or increase in labour supply, depending on the relative strength of the substitution and income effects. Earnings-related benefits or a NIT will have a similar influence. Where benefits are withdrawn by £1 for each £1 increase in earnings there will be an unambiguous reduction in labour supply. Categorical benefits for unemployment, sickness and similar contingencies may have a similar effect by inducing voluntary benefit participation. Benefits which are unrelated to work like a NIT income guarantee or Child Benefit will have a pure income effect on behaviour, leading to some reduction in labour supply.

Thus the influence of social security measures on work behaviour depends crucially on the magnitude of the substitution and income effects: in some cases on both effects, in other situations on the income effect alone. These two effects in turn depend on household preferences and can only be determined by empirical measurement.

By providing Retirement Pensions and other benefits the social security system may bring about some reduction in saving. But the fall in saving will be much smaller than total NI contributions in view of the substantial redistributive element in the system. It provides high earnings replacement ratios for low earners who would not save much in any case and low replacement ratios for high earners who are responsible for the bulk of savings. Moreover, the social security system brings about an offsetting increase in savings by inducing earlier retirement. Higher retirement benefits, the earnings rule and earnings-related benefits will all bring about earlier and longer retirement which in turn will provide an incentive for increased saving. Again, whether the saving reduction effect of social security will dominate the saving-inducing influence is an empirical matter.

The previous two sections dealt mainly with the initial effects of social security on labour supply and savings behaviour. They focused on a single market and considered how it in isolation would be affected by various measures. Where induced changes in factor supplies are small relative to aggregate supply in the long-run, or to short-term variations in total factor supplies, this partial analysis is satisfactory. In these circumstances the initial and final effects will be similar.

However, Section 2.3 showed that the social security sector provides the primary source of income for up to a quarter of the population and amounts to about one-tenth of national income—it is of roughly the same importance as private saving. It follows that many aspects of social security provision will have far-reaching consequences throughout the economy which violate the implicit *ceteris paribus* assumptions made in the earlier analysis. Partial equilibrium and initial incidence effects may yield a quite misleading picture of the ultimate outcome. It is therefore necessary to go beyond the impact of measures on a single factor and to consider how two or more markets will be influenced by the changes under consideration. This more realistic analysis will be exceedingly complex. Ideally it requires a model of the entire economy and while it is clear how the analysis can be carried out in principle its practical implementation is much more difficult.

The emphasis here will be on the illustration of some of the wider consequences of social security measures rather than a more complete catalogue of the ultimate effects. Two issues will be examined. The effect of National Insurance contributions provides a good example of how the initial incidence of measures differs from their nominal effect and demonstrates very clearly the importance of consequent changes beyond the labour market in determining final incidence. The implications of a reduction in savings stemming from the unfunded basis of financing social security yields an insight into the way in which capital market changes can feed back into the labour market and ultimately undo in part the original intent of social security.

As in the previous section NI contributions will be viewed as current transfers: to the extent that they are regarded as inter-temporal transfers by households to themselves the effects considered below will be diminished. Assuming that the labour supply curve is upward-sloping the introduction of, or more realistically, increases in National Insurance contributions will bring about an upward shift between the earnings floor and ceiling. The employer has to pay contributions of 8·75 per cent of the employee's earnings for each hour of work while the employee contributes a further 5·75 per cent, giving 14·5 per cent in total. Thus each hour involves an additional 14·5 per cent in total wage costs to employers if the same supply of labour is to be brought forward and the original supply curve S_1S_1 in Figure 4.7 is shifted upwards by this proportion to give the new curve S_2S_2. Given the employers' demand curve for labour DD, the original equilibrium wage rate W_1 and hours worked H_1 will change with the shift in the supply curve to yield the new equilibrium W_2H_2.

The partial equilibrium analysis in Figure 4.7 shows that the initial incidence of contributions on employers and employees will generally differ from the nominal incidence of 8·75 and 5·75 per cent respectively. The increase in the wage rate OW_2-OW_1 indicates the extent to which contributions are borne by employers and OW_1-OW_2' shows how far they fall on employees through a reduction in the net wage rate. The less elastic the demand curve relative to the supply curve the greater the incidence on employers and the smaller

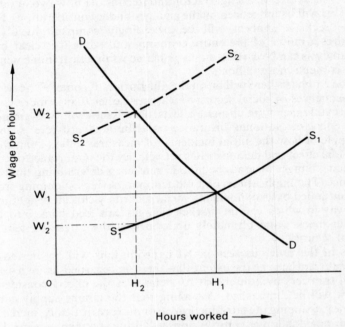

FIGURE 4.7   *A partial equilibrium analysis of the incidence of National Insurance contributions*

the fall in net wages of employees: the converse holds the more elastic the demand curve relative to the supply curve. For example, Brittain (1971; 1972a; 1972b) argues that the labour supply curve is inelastic for institutional reasons and therefore social security contributions are borne mainly by employees. The true initial incidence of contributions is determined by the elasticities of labour demand and supply.

This simple analysis of incidence focuses on the way in which contributions alter the quantity of labour supplied at any given wage

rate. It implicitly assumes that this change in the supply of labour
will be sufficiently small to leave unaltered the equilibrium quantity
and price of capital and the marginal products of labour and capital
in production (Feldstein, 1972b). Suppose this is not the case and
the reduction in labour supply leads to a substitution of capital in
production and a rise in its price. Production technology will be such
that the output per unit of capital and labour will also change, leading to a shift in the derived demand for labour curve DD in Figure
4.7. Thus the new equilibrium will differ from W_2H_2 and the final
incidence of contributions will be determined by these consequent
changes in the rest of the economy.

A reduction in saving stemming from the substitution of current
social security transfers for funded private insurance will have a
similar effect on capital markets. Capital will be in shorter supply
than would otherwise be the case and the rate of return on financial
assets will increase. This higher return will encourage saving so the
equilibrium effect of social security on the volume of saving will be
less than the initial leftward shift in the savings supply schedule
would suggest. Paradoxically, the reduction in saving and increased
rate of return resulting from the unfunded nature of social security
will mainly benefit higher income groups who are responsible for
the major part of aggregate saving.

Moreover, under certain plausible assumptions this improved
return to savers will be at the expense of wage earners and the total
effect will be concentrated on the middle of the income distribution
where earnings constitute the main source of income. Provided
labour is not a perfect substitute for capital and is not in excess
supply at the prevailing wage rate the higher cost and more limited
supply of capital will bring about a reduction in output due to the
lower capital per worker (Feldstein, 1975; and Boskin, 1976): the
labour demand curve DD would shift to the left. Hence there will
be a reduction in the wage rate to the detriment of earners—especially low earners who depend largely on wage income and are one
of the groups which social security is designed to help.

This wider analysis of the effect of NI contributions and of the
unfunded nature of finance also applies to other aspects of social
security measures. Higher benefits and higher marginal tax rates induce a reduction in labour supply if the substitution effect dominates
the income effect. The expenditure side of the social security sector
will therefore tend to have an adverse effect on labour supply in the
same way as contributions. While social security may lead to some
reduction in savings it will also bring about an increase in the consumption expenditure of beneficiaries and so expand aggregate

demand in the short-run to the benefit of wage earners. Golladay and Haveman (1976) have traced the initial impact of a NIT in the US on the structure of output and distribution of income. Although the distribution of net transfer income was of greatest benefit to low income groups the resulting increase in consumption expenditure was small for many prominent low income occupations. In consequence there was a second-round distributional effect whereby the earnings of higher income groups increased by more than the earnings of lower income groups. Measures may not have the intended effects and the ultimate outcome of major changes can only be appreciated by quantifying their influence on labour, capital and product markets paying special attention to the distribution of costs and benefits between income groups within each of these three broad spheres of economic activity. These more general ramifications throughout the economy are complex and need to be analysed with care: in addition to effects on economic efficiency they include the distributional impact of measures which in turn entails distributional judgements.

4.5   Distributional judgements

The emphasis so far in this chapter has been on the influence of social security on factor markets and hence on the level of national output and income: measures may reduce the available supply of labour and the stock of capital, leading to a reduction in economic efficiency. But economic efficiency is not the only objective of economic policy: the size of the social security sector is evidence of the importance which is also attached to distributional objectives. There is a direct conflict between equity and efficiency which has to be reconciled and this section considers the framework within which the trade-off between the two can be considered. Two alternative approaches have been adopted in the literature.

The first approach, which is relatively recent, is based on the Pareto criterion discussed in Section 3.2. Interpersonal comparisons of utility are replaced by a test of whether a change will make at least one household better-off without making others worse off— a Pareto improvement—the evaluations being performed by the individual households themselves. Where none can be made better-off without making others worse off Pareto optimality is attained. Hochman and Rodgers (1969) combined the Pareto criterion with interdependent utility functions whereby the welfare of one household enters into the utility function of another. On this basis they demonstrated how income redistribution could be integrated with allocative efficiency within the Paretian framework. Mayer and Shipley (1970), Musgrave (1970), Goldfarb (1970) and Hochman and Rodgers (1970) have extended and refined this approach. It has also been applied by Zeckhauser (1971) in evaluating the relative merits of contingency benefits, a negative income tax and wage subsidy—although the conclusions of that analysis have been weakened by Schlenker (1973) and questioned by Garfinkel (1973a).

The second approach to the integration of equity and efficiency considerations has been followed over a much longer period. It is also adopted in the recent literature on optimal taxation which is surveyed by Sandmo (1976), Atkinson and Stiglitz (1976) and Bradford and Rosen (1976). The objective of economic policy is viewed as the maximization of a social welfare function which is the sum of individual household utilities. In the simplest additive and independent case, where social welfare is the unweighted sum of individual utilities, an additional £1 of income to a rich household adds as much to social welfare as an extra £1 to a poor household. Equity considerations can be introduced by attaching explicit distributional weights to households with different utilities. A larger weight may be judged desirable for a household with low utility while a lower weight is considered appropriate for a high utility household. Where utility functions are identical households will consume the same combination of goods and services at a given income level, and distributional weights will decline with increasing income.

In Section 3.3 it was shown that differences in consumption patterns and incomes could arise at the same standard of living or utility level from variations in household circumstances. Adjusting consumption by commodity scales and incomes by an income scale provided a means of allowing for heterogeneous household types. Adopting equivalent income rather than money income in the present context assumes that household utility functions only differ by virtue of variations in household characteristics captured by the commodity scales. It also involves the judgement that actual household behaviour as reflected by the commodity scales is acceptable or desirable. Subject to these qualifications equivalence scales, and the use of equivalent income rather than money income, provides a means of integrating horizontal and vertical equity with efficiency considerations.[1]

[1] In contrast, Atkinson and Stiglitz (1976), Bradford and Rosen (1976) and Musgrave (1976) note that there may be a conflict between the maximization of social welfare and the principle of horizontal equity. This has been avoided above by treating horizontal equity as more basic and prior to the question of vertical equity and

The social marginal utility of income may therefore be judged as diminishing with increasing equivalent income. An extra unit of income to a poor household adds more to social welfare than an extra unit to a rich household: a larger increment to the money income of a large household is required to bring about the same increase in social welfare as in a small household. In the inequality index proposed by Atkinson (1970) different values of a single parameter imply different weights in the social welfare function—varying degrees of inequality aversion. Atkinson (1973) shows that it includes as polar cases the simple or unweighted addition of individual incomes and at the other extreme the maximin criterion advanced by Rawls (1974) where only the income of the poorest member of society matters: the interdependence of utility is further considered by Feldstein (1976b). This approach has been widely adopted in the optimal taxation literature and can be used to demonstrate that income transfers from rich to poor may add to social welfare. Income transfers can involve a reduction in aggregate income and social welfare but may nevertheless be optimal due to the offsetting increase in social welfare stemming from redistribution. Using the same framework Feldstein (1972a) and Wilson (1977a) show how distributional considerations modify the usual public enterprise pricing rules: marginal cost pricing is no longer optimal.

The trade-off between equity and efficiency can be visualized in terms of Figures 3.1 to 3.3. Efficiency, or the size of national income, is recorded on the vertical axis and equity, measured in terms of a given set of distributional weights applied to a range of hypothetical income distributions associated with increasingly redistributive transfers, is depicted on the horizontal axis. The budget line represents the various feasible combinations of national income and redistribution: at one extreme national income can be maximized with no income transfers while at the other extreme extensive redistribution is associated with a reduced level of national income. The social indifference curves represent different levels of social welfare and any given level can be obtained with different combinations of efficiency and equity. Maximum social welfare is obtained at the point of tangency between the national budget line and the highest social indifference curve: this optimum requires the sacrifice of some

---

efficiency but this approach is not entirely satisfactory. For example, it could result in relatively high money incomes for large families which would have adverse efficiency effects and might lead to lower benefit levels for all families. Treating horizontal equity as prior therefore ignores potential trade-offs between horizontal equity, vertical equity and efficiency objectives. Ideally horizontal equity, vertical equity and efficiency considerations should be simultaneously reconciled with one another.

national income in favour of greater equity. The distributional weights are critical. In the situation where inequality aversion is minimal, the weights show little change with increasing incomes and the social welfare function approaches the simple sum of individual incomes. The budget line would be steeply sloped and the optimum implies a very limited amount of redistribution. A high degree of inequality aversion involves a less steeply sloped budget line, a reduction in national income and more redistribution. These distributional weights require a value judgement of the second type distinguished in Section 1.4 and emphasize the fundamental ethical basis of analyses which deal with either allocative efficiency or distribution.

From the viewpoint of this study the use of distributional weights is preferable to the Pareto criterion. Although the Paretian approach avoids the difficulty of interpersonal comparisons, Section 3.3 showed that these were inevitable where horizontal equity is involved so this advantage is of no consequence in the present context. And, as Mishan (1972) notes, treating redistribution as an externality entering individual utility functions raises the major operational disadvantage of the need to know the interdependence between the single units. The idea of utility interdependence may also be incorporated in the social welfare function approach although the practical difficulty of determining the nature of the inter-relationship between households or groups of households remains.

The introduction of distributional weights requires explicit value judgements about the rate of decline in the marginal social utility of income. This too poses serious practical problems which have been circumvented by making a range of assumptions about the weights attached at different points in the distribution. But the difficulty does not arise where the purpose of the analysis is to promote consistent distributional judgements between a number of proposals. Nor does it arise in the comparison of new and existing measures since, as Le Grand (1975) has shown, the latter embody implicit distributional weights although they may reflect efficiency as well as distributional considerations. Indeed the practical difficulty may turn out to be which set or combination of existing distributional judgements to adopt out of the many available.

From an institutional point of view the social welfare function and distributional weights represent a highly simplified conceptualization of the distributional decision-making process. Buchanan and Bush (1974) stress the political context of such decisions and argue that to be viable redistribution must benefit at least half the enfranchised population. The evidence that middle income groups benefit more from transfers than low income groups is cited in support of this argument. In a similar vein a more elaborate model of redistribution within a framework of majority voting is examined by Denzan and Mackay (1976). Further development of this method may, in the longer term, provide an alternative approach to the analysis of equity and efficiency considered here.

4.6 Complications

The models of choice between work, leisure, income and saving which formed the basis of this chapter represent a highly simplified description of the real world. The implications of a few more realistic features of households, labour and capital markets need to be considered.

The models are based on the axiom that households maximize utility and this raises the question of what factors contribute to household utility. The assumption in Chapter 3 that market goods and services generate utility may be more plausible than the supposition that work generates disutility. Work has important social dimensions as well as economic characteristics: the work ethic and the stigma associated with unemployment or the receipt of benefits may generate disutility from leisure consumption or from leisure exceeding a certain level. Indeed some people may enjoy work just as much as leisure, while involuntary unemployment is evidence of an excess supply of leisure: in both cases it is hardly appropriate to classify the two as opposites. However, the first considerations may simply reflect more 'concentrated' and 'rectangular' preferences than the indifference curves discussed in this chapter. This would mean that beyond a narrow range of work and leisure hours the desire to substitute one for the other is limited. This would help to explain the heavy concentration of hours worked within a relatively narrow band around 40 hours compared with the potential range of 1 to 80 hours per week. Involuntary unemployment is more difficult to deal with in the sort of framework developed earlier and we return to this point below.

In a world of uncertainty ideas about future consumption requirements will be nebulous and saving, or deferred consumption, may contribute to household utility in only the vaguest way. Yet that saving occurs at all is evidence of a telescopic facility which is not entirely defective although in addition to the precautionary and retirement motives stressed in Section 4.3, Blinder (1976) and Ishikawa (1975) focus on bequests and human capital formation, notably in the form of training and formal education. The choice between consumption and saving will therefore be much more complex and involved than Figure 4.6 would suggest without necessarily invalidating the essential conclusions of that analysis.

Section 3.5 noted that the household may not behave as a decision-making entity and much of that discussion is equally applicable to the work and saving decision processes. The assumption that the household is a single unit is less plausible where there is more than one earner or potential worker and least acceptable where there are several. Each worker will make choices between work and leisure, consumption and saving, which are in part independent of the rest of the household. Becker's (1965) household production model, in which market goods are combined with the time of household members to produce final consumption goods, provides a framework for analysing and understanding the inter-related work decisions of households, especially of husbands and wives. Pollak and Wachter (1975) have pointed out that this model is unsatisfactory where there is joint production—or joint consumption in terms of Sections 3.3 and 5.3. The approach is not feasible in this study in any case because we do not have the requisite information on time allocation or data on the characteristics of non-market workers to allow estimates of the opportunity cost of working in the home. This is an area in which much further work needs to be done.

Institutional features of labour and capital markets will invalidate some of the assumptions made in the earlier analysis. Returns on saving will vary with the amounts involved and the wage rate will not necessarily be constant where weekly hours of work vary. Overtime rates are generally higher than standard rates of pay while wage rates for part-time workers are usually lower than for full-time workers: the budget line in Figure 4.1 would become a series of increasingly steeply sloped linear segments with higher incomes. On the other hand the progressive income tax schedule will introduce decreasingly sloped linear segments. Fixed costs for learning, training and hiring may partly account for increasing wage rates with longer hours of work. Information and transaction costs will have a similar effect on the budget line between current and future consumption.

Education and on-the-job training will be associated with non-competing groups of workers who differ in productivity in various occupations. The result will be a range of budget lines with different slopes and a worker will only be employed in a specific job within a limited range of productivities, thereby excluding many potential earners. Disequilibrium in the labour market goes well beyond the mismatching of skills and jobs: it is reflected in more general unemployment. Lack of employment opportunities for either specific occupational groups or for workers as a whole means that the horizontal benefit line in Figure 4.5 is extended to form the entire budget line. In the absence of Unemployment Benefit or Supplementary Benefit unearned income would yield a parallel budget line and a much lower standard of living for most workers. Deficient aggregate demand will reduce investment and disequilibrium in capital markets may mean that saving will not necessarily result in an increased capital stock.

Most earners incur expenses which would not arise if they did not work. Travel costs, protective clothing, union dues and the additional costs of eating outside the home are typical work expenses, although in some cases they may be partly or wholly subsidized by employers. Work expenses can be incorporated in the earlier framework by expressing the wage rate for earnings net of these costs. Transaction costs play a similar role in capital markets and can be accommodated in the same way.

Due to the time and trouble involved in acquiring information about earnings and the return on capital assets households may only be fully aware of one point on the budget line. For similar reasons only one area of the indifference curve may be known. In an equilibrium situation these information costs are immaterial but where conditions change they create problems. It will take time to appraise the new situation, time to decide on the appropriate adjustment and still more time to put the change in work or saving into effect. Where knowledge is imperfect a certain amount of trial and error may be involved in the adjustment process.

Information and adjustment costs provide one basis for dynamic theories of work and savings behaviour which are extensions of the dynamic consumption theory mentioned in Section 3.6. In the long run the analysis of the earlier sections remains valid but in empirical work successive disequilibrium states may be observed with little discernible relationship between wage rates and hours of income and saving. Behaviour will also reflect accumulated work experience, social class, education and a host of similar factors. As noted in Sections 4.2 and 4.3 preferences for consumption, leisure and saving may vary over the life-cycle, with greater emphasis on income and the acquisition of durable assets in the early stages and more concern about financial assets and leisure in later years.

The various complications considered in this section make the earlier analysis exceedingly complex. The interaction between capital, labour and output markets becomes too involved for verbal or geometric analysis. Yet clearly many of the complications can be accommodated within the framework developed in earlier sections and most of the results obtained there apply in more complex and realistic situations. The highly abstract approach which has been adopted is a rich source of testable hypotheses and quantifiable relationships between social security measures, work and savings behaviour.

4.7 Summary

Due to the size of the social security sector it may have a considerable influence on economic efficiency—the level of national output obtained with a given resource endowment. Several measures may influence the supply of labour—contributions, taxes, benefit levels, benefit withdrawal rates, cumulative marginal tax rates and so on. In considering how the choice between work and leisure may be distorted by social security it was convenient to distinguish between voluntary and involuntary benefit participants. While this demarcation was analytically useful it may prove to be of limited practical application due to the difficulty of distinguishing the two categories except in the case of the retired, where voluntary participation is numerically important.

The substitution of social security retirement and other benefits for private insurance may lead to a reduction in saving due to the replacement of funded income by current transfer payments. The higher propensity to save among the rich and much lower earnings replacement ratios for the better-off, coupled with the horizontal transfers involved, should together limit the adverse effect of social security on saving. Thus contributions will tend to lead to a fall in current consumption rather than to a decline in savings. Furthermore, the provision of retirement benefits will induce earlier and longer retirement leading to an increase in private saving.

The influence of social security measures on capital or labour markets will ultimately feed through to other sectors of the economy. A reduction in labour supply stemming from higher contributions or higher benefits will bring about a substitution of capital for labour. These consequent effects will, in turn, influence returns to labour and capital and may partly offset the intended outcome of the original measures.

Equity and efficiency objectives can be reconciled in a social welfare function which incorporates explicit distributional weights. Although these involve value judgements using a range of weights, or adopting the weights embodied in existing measures, this approach is operationally feasible. While it was suggested that horizontal equity could be dealt with first, leaving vertical equity and efficiency to be determined by the maximization of social welfare, it is recognized that this approach is not ideal. Further work needs to be done to show how horizontal equity, vertical equity and efficiency can be reconciled with one another.

The analysis of labour supply and saving indicated that both leisure and future consumption enter the household utility function. Taussig (1973) includes these and other factors in measuring the distribution of economic welfare in the US. Studies in this area have also made use of Becker's full income concept which implies that incomes of £40 and £30 for two earners yield the same welfare as an income of £40 for one earner when the second person withdraws from the labour market, since the opportunity-cost of home production is £30 in the latter case. However, the value of home production may be much lower. Others have argued that current incomes may be low because, for example, individuals are undergoing education and acquiring human capital which will enhance their lifetime incomes. Garfinkel and Haveman (1974) have therefore adopted a measure of earnings potential as a better indicator of living standards. In later chapters current weekly income alone modified to take account of the imputed rental of owner-occupied housing is adopted as the measure of economic welfare in households (Section 6.2). This seems appropriate in a study of social security for the reasons set out in Section 3.6: it also has the advantage of presenting fewer practical problems than wider definitions of living standards. Again this is an area where much further research needs to be done.

5. Horizontal Equity and Equivalence Scales

5.1 Introduction

The description of social security in Britain indicated that horizontal equity was an important objective of the system (Section 2.8). A conceptual framework was therefore developed in Chapter 3 for measuring living standards in households differing in composition and other characteristics. But greater equity is not the only objective of social security and the wider economic system. These ideas of equity were therefore integrated with notions of efficiency in Chapter 4 and the behavioural response of households was shown to be a potentially important issue. But the results obtained so far have been qualitative rather than quantitative: for most practical purposes the magnitudes of the various effects are more important than their direction. The remainder of the study will be largely concerned with applying the theoretical framework sketched in Chapters 3 and 4 in quantifying these aspects of social security. This chapter will focus on the question of horizontal equity: it will present estimates of equivalent commodity and income scales derived from household expenditure data.

5.2 Method and data

A change in household consumption stemming from differences in circumstances could, according to the analysis of Section 3.3, be decomposed into three distinct influences:

(i) a direct effect or commodity scale,
(ii) a price substitution effect,
(iii) an income effect or income scale.

Ideally we require estimates of all three separate influences on household commodity consumption. These would allow us to analyse the impact on living standards of changes in household circumstances, money incomes and market prices. Variations in any one of these three factors influences household utility and it is desirable to know the direction and magnitude of the effect.

The method used to estimate the equivalent commodity scales in this study unfortunately does not allow the direct and quasi price substitution effects to be disentangled. However, the estimates are based on cross-sectional data so that it can be assumed that market prices of goods and services are approximately constant. The price substitution effect for a commodity will therefore be constant for any specific household circumstance, e.g. an additional child. Thus the estimated commodity scales are a composite of the direct effect and the price substitution effect of a change in household circumstances. This means that in the case of a commodity which is entirely jointly consumed, or not consumed by a certain type of individual, the direct effect will be zero, whereas from Figures 3.6 and 3.7 the price substitution effect will lead to an increase in consumption by the household. As a result the composite commodity scale will be positive indicating an increase in consumption due to the price substitution effect. In the case of children, housing services may approximate a jointly consumed commodity while alcohol or tobacco will not be consumed by younger children although the composite commodity scales for all three goods would be positive.

The income scale is derived from the composite commodity scales and shows the income required to obtain a given standard of living after the price substitution effects have taken place (Section 3.3). Thus both the composite commodity and income scales relate to a given set of relative market prices and are not appropriate for different market price regimes. Nor can they be used to evaluate the impact of changing relative prices. A rather different approach will therefore be taken in considering the horizontal effects of relative price changes in Chapter 8.

The estimates also differ from the theory developed in Section 3.3 in a second respect. The income scale is given by the commodity scales weighted by their budget shares. As budget shares vary with income, for example, food tends to decline with increasing income *ceteris paribus*, the income scale will also vary with income. The method used to estimate the scales reported below has imposed a constant income scale at all income levels. This approximation, although computationally convenient, means that the income scales do not correspond exactly with the concepts discussed earlier.

The method itself is involved and will not be described here: a detailed description is given in McClements (1977b), while there is a less technical presentation in McClements (1977a). It is a modified version of the approach suggested by Prais and Houthakker (1955) and adopted by Singh and Nagar (1973). Very briefly, it involves starting with arbitrary but approximate commodity scales which are then improved in a two-stage iterative regression process using household expenditure data.

The estimated commodity and income scales in this chapter are based on information recorded in the 1971 and 1972 Family Expenditure Survey (FES). The FES, which covers about 7000 responding households annually, is described in HMSO (1973), *Family Expenditure Survey: Report for 1972*, while the sampling, fieldwork and questionnaire used in the survey are given in Kemsley (1969). A household expenditure unit, which is defined as individuals sharing living and eating arrangements, is used throughout. The use of a smaller unit would raise all the difficulties of involuntary and voluntary income sharing discussed in Section 3.5. The expenditure data are mainly averaged over the two-week survey period, although regular but infrequent payments are converted to a weekly amount. For owner-occupied or rent-free dwellings a rental is imputed on the basis of ratable value but the FES contains insufficient information to allow the flow of consumption services from other durable goods to be calculated.

A ten-commodity classification of goods and services is adopted below. Comparison of raised FES figures with national accounts estimates indicates a very considerable under-recording of alcohol expenditure and a less marked under-reporting of tobacco: this may affect the scales for these commodities. Moreover, some items of income, notably from investments, are also under-recorded and will affect some of the results discussed in Chapters 6 and 7. In this chapter total expenditure is utilized rather than income to take account of the imputed rental for housing.

5.3 Joint consumption and economies of scale

Before going on to present the results for children, adults and pensioners in the next three sections we need to clarify what is meant by joint consumption, how it relates to economies of scale and discuss the manifestation of these phenomena in the estimated commodity and income scales.

In Section 3.3 joint consumption was defined as the consumption of a unit of a good or service by two or more individuals in the household where the satisfaction derived by one person did not reduce that obtained by another. Housing services and durables are good illustrations of joint consumption. Two adults can share a kitchen, bathroom and living room obtaining the same standard of living as a single adult using the same facilities. Similarly, two people can watch a television or share a refrigerator.

Joint consumption arises for two related reasons. First, units of a good or service may be indivisible. It is not possible to have half a kitchen, bathroom, living room, television set or refrigerator—they come in single units. And second, by virtue of their indivisibility, it is not possible to attribute consumption entirely to one individual or another. If one individual left the household consumption of indivisible commodities would remain unchanged. Consumption could then be attributed to the remaining individual. But to whom should it be attributed in the two-or-more person household? Thus indivisibility and non-excludability give rise to joint consumption and it was essentially because of this phenomenon that the household unit was adopted in Section 3.5. Jointly consumed goods within the household have the same attributes as collective or public goods at the national level (*see* Section 9.2) and pose very similar problems of measurement and analysis.

At the other end of the spectrum there are goods which are divisible and can be attributed to individuals. Most household food and clothing consumption could, in theory, be allocated among household members although it might be difficult to do so in practice. But even here there may be an element of joint consumption. Food wastage in preparation and cooking may account for a declining proportion of the food budget with increasing household size at the same standard of living. Certain items of clothing may be shared, and so on. Two adults may be able to share the same kitchen or refrigerator to obtain the same standard of living. In practice the great majority of commodities will fall somewhere between the two extremes of pure joint consumption and entirely separable consumption. Most goods will be partly but not entirely attributable to individuals.

Economies of scale in household consumption are a manifestation of joint consumption—doubling household size does not result in a two fold increase in consumption at the same standard of living. If two identical individuals can share indivisible items like furniture or a refrigerator then joint consumption will be reflected by a zero commodity scale for the second adult—although the composite commodity scale discussed in Sections 3.5 and 5.2 will be positive. Thus a zero direct effect, or simple commodity scale, would indicate pure joint consumption or total economies of scale for the good in question and would tend to be reflected by a small positive composite commodity scale. The income scale for the second adult would also

reflect the overall economies of scale in consumption between one-
and two-adult households.

Measuring joint consumption and economies of scale is more difficult in practice because the individuals in the population are not
identical. Their needs vary in consequence, and it is not always possible to determine whether it is these differences in individual preferences or joint consumption which give rise to a small or zero commodity scale. Does a small housing scale for a first child reflect joint
consumption or the limited housing requirements of the child? A
zero alcohol and tobacco scale for a child will be due to the fact
that it does not consume these commodities. But how do we interpret
small alcohol and tobacco scales for women? They may have different preferences from men, and it would be wrong to confuse these
with joint consumption.

Clearly joint consumption and economies of scale can only be un-
ambiguously determined where we are dealing with identical individuals. Thus it is possible to think in terms of economies of scale
in family size and to measure it by comparing one, two, three-
and four-or-more-child families. But otherwise it is less straightforward. Children have different needs from married couples so it
is difficult to measure economies of scale for the first child. When
considering joint consumption in married-couple households compared with single men or women account needs to be taken of differences in preferences between men and women. In what follows
the term 'economies of scale' will be confined to comparisons
between identical individuals, or between commodity scales for individuals who are assumed to be similar in terms of having identical
needs.

5.4 Children

Casual observation suggests that an adolescent consumes much
more than a baby. And as a consequence of joint consumption of
commodities like housing a second, third or fourth child may not
involve as much overall additional expenditure as a first child of the
same age. How much more than a baby does an older child require?
How marked are economies of scale in additional children? This section considers these two basic issues. There are, of course, many
further questions which could be posed. Requirements may vary by
sex as well as by age. The sex of adjacent births in the family may
influence household expenditure on clothing and footwear while the
temporal spacing between successive children could have a similar

effect. These further questions have not been considered here because they are judged to be relatively unimportant compared with the effects of age and numbers of children.

Estimated commodity and income scales by age of child are shown in Table 5.1, a child being defined as an individual under 19 and in full-time education or under 5 years of age. The composite commodity scale for housing, at about 20 per cent of the married-couple scale, is roughly similar across age groups whereas the fuel scale increases gradually with age. A much more marked increase is evident

Table 5.1

Estimated equivalence scales by age of child
(married couple = 1.00)

| Commodity | Age of child in years | | | | | | | Budget share |
	0–1	2–4	5–7	8–10	11–12	13–15	16–18	
1. Housing	0·17	0·17	0·22	0·20	0·21	0·18	0·22	0·13
2. Fuel	0·12	0·16	0·17	0·18	0·14	0·19	0·15	0·07
3. Food	0·05	0·18	0·24	0·25	0·28	0·30	0·42	0·30
4. Alcohol	0·00	0·05	0·05	0·04	0·01	−0·01	0·07	0·05
5. Tobacco	0·03	0·02	0·03	0·03	−0·02	−0·01	0·09	0·06
6. Clothing and footwear	0·08	0·17	0·26	0·31	0·34	0·42	0·50	0·07
7. Durables	0·24	0·28	0·28	0·34	0·36	0·40	0·40	0·05
8. Other and miscellaneous	0·07	0·22	0·21	0·28	0·32	0·37	0·48	0·08
9. Transport and vehicles	0·15	0·23	0·24	0·29	0·33	0·33	0·50	0·12
10. Services	0·10	0·23	0·23	0·29	0·36	0·41	0·53	0·07
Income	0·09	0·18	0·21	0·23	0·25	0·27	0·36	1·00

in the food scale which increases fivefold between the youngest and the oldest age group. A food scale for a 16–18-year-old of 42 per cent of a married-couple scale is quite plausible if allowance is made for some economies in household food consumption with increasing family size. Too much importance cannot be attached to the commodity scales for alcohol and tobacco in view of the large recording errors in the data. Nevertheless they are generally small but positive, which is consistent with a zero direct effect and a positive price substitution of household consumption towards these commodities if living standards are held constant (Sections 3.3 and 5.2).

Like the food scale, the clothing and footwear scale increases quite rapidly with age and for older children it amounts to half the married-couple scale. In the younger age groups the durables scale is highest of all the commodity scales in absolute terms: it increases gradually up to the 5–7-year age group and more rapidly thereafter. For teenagers the durables scale amounts to 40 per cent of the married-couple scale. The commodity scale for other goods and miscellaneous expenditure, which includes children's pocket money, displays a marked increase with age to about half the married-couple scale for the oldest age group. The scales for transport and vehicles and services are higher than for other goods in the younger age ranges but increase less rapidly with age to about the same level for the oldest age group.

For commodities like housing and fuel the composite scales are roughly similar for all age groups; for durables and transport they increase gradually with age; while for food, clothing, other goods and services there is a more marked increase with age. The commodity scales weighted by the equivalent budget shares yield the income scale which reflects the broad pattern of results discussed above. Food, with an equivalent budget share of 0·30, predominates the income scale, followed by housing and transport with weights of 0·13 and 0·12. The income scale increases from about 9 per cent of the married-couple scale for a baby aged 0–1 years to about 36 per cent in the 16–18-year age category, although less confidence should be placed in the latter estimate because of the smaller numbers of children in the age range and the tendency for them to be in richer households. This fourfold increase in the income scale does not occur regularly with age. The greatest increases arise between the first two and last two age groups—from 0·09 to 0·18 in the first case and from 0·27 to 0·36 in the latter case. These increases are as great in absolute terms as those which occur over the four groups covering the 5–15-year age range.

Economies of scale in family size were investigated by estimating separate scales for married couples with one, two, three and four to six children: these results are presented more fully in McClements (1977b). The main evidence of economies of scale was for housing, with some slight indication for a few other commodities. And while the savings on housing were substantial when measured in terms of the additional housing requirements imposed by a third or fourth child compared with the first, they are negligible in terms of the income scale. If there are marked economies of scale in family size then they must arise with either the first child or with the fifth and subsequent children.

5.5 Adults

The requirements of pensioner and non-pensioner adult households may be influenced by differences in work status with pensioners spending less on food, clothing or travel and more on fuel and services. Households without children will therefore be considered as two separate groups—adults and pensioners. This section will focus on adult non-pensioner households which are defined as those with no dependent children and containing one or more adults who do not record their economic position as retired, although this criterion

Table 5.2

Equivalence scales for 1-man and 1-woman households
(married couple = 1.00)

Commodity	1 man	1 woman	Budget share
1. Housing	0·70	0·81	0·15
2. Fuel	0·47	0·64	0·08
3. Food	0·54	0·48	0·29
4. Alcohol	0·96	0·17	0·04
5. Tobacco	0·77	0·23	0·05
6. Clothing and footwear	0·33	0·38	0·08
7. Durables	0·38	0·49	0·05
8. Other and miscellaneous	0·46	0·52	0·08
9. Transport and vehicles	0·71	0·46	0·09
10. Services	0·56	0·66	0·09
Income	0·57	0·53	1·00

resulted in about half the one- and two-woman adult households containing Retirement Pensioners. Three questions about adult households are considered. How do single-adult households compare with married couples? Do two men or two women living together differ from a married couple? And do the third and subsequent adults in a household exhibit economies of scale?

Although social security policy does not provide different benefits for men and women, recorded consumption of tobacco and alcohol is much higher among males. In recognition of this difference in expenditure patterns single-adult households are classified by sex and the estimated equivalence scales are recorded in Table 5.2.

The composite commodity scales for housing indicate that a single adult incurs 70 to 80 per cent of a married couple's expenditure on housing at the same standard of living. Moving from one-adult to a two-adult household involves an additional 25 to 45 per cent expenditure on housing—not much more than the first or second child requires. Clearly there are substantial economies of scale in housing consumption. The commodity scale for fuel is much lower for single men than for single women, reflecting the high proportion of retired among the female group. Conversely, the food scale for women is lower due to age as well as the lower nutritional requirements of females. Because of the large recording errors in alcohol and tobacco expenditure these scales should be interpreted with caution. Taken at face value they indicate that single men consume almost as much alcohol as married couples and about three-quarters of the tobacco. If the division of alcohol and tobacco consumption within married-couple households is similar to this pattern between one-man and one-woman households, and the fact that the estimates add to about unity lends credence to this supposition, then it carries interesting implications for the question of intra-household distribution discussed in Section 3.5.

Of the remaining commodity scales all but transport and vehicles are higher for the single-woman household. Clothing and footwear, durables, other goods and services are more likely to be needed by women, whereas vehicles tend to be associated with men. However, while this pattern of results may accord with our intuitive notions it may also be influenced by the high proportion of retired among the single-woman households.

Despite higher expenditure on housing and fuel, the equivalent income scale for a single woman is lower, at about 53 per cent of the married-couple scale, than the scale of 57 per cent for a single man. This is mainly a consequence of lower expenditure on food, alcohol, tobacco and transport by the female households. These estimates may reflect, in part, the large number of female pensioner households in the sample and need to be treated with caution for this reason. Finally, the results also suggest that one man and one woman living in separate households need 110 per cent of the income of married couples to obtain the same standard of living. Furthermore, two men or two women living in separate households require additional income of 6 to 14 per cent compared with a married couple living together. If two-men or two-women households have similar requirements to a married couple then living together would involve economies of scale of this magnitude.

The expenditure of two-men and two-women households provides the basis for Table 5.3: the commodity and income scales display the same broad pattern as before. Thus two men or two women living together have similar housing requirements to a married couple. The lower fuel needs of two-men households and higher scale for two women households probably reflects greater labour market participation among the first category and the large number of retired in the second. These same factors will account for the opposite pattern in the food scales, although both are lower by 6 to 12 per cent compared with the food scales for single-man or -woman households respectively (Table 5.2). The most obvious explanation of the disparity is that there are economies of scale of this magnitude in food consumption between one- and two-adult households.

Table 5.3

Equivalence scales for 1 man or 1 woman in 2-men or 2-women households (married couple = 1.00)

Commodity	1 man in 2-men households	1 woman in 2-women households	Budget Share
1. Housing	0·50	0·53	0·14
2. Fuel	0·44	0·54	0·07
3. Food	0·51	0·42	0·27
4. Alcohol	1·07	0·15	0·05
5. Tobacco	0·72	0·24	0·05
6. Clothing and footwear	0·34	0·48	0·08
7. Durables	0·40	0·52	0·05
8. Other and miscellaneous	0·34	0·50	0·08
9. Transport and vehicles	0·66	0·37	0·12
10. Services	0·49	0·53	0·09
Income	0·52	0·44	1·00

As before, the alcohol and tobacco scales are much higher for men than for women—two men consume about twice as much alcohol, and one and a half times as much tobacco as a married couple. Of the remaining scales only the one for transport and vehicles is higher for men than for women and this parallels the earlier results. The larger commodity scales for food, alcohol, tobacco and transport result in an income scale which is higher for men than for women in two-adult households. Again, the higher proportion of retired women may be influencing the estimates and the comparison between the two groups should be made with care. But contrasting the income scales in Table 5.3 with those in Table 5.2 suggests that for households composed of two men expenditure behaviour is very similar to that of a married-couple household if an allowance is made for the apparently male-dominated nature of alcohol, tobacco and transport consumption. Furthermore, doubling the income scales in both tables suggests that two men or two women living together involve economies of scale in overall expenditure of 10 to 18 per cent, which is broadly in line with the estimate of 6 to 14 per cent derived from Table 5.2 alone.

Economies of scale are further investigated in multi-adult households using two sub-samples drawn from the 1971 and 1972 FES which are composed of married couples, three- and four-adult households. These differ from the earlier samples in that the great majority of the three- and four-adult households contain children

Table 5.4
Equivalence scales for third and fourth adults
(married couple = 1.00)

Commodity	Third adult	Fourth adult	Budget share
1. Housing	0·18	0·06	0·13
2. Fuel	0·32	0·26	0·06
3. Food	0·47	0·40	0·26
4. Alcohol	0·53	0·60	0·05
5. Tobacco	0·47	0·49	0·05
6. Clothing and footwear	0·56	0·48	0·08
7. Durables	0·41	0·35	0·05
8. Other and miscellaneous	0·40	0·30	0·08
9. Transport and vehicles	0·43	0·43	0·15
10. Services	0·46	0·39	0·09
Income	0·42	0·36	1·00

who are no longer dependant and this age factor may affect comparison with the previous results. The estimated equivalence scales are shown in Table 5.4 and the most marked feature of the results compared with Table 5.2 is the evidence of economies of scale.

A third adult adds 18 per cent to the married-couple housing scale while the fourth adult adds only 6 per cent. This first result is in line with the housing scale of about 20 per cent for children in Table 5.1 but the second suggests greater economies of scale than revealed in the estimates for children. Quite definite economies of scale are also evident from Table 5.4 for fuel, food, durables, other goods and services. For housing and durables the apparently contradictory evidence for adults and children may be due, in part, to differences in decision-making behaviour where households are composed of dependent and non-dependent children. There may also be life-cycle factors involved with expenditure behaviour anticipating the imminent departure of some members from the household. The absolute size of these various scales is broadly similar to those for the 16- to 18-year-old age range in Table 5.1. The income scales of 0·42 and 0·36 for the third and fourth adults respectively are also consistent with the results for older children. From Table 5.2 we can deduce that the second adult in a married-couple household adds 0·43 to 0·47 to the married couple's income scale, and the income scales of 0·42 and 0·36 in Table 5.4 are also in line with these earlier results.

5.6 Pensioners

Pensioner households, defined as one- and two-adult units where the head records his or her economic position as retired, may differ from adult households for a variety of reasons. Retirement may influence food consumption, most work expenses are not incurred, and because pensioners remain at home for most of the day, fuel and some other items of expenditure may be higher. If expenditure on durable commodities has a life-cycle dimension, then the expenditure of pensioner households will be influenced accordingly—although the imputation of a rental for housing services (Section 5.2) should partly circumvent the problem of capital accumulation and consumption.

These considerations, the earlier results, and the description of the social security system in Chapter 2, suggest three questions about pensioner households. What relative incomes are required by single- and married-couple pensioner households to obtain similar standards of living? Do the consumption of single male and female pensioners follow the pattern shown in the previous section? Is there evidence of changing requirements with age? The first question is of considerable practical importance given the large number of pensioner households in the population and the various measures aimed at this group. Single-pensioner households include a majority of females and while the second issue is more academic since males and females are usually treated equally, it may help to elucidate the first question. The extent to which needs change with age may also help to throw some light on the first two questions and is an important issue in its own right.

The relative requirements of single- and married-couple pensioners households are examined in Table 5.5. At the same standard of living the single pensioner spends about 80 per cent of the married couple on housing and about two-thirds as much on fuel. The food scale is over half, while for both tobacco and alcohol it is under half, of the married-couple scale. The clothing and footwear scale, at 41 per cent, is also low; both other and miscellaneous and transport and vehicles expenditure are over half, and the services scale amounts to 70 per cent, of the married-couple scale. The income scale suggests that the single person requires about 61 per cent of a married couple's income to obtain the same standard of living.

Like the estimates for adults the results in Table 5.5 point to considerable economies of scale in housing, fuel and services, with more

Table 5.5
Equivalence scales for single pensioners
(married couple = 1.00)

Commodity	Single pensioner	Budget share
1. Housing	0·83	0·19
2. Fuel	0·67	0·11
3. Food	0·54	0·33
4. Alcohol	0·49	0·03
5. Tobacco	0·47	0·05
6. Clothing and footwear	0·41	0·06
7. Durables	0·50	0·04
8. Other and miscellaneous	0·55	0·08
9. Transport and vehicles	0·55	0·05
10. Services	0·70	0·08
Income	0·61	1·00

limited economies in food, other goods, transport and services. However, about two-thirds of the single pensioner households are female and the results in Table 5.5 are more similar to those for women in Table 5.2.

The difference between single male and female households is investigated further by distinguishing between the two types of single-pensioner household, and the estimated equivalence scales are given in Table 5.6. The results reflect the same pattern as shown for adults in Table 5.2: women have higher scales for housing, fuel, clothing, durables, other and miscellaneous goods, and services; while their alcohol and tobacco scales are much lower than for men. Again these results provide some insight into the possible distribution of consumption within the married couple household. The male pensioner income scale, 0·57, is the same as for the male adult in Table 5.2, but the single-female scale of 0·62 is considerably higher than the 0·53 shown earlier. This is mainly due to the higher housing and food scales in the pensioner's case. The single female pensioner results are probably of greatest applicability in view of the disproportionate number of this household type.

The third question, possible changes in requirements with age, is examined by classifying married-couple households into four age groups—under 30 years, 30 to 49 years, 50 to 64 years and 65 years or more. Families had to be included to obtain an adequate sample

Table 5.6

Equivalence scales for single male and female pensioners
(married couple = 1.00)

Commodity	Single man	Single woman	Budget shares
1. Housing	0·75	0·92	0·19
2. Fuel	0·66	0·71	0·10
3. Food	0·53	0·54	0·32
4. Alcohol	0·76	0·36	0·03
5. Tobacco	0·89	0·18	0·05
6. Clothing and footwear	0·21	0·38	0·07
7. Durables	0·34	0·55	0·04
8. Other and miscellaneous	0·51	0·54	0·07
9. Transport and vehicles	0·54	0·53	0·05
10. Services	0·50	0·75	0·09
Income	0·57	0·62	1·00

and children were classified according to four age ranges based on the results of Table 5.1: 0–1 years, 2–10 years, 11–15 years and 16–18 years. The estimated commodity scales for married couples, taking the oldest age range as the reference group, are shown in Table 5.7. Fuel needs are generally lower among younger households, whereas food requirements are higher. Younger households also spend more on durables and vehicles than older households. But the main conclusion to be drawn from Table 5.7 is that while expenditure patterns do vary with age, the overall effect in terms of income is negligible. The main differences in expenditure patterns, as reflected in the budget shares of Tables 5.5 and 5.6 compared with the earlier tables, is due to the lower income, on average, in pensioner households

Table 5.7

Equivalence scales for married couples classified by age of household head (married couple aged 65 or over = 1.00)

Commodity	Age of household head			Budget shares
	< 30	*30–49*	*50–64*	
1. Housing	0·99	0·96	0·96	0·16
2. Fuel	0·87	0·88	1·03	0·08
3. Food	1·01	1·02	1·08	0·29
4. Alcohol	1·12	0·96	1·03	0·04
5. Tobacco	1·07	1·02	1·09	0·05
6. Clothing and tobacco	0·97	1·03	0·98	0·07
7. Durables	1·04	1·00	0·96	0·05
8. Other and miscellaneous	1·02	1·08	1·00	0·08
9. Transport and vehicles	1·05	1·03	0·99	0·11
10. Services	0·95	1·01	1·03	0·08
Income	0·99	1·00	1·02	1·00

rather than any more fundamental difference in expenditure behaviour.

This conclusion may minimize age effects because it is based on married-couple households. Some of the differences between single-male and -female pensioner households evident from Table 5.6 may in fact reflect the greater average age of the female pensioners. This could result in higher fuel and services scales, for example. And a higher proportion of the single females are surviving spouses which may account in part for the larger housing scale: consumption of housing services has not been adjusted after the death of a husband. For these reasons a comparison of single adults, or possibly single females and males, classified by age might yield more marked age variations in the scales.

5.7 Summary of results

The results for children, adults and pensioners are in broad agreement. Many of the commodity scales for a dependent child aged 16–18 years are similar to those estimated for a third or fourth adult. In the case of food, the scale for a 16–18-year-old child is 0·42 compared with 0·47 for a third adult and 0·40 for a fourth adult. The food scale for the single adult and single pensioner is somewhat higher, at up to 55 per cent of the married couple's consumption, reflecting some economies of scale in food consumption. The scales for clothing and footwear, and for durables, are also broadly comparable between the oldest child and the third or fourth adult. A major difference arises in the alcohol and tobacco scales, which are very much higher for third and fourth adults who are mainly non-dependent offspring living with their parents. This, like the difference in these scales for men and women discussed in Section 5.5, may reveal something of the decision-making process of the two types of household and the consequent distribution of consumption within the household. Alternatively, it may also reflect the large recording errors which are known to exist for these two commodities.

The results for adult households are very much in line with the estimates for pensioners. There are quite marked economies of scale in housing with the single adult or pensioner requiring 70 to 80 per cent of the married-couple scale at the same standard of living. Less marked economies of scale are evident in fuel and services expenditure; these scales are generally higher for single females in contrast with alcohol, tobacco and vehicles, which are male-dominated. However, these differences will also reflect the greater labour force attachment of male adults.

The evidence on joint consumption is broadly consistent for family, adult and pensioner households. The commodity scale for housing is relatively small for all individuals compared with the first adult. The limited economies of scale in housing with increasing family size are something of a puzzle compared with the marked evidence for the fourth adult and the explanation may lie in life-cycle aspects of housing consumption. Fuel economies of scale are also evident but the picture is complicated by some differences between males and females with the requirements of the latter being greater than the former. Similar, but even more marked variations are apparent for the services scales. The transport and vehicles scale also displays some evidence of joint consumption which one would expect for the vehicles component of this group, but again the picture is complicated by a marked difference between males and females. Perhaps the most surprising result is the evidence of very little joint consumption of durables. This may be partly due to the definition of durables which include many smaller items in addition to the usual household durables but exclude any of the latter which are hired and therefore fall in the services group.

For commodities like food, clothing and footwear, other goods and miscellaneous expenditure, there is evidence of limited, if any, joint consumption. Again this is consistent with casual observation: there may be some economies in buying larger packets of food and cooking together for larger households but they are limited compared with housing, services or fuel.

This broad pattern of commodity scales is reflected in the income scales. For most policy applications of the results the sex differences in expenditure behaviour are irrelevant as men and women are treated equally. These are therefore ignored in Table 5.8, which summarizes the income scales for different types of individual. Because there is a relatively small number of single-adult households in the non-pensioner population the single-pensioner result is applied to this group. Section 2.6 indicated that some of the relativities embodied in social policy measures related to income net of housing expenditure and another row is therefore included, giving the income scale net of the housing scale. The greatest difference between the income scale and the income scale net of housing arises for single-adult households where there are very considerable economies in housing consumption.

5.8 Comparison with other estimates

It is instructive to compare the results with other estimates in the literature. These other estimates have been obtained using different approaches; they relate to different price regimes and in one case to a different country, so the scales may differ for these reasons. By far the most comprehensive British estimates are incorporated in the household budgets which provide the basis for the recommendations of the Beveridge Report (HMSO, 1942, Cmd 6404). Stark (1972) bases his equivalence scales on a geometric mean of three other scales, one of which is derived from the Beveridge Report's budgets. The third set of scales relate to the US (Orshansky, 1965): they are based on the cost of providing a low-cost diet multiplied by a factor of three for households of three or more persons, by 3.7 for two-person households, while one-person households are attributed a proportion of the two-person scale. Thus the third set of scales is largely based on a food budget for larger households modified by factors to account for diseconomies in smaller households.

The equivalence scales implicit in the Beveridge Report subsistence budgets are shown in Table 5.9 together with the married-couple budget shares for the various commodities. The subsistence budget ⁰shares for other household types generally show an increasing proportion devoted to food and a declining share going to housing and fuel with increasing household size. This reflects the underlying

Table 5.8

Summary of equivalent income scales including and excluding housing

Scale	Dependent child aged (years)							Adult			Married couple
	0–1	2–4	5–7	8–10	11–12	13–15	16–18	Fourth	Third	Single	
Income scale net of housing	0·07	0·18	0·21	0·23	0·26	0·28	0·38	0·40	0·45	0·55	1·00
Income scale	0·09	0·18	0·21	0·23	0·25	0·27	0·36	0·36	0·42	0·61	1·00

Table 5.9

Equivalence scales implicit in Beveridge Report subsistence budgets

Commodity	Child aged				Non-dependant 16–17 years	Single adult	Married couple	
	0–4 years	5–9 years	10–13 years	14–15 years			Scales	Budget shares
Housing	0·00	0·00	0·00	0·00	0·15	0·65	1·00	0·31
Fuel, etc.	0·06	0·06	0·06	0·06	0·00	0·63	1·00	0·13
Food	0·35	0·46	0·54	0·58	0·58	0·54	1·00	0·41
Clothing	0·19	0·28	0·33	0·42	0·50	0·50	1·00	0·09
Margin	0·00	0·00	0·00	0·00	0·75	0·75	1·00	0·06
Income	0·16	0·22	0·26	0·28	0·38	0·59	1·00	1·00

Source: HMSO (1942), Cmd 6404, paras. 222, 226 and 227–8; budgets for non-pensioner households and single males have been used in constructing the table.

assumption that the latter commodities are, by and large, jointly consumed. Comparing Table 5.9 with the commodity scales in Tables 5.1 and 5.5 some very marked differences are apparent. The housing scale for children is about 0·20 in Table 5.1, whereas it is assumed to be zero in Table 5.9. The estimated fuel scale is two to three times the Beveridge allowance although this may reflect a change in life styles between 1938 and 1971–72. The food scale is much lower for the younger age groups in Table 5.1 and although it increases quite rapidly with age, it only amounts to 30 per cent of the married-couple scale for the 13- to 15-year age group compared with 58 per cent in the subsistence budget. As the Beveridge food allowance was based on attaining recommended dietary levels, the divergence may reflect a difference between nutritional theory and household behaviour. The clothing scales are nearly identical in the two tables although the Beveridge clothing budget was based on the subsistence allowance for food. The overall effect in Table 5.9 is that the income scales are very close to the estimates in Table 5.1: the quite different commodity scales for children and implicit budget shares combine to yield income scales which are very similar.

Comparing Table 5.5 and the single-adult column in Table 5.9 reveals a less marked difference in the commodity scales. The subsistence allowance for housing is lower than the estimated equivalence scale although the fuel and food scales are similar. The overall effect is a Beveridge recommendation somewhat lower, at 0·59, than the estimated income scale of 0·61 in Table 5.5.

Comparisons between the equivalence scale estimates and the Stark (1972) and Orshansky (1965) figures are more difficult because the latter studies do not distinguish children by age. For comparative purposes the scales for a child aged 8–10 years are adopted and it is assumed that in households with three or more individuals the additional persons are children. As two of the three scales on which the Stark (1972) geometric mean is based related to income net of housing, the equivalent income scale net of housing is also shown in Table 5.10. The income scales implicit in the Beveridge subsistence budgets are included to complete the picture and a child income scale of 0·24 is assumed being midway between the scales for a 5–9-year-old and a 10–13-year-old in Table 5.9.

The main difference between the various income scales in Table 5.10 occurs for the single-adult household. If the Stark (1972) scale is net of housing expenditure then at 0·63 it is high compared with the estimated income scale net of housing which is 0·55. The Orshansky (1965) scale for a single adult is also considerably higher than the equivalent income scale. On the basis of nutritional

Table 5.10
Comparison of estimated equivalent income scales with scales implicit in other studies

	Single adult	Married couple	Married couple with			
			1 child	2 children	3 children	4 children
Income scale net of housing	0·55	1·00	1·23	1·46	1·69	1·92
Income scale	0·61	1·00	1·23	1·46	1·69	1·92
Beveridge Report	0·59	1·00	1·24	1·48	1·72	1·96
Stark (1972)	0·63	1·00	1·31	1·56	1·75	2·00
Orshansky (1965)*	0·69	1·00	1·16	1·48	1·72	1·93

* Based on low-cost non-farm budgets for all households under 65 years of age.

requirements the US estimates also show scales for pensioner households which are up to 10 per cent below those for non-pensioners. Our estimates in Table 5.7 indicate that in younger households food requirements are 1 to 8 per cent higher than in pensioner households. However, for commodities as a whole, and hence for the income scale, there is no evidence that pensioners' needs are lower. Any reduction in the food scale is offset by higher requirements for fuel and other commodities. It is clear from this comparison that the different approaches can lead to very different estimates of commodity and income scales.

5.9 Conclusions

It could be argued that the estimates of equivalence scales presented in this chapter show what households actually do, not what they ought to do and that in consequence the results are irrelevant to social policy. It is true that the estimates are based on actual household behaviour although, because of methodological limitations and data inadequacies, they are undoubtedly less exact than we would like. But actual behaviour may be considered an inadequate guide for policy action for two reasons.

First we may have ideas about what 'ought' and what 'ought not' to be consumed by others and by the poor in particular. Alcohol and tobacco may be considered undesirable, whereas food, housing and clothing may be viewed as suitable. A judgement of this kind would seem to underlie the Beveridge subsistence budgets for they only covered housing, fuel, food and clothing with a small margin for other goods and wastage. The difficulty with this view is that it also implies that cash benefits, the basis of the social security system, are not an appropriate instrument. Short of reforming beneficiaries, the only way to ensure that they spend their incomes as the 'ought' is through the provision of benefits-in-kind. And as we saw in Section 3.4 determining what households of different composition 'ought' to spend on one or more commodities is fraught with difficulty. It would certainly seem to involve judgements of the first type discussed in Section 1.3 which lie beyond the domain of economic analysis.

The second reason which some would advance for discarding actual behaviour is that the existing behavioural pattern is unduly constrained. The incomes of pensioners are generally low and since most receive Retirement Pensions the estimated equivalence scales may simply reflect existing relativities. If all pensioners had no other source of income, or if another group like families with young children or one-parent families were universally poor, there would be considerable force in this argument. However, in the next chapter, which considers the distribution of living standards for different household types, we see that this is not the case. While some groups may be poorer than others on average, there is a wide dispersion of living standards within each category. Moreover, the estimated equivalence scales are based on all households in the income distribution, not just poor households.

Yet there is some substance in the argument that actual household behaviour does not always yield a guide for policy decisions. While measures may, by and large, be framed to reflect existing values and behaviour, some instruments are designed to bring about change. To the extent that interest is centred on society as it is, then clearly actual household behaviour is important. But where measures are designed to change society and modify behaviour, then what people actually do may be less relevant. Distribution within the household and the different expenditure patterns of males and females are cases in point. These aspects of actual behaviour may be consciously judged to be undesirable and measures taken to modify human action. In one case it may involve paying equal benefits to men and women, whereas in another it may require the payment of benefit to the mother rather than the father of the child. Yet in both illustrations actual household behaviour is of some importance—it needs to be known and understood before the desired action can be taken.

For most purposes we can conclude that actual household behaviour, as reflected in equivalent commodity and income scales, is important in formulating social security measures. And the approach adopted in this chapter would seem to have some advantage over alternative methods which have been adopted in the literature. As Section 3.4 pointed out, it involves fewer difficult judgements in at least three important areas and, as we have seen, these can influence results to a considerable extent. But actual household behaviour is not the only consideration taken into account in formulating some social security measures.

6. Vertical Equity and Household Characteristics

6.1 Introduction

The estimated equivalence scales reported in the previous chapter will be used in this and the next three chapters to examine the distribution of living standards and show how they are influenced by transfers, subsidies, prices and goods provided by the public sector which are allocated by non-market mechanisms. In so doing not only are inter-household type welfare comparisons necessary, but averages for equivalent income quintile groups are given and these imply that living standards can be measured cardinally within quintiles (Section 3.2). The division of the equivalent income distribution into groups containing equal numbers of households is in the spirit of the relative approach discussed in Section 3.4 and quintiles are adopted largely for presentational convenience. However, it does avoid explicit distributional judgements of the type discussed in Section 4.5, leaving the reader free to attach whatever weights are deemed appropriate in comparing quintile averages. In this chapter the emphasis will be on the vertical distribution of living standards in households of different types. Subsequent chapters will consider the impact of income transfers, prices and non-market goods on living standards. Throughout Chapters 6 to 9 the emphasis will be on the measurement of initial incidence effects on the basis of prevailing behaviour as recorded in the 1975 FES. No account will be taken of the possibility that observed behaviour may be conditioned to a greater or lesser extent by the factors being studied. This approach is convenient because we know very little about the quantitative importance of behavioural responses to the British social security system. Chapter 10 goes on to consider in more detail potential behavioural response and reviews the available evidence on this important subject.

In Chapters 6 to 9 current income is adopted as the basic definition from which the various distributions are derived. Despite its limitations this measure is preferred over alternatives like annual, permanent or lifetime income for the reasons discussed in Section 3.6. The decisive argument for using current income is that it provides the closest approximation to the operational concepts embodied in the social security system. The household will also be utilized as the basic unit of analysis. Although it does not always correspond with the benefit unit it avoids difficult assumptions about the extent of involuntary and voluntary income sharing within the household.

6.2 Data

The distributions of living standards in Chapters 6 to 9 are based on the 1975 FES which covered 7203 households: the results are summarized in HMSO (1976), *Family Expenditure Survey 1975*. Although the equivalent income scales in Table 5.8 were based on the 1971 and 1972 FES, they have been applied to the 1975 data. The absolute level of prices changed quite dramatically over this period, but changes in relative prices were less marked. Thus the equivalent income scales based on the 1971–72 price regime should not be too unsuitable when applied to the 1975 data and provide the best available estimates.

Unless stated otherwise all the figures derived from the 1975 FES in this and subsequent chapters are based on FES sample numbers for the UK. No adjustments are made for response bias which leads to under-representation of older households and too many children—*see* Kemsley (1975) for other factors associated with the response rate. From a comparison of the number of individuals in the FES with non-institutional home population figures a simple raising factor of 2765 can be applied to obtain household population figures. Nor has any adjustment been made for reporting errors. Where either response bias or reporting errors are thought to be important they will be mentioned but in general they do not affect the broad conclusions to be drawn from the sample survey numbers.

In Chapter 5 Total Expenditure was used rather than income to ensure that commodity expenditure added up. From now on a net household income concept will be used in measuring standards of living. Ideally we require the best available indicator of potential command over market goods and services. Thus it should exclude statutory deductions but include benefits-in-kind, public and private, at their value to consumers. Income is defined as gross household income in the last week or month prior to the FES survey period net of income tax and employee National Insurance contributions.

Income in kind is included, as is the imputed value of Free School Meals, self-supply goods and Rent and Rate Rebates and Allowances. These items are valued at market prices which will, in general, be higher than their value to consumers (Section 9.2). Retail prices increased by 25 per cent during 1975 so that the volume of market goods and services which a given money income would purchase fell accordingly. Net money income of households surveyed throughout the twelve-month period is therefore adjusted to December 1975 prices using the Retail Price Index. The use of a single index is not ideal as Section 8.4 will show, but it provides a means of getting closer to the desired measure than money income in different months of the year.

Rent-free and owner-occupied housing pose special difficulties. Some households in these categories will enjoy quite a high standard of accommodation although they pay nothing or very little for it: others with recently acquired mortgages will be incurring large payments for the same volume of housing services. The imputed rental for housing services, calculated as described in HMSO (1976), *Family Expenditure Survey 1975*, Appendix 3, is therefore added to net income. But for those households with mortgages, interest payments are deducted from net income. None of these adjustments is ideal, but they are judged as giving the best available approximation to the household's command over market goods and services.

6.3 Distribution of living standards

Household net income, as defined in the previous section, is divided by the appropriate household equivalent income scale to yield household equivalent net income. For convenience throughout the rest of the study household net income and household equivalent net income will be simply referred to as money income and equivalent income respectively.

The household equivalent income scale is based on Table 5.8, the estimated scales being multiplied by the number of each type of individual in the household and summed over all individuals. Thus a married couple with two children aged 11–12 years has an income scale of 1·50 while a single-adult household has an income scale of 0·61, and so on. Dividing money income by the equivalent income scale yields equivalent income. It represents the money income which households of different composition would require to obtain their existing standard of living if they consisted of a married couple alone. In the case of a single adult a money income of £30.50 per week yields an equivalent income of £50. For a married couple with two children aged 11–12 years a money income of £75 is required to provide the same standard of living or equivalent income as a married couple with a money income of £50.

Thus equivalence scales provide a convenient method of calibrating living standards in households of different size and composition: 'rich' and 'poor' and all points between the two extremes can be defined quite simply in terms of equivalent income. By concentrating on equivalent income we can focus on the vertical distribution of living standards. Changing from a money to an equivalent income basis has a quite marked effect on the shape of the distribution (Figure 6.1). The distribution of equivalent income or living standards, which averaged £52, is much more peaked and has a thinner and shorter upper tail than money income. There is a correlation between household size and money income so the distribution of living standards is more equitable than money income would suggest because requirements also increase with household size.

Nevertheless there remains a very considerable gap between the upper and lower ends of the equivalent income distribution: the lower quintile is less than half of the top quintile and the mean of the top group is almost four times the mean of the bottom quintile. But note that even with inter-household type comparisons and cardinal utility we cannot say that the top quintile enjoys twice the standard of living of the bottom quintile or that the average in the top is about four times that in the bottom group. To make statements of this nature, or of the kind made in the previous paragraph contrasting the money and equivalent income distributions, requires an additional assumption about the marginal utility of equivalent income—that it is constant across the equivalent income distribution. Such an assumption is entirely arbitrary (Section 4.5), and is not required for the purpose of this or the next two chapters although distributional judgements arise in Chapter 9 and will be further discussed there. In the meantime it is only necessary to accept that a higher equivalent income is indicative of a higher standard of living without quantifying the extent of the improvement.

The distinction between persons, tax and household units was drawn in Table 2.1 and the definition of the appropriate unit of analysis was discussed at some length in Section 3.5. The distribution of persons, family units and households, classified into single and multiple tax unit households, is shown in Table 6.1 by household equivalent income quintiles. The family unit is defined as a nuclear family and does not correspond with the tax unit definition in Table 2.1: basically the family unit consists of a single person or married

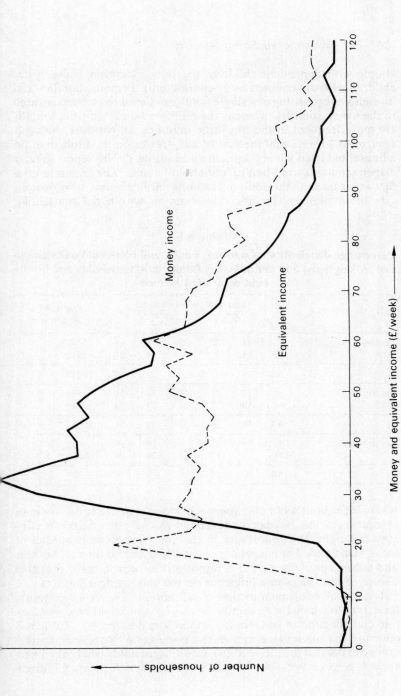

FIGURE 6.1 *The distribution of money and equivalent income,*[1] *1975*

Money income

Equivalent income

Money and equivalent income (£/week) ——

Number of households

[1] The equivalent income quintiles are £31·35, £40·83, £51·77 and £67·49 while the quintile means are £25·31, £35·93, £46·17, £58·89 and £93·87.

couple with dependent children, the only exception being foster children who are counted as a separate unit. Persons, families and households consisting of a single family unit tend to be concentrated in the lower quintiles, whereas the multiple family unit households are more frequent in the top three quintiles. In contrast, Morgan *et al.* (1962) found that inequality was greater on an adult than on a household basis while Fiegehen and Lansley (1976) report greater dispersion in tax unit than in household income. The apparent conflict arises because the adult or tax units implicitly assume no voluntary or involuntary income redistribution within the household,

Table 6.1

Percentage distribution of persons, family and household units classified by single (S) and multiple (M) family unit households and household equivalent income

Unit		Equivalent income quintile					Total number (100 per cent)
		1	*2*	*3*	*4*	*5*	
Persons	S	21	22	23	18	16	14342
	M	11	17	23	28	21	5912
	All	18	21	23	21	17	20254
Family units	S	23	21	19	18	19	5602
	M	10	15	23	29	24	3630
	All	18	19	21	22	21	9232
Households	S	23	21	19	18	19	5602
	M	10	15	23	28	24	1601
	All	20	20	20	20	20	7203

whereas the household unit approach adopted in Table 6.1 assumes complete sharing. Neither of these polar cases is correct and the contrast highlights the importance of the unit of analysis in studies of living standards. The household unit will be adopted throughout this and subsequent chapters: it is important to bear in mind that this choice of unit has some influence on the various distributions.

The overall equivalent income distribution in Figure 6.1 conceals the extent to which living standards vary by household type. A nine-fold classification of households is therefore presented in Table 6.2 covering the main categories in the population. Pensioner households are defined as one- and two-adult households where the head exceeds pension age—60 years for women and 65 for men. Children are individuals under the age of 16 or under 19 years and in full-time education: all other persons are classed as adults. Due to the use of a household unit a substantial minority of one-parent families fall in the 'other households with children' category, and because of the small numbers one-parent households are subject to larger sampling errors than other groups.

Three broad conclusions can be drawn from Table 6.2. First, pensioners as a whole are very poor, with about two-fifths falling in the poorest 20 per cent of all households. And single pensioners are marginally poorer than married-couple pensioner households. Second, non-pensioner adult households without children are relatively

Table 6.2

Percentage distribution of household types by equivalent income

Household type	Equivalent income quintile					Number of households (100 per cent)
	1	2	3	4	5	
Single adult	16	12	14	21	38	471
Two adults	8	10	15	26	41	1460
Other adult households	7	9	22	29	33	656
One-parent families	50	20	13	10	7	164
Two adults, 1–2 children	12	21	32	23	13	1636
Two adults, 3+ children	27	32	23	12	6	521
All other households with children	13	21	25	28	13	592
Single pensioner	44	31	11	8	7	971
Married-couple pensioner	39	28	14	11	8	732
All households	20	20	20	20	20	7203

rich: about two-fifths fall in the richest quintile. Finally, households with children are, on average, neither rich nor poor but fall between the adult and pensioner groups. And within families as a whole single parents are by far the poorest, being even worse off than single pensioners. Larger families with three or more children are also poorer than small families or multi-adult households with children. Coverdale (1976) has carried out a more detailed analysis of the characteristics of the poorest quintile.

Thus pensioners on the whole are poorest, families have an intermediate standard of living and adult households as a group are richest. But going beyond these generalizations, there is a very wide distribution of living standards within each of the three groups or within the nine household type classification in Table 6.2. Some pensioners and one-parent families are in the richest quintile while some two-adult households are in the poorest 20 per cent. There is no categorization by household type which corresponds exactly, or even closely, with living standards.

6.4 Families

The 2913 households with children in Table 6.2 will be considered in more detail to determine some of the factors associated with variations in family living standards. From the results in Section 5.4 it seems that in addition to household income, numbers of children and their ages may be important. But these three factors are not independent. One would expect the earnings of the mother to fall with increasing family size due to a lower likelihood of being in the labour force. On the other hand labour market participation of mothers will tend to increase with the ages of children generally and with the age of the youngest child in particular. However, the requirements of children increase with age. There is also a greater chance that, as a child grows older, there will be two or more earners in the household as more senior siblings enter the labour market. The importance of these various factors cannot be determined *a priori*: it is largely an empirical matter. These questions are investigated using the 1975 FES and it is important to remember that the situation may change gradually over time with the evolution of labour market and household behaviour.

The distribution of family size by equivalent income quintiles is shown in Table 6.3. The proportion of each family size in the bottom or second quintile generally increases with number of children:

Table 6.3
Percentage distribution of families of different size by equivalent income

Family size— number of children	Equivalent income quintile					Number of household (100 per cent)
	1	*2*	*3*	*4*	*5*	
1	12	17	28	28	16	1028
2	15	23	31	21	10	1207
3	20	33	25	14	7	438
4	38	29	21	8	4	154
5	59	34	6	0	0	64
6+	68	23	9	0	0	22
All families	17	23	28	21	11	2913

larger families are much more likely to be poor. Yet family size is not an effective way of identifying poor children due to their concentration in smaller families. About four-fifths of all children live in families with three or fewer children and only around 30 per cent of children in the bottom two quintiles are to be found in larger families.

Some of the main sources of income within the household, classified by family size, are given in Table 6.4. For two- and three-child families the gross earnings of the household head account for about three-quarters of the total, but in the case of five-child families it

Table 6.4

Sources of income and labour force participation of second adult for families of different size

Number of children	Per cent of gross income from:				Labour force participation of second adult[1] (per cent)
	Earnings of head	Earnings of second adult	Unearned income	Social security benefits	
1	69	14	3	4	50
2	76	12	2	5	57
3	75	11	2	6	62
4	70	10	1	13	49
5	51	12	1	25	35
6+	68	9	1	19	18
All families	73	12	2	5	55

[1] Relates to 2104 married couple households only

is as low as half of household income. This is partly a consequence of increasing social security income—due to a higher probability of being on short- or long-term benefits and to family-size related Family Allowances. Gross unearned income and the earnings of the second adult both decline with increasing family size. The final column of Table 6.4 shows the labour force participation of wives in the 2014 families where the adults consisted of a married couple alone. The declining contribution of the second adult with increasing family size is partly due to a substitution of part-time work or self-employment for full-time employment as well as to a fall in labour force participation *per se*. The remainder of household income comes from a diverse range of sources including the earnings of other adults, benefits-in-kind, and the imputed value of rent-free or owner-occupied accommodation.

The estimated equivalence scales in Table 5.1 showed a fourfold increase between the youngest and oldest age groups. The distribution of living standards will, other things being equal, tend to reflect this fact by showing a higher concentration of younger children in richer households. However, there is likely to be a higher concentration of older children in families with adult siblings while the typical earnings profile for men tends to increase with the ages of their children. Moreover, the mother is more likely to work as the child grows older.

These possibilities are examined by considering households classified by the age of the youngest child (Table 6.5). Excluding the

Table 6.5

Percentage distribution of households classified by age of youngest child and equivalent income

Age of youngest child (years)	Equivalent income quintile					Number of households (100 per cent)
	1	2	3	4	5	
0–1	19	25	30	16	10	534
2–4	22	27	27	17	6	704
5–7	20	24	26	21	9	511
8–10	16	22	27	22	13	444
11–12	12	23	28	22	15	260
13–15	8	13	29	33	17	378
16–18	5	13	24	39	18	82
All ages	14	25	26	22	13	2913

youngest age range, there is a falling proportion of households in the lowest quintile as the age of the youngest child increases and conversely in the top quintile. But aside from the top and bottom quintiles there is practically no association between the age of the youngest child and living standards: the overall relationship is a very loose one. Some of the factors contributing to this loose relationship are evident from Table 6.6. The share of the household head's earnings falls, while that of the second adult increases markedly, with the age of the youngest child. The contributions of gross unearned income and social security benefits are relatively unimportant. The final column of Table 6.6, which again refers to the 2104 married-couple households in the sample, displays a threefold increase in labour force participation as the youngest child in the family grows

Table 6.6

Sources of income and labour force participation of second adult for families classified by age of youngest child

Age of youngest child	Per cent of gross income from:				Labour force participation of second adult[1] (per cent)
	Earnings of head	Earnings of second adult	Unearned income	Social security benefits	
0–1	87	4	2	5	29
2–4	80	8	1	6	47
5–7	73	14	2	5	65
8–10	69	15	2	6	71
11–12	63	19	2	5	75
13–15	58	18	4	4	76
16–18	59	18	5	3	80

[1] Relates to 2104 married couple households only

older. One interesting feature of the constituent elements which lie behind this column is the extent to which self-employment is substituted for by part-time or full-time employment as the youngest child grows older. Self-employment accounts for over half of the labour force participation in the youngest age range and for very little in the oldest age groups.

In conclusion, this analysis of living standards in households with children shows that larger families are more likely to be poor than smaller families. The ages of children are relatively unimportant, as there is a very loose connection with the age of the youngest child. One important reason why families become better-off as the

Table 6.7

Percentage distribution of adult households

Household type	Equivalent income quintile					Total number (100 per cent)
	1	2	3	4	5	
One adult	16	12	14	21	38	471
Two adults	8	10	166	26	41	1460
Married couple with non-dependent children	6	8	20	31	35	462
Other	8	11	28	25	28	194
All-adult households	9	10	17	26	38	2587

youngest child grows older is the threefold increase in the labour force participation of the mother and the even greater rise in her proportionate contribution to household income.

6.5 Adults

In this section we consider the living standards of the next largest of the three broad groups in the population—the 2587 households headed by adults and composed of adults and pensioners. Adults are defined as individuals below pension age and not in full-time education if over the age of sixteen. This is a rather heterogeneous group of households. The two-adult households fall mainly into two distinct categories: married couples who have not yet had children and those with completed families who have left home. This group

Table 6.8

Sources of income in adult households

Per cent of gross income from:	*Equivalent income quintile*					*All households*
	1	*2*	*3*	*4*	*5*	
Earnings of head	27	52	57	60	63	60
Earnings of second adult	7	8	11	19	22	19
Earnings of other adults	2	7	11	10	6	7
Total earnings	36	67	79	89	90	86

constitutes the richest group in the household population: two-fifths are in the top quintile (Table 6.7).

The main reasons for the affluence of adult households can be seen with the aid of Table 6.8, which shows sources of gross earnings within the household. Earnings as a whole account for 86 per cent of gross income, so adult households obtain a somewhat higher proportion from employment compared with the entire population where four-fifths of gross income is earned (*see* Table 7.1). The household head accounts for three-fifths of gross income in adult households while the second adult contributes a further one-fifth. Subsequent adults are relatively unimportant in the group as a whole although they do make a sizable contribution in households of more than two adults. Their share of gross income is highest in the middle quintile, reflecting a higher proportion undertaking full-time education in richer households.

Thus adult households are generally well-off for four basic reasons. First, earnings of both the head and second adult make a greater proportionate contribution than in households as a whole. Second, this arises in part because adult households are typically small so that a given money income yields a higher standard of living. Third, where household size is greater there are substantial economies of scale, as Section 5.5 showed. Finally, associated with this greater size is the increasing likelihood that the second and subsequent adults will also have earned incomes. Some adult households are nevertheless poor, mainly due to the absence of earned income, and again these are to be found in all household types.

6.6 Pensioners

Finally, living standards and some of the determining factors are considered for the third group of 1703 households consisting of a single person or man and woman where the head is over pension age. Although this is the smallest of the three broad categories of household types in the population it is also one of the most homogeneous in terms of composition. The single-pensioner households are further differentiated by sex, and within each of the three categories they are divided into those with a head under and over 75 years. Table 6.9 shows the distribution of these six pensioner household types by equivalent income. While pensioners as a group are generally poor, single males and females are poorer on average than one-man–one-woman households or 'married couples'. The age of

Table 6.9
Percentage distribution of pensioner households by equivalent income

Household type		Equivalent income quintile					Number of households (100 per cent)
		1	*2*	*3*	*4*	*5*	
Married couple—head aged 65–74		36	30	14	12	8	556
	—head aged 75+	48	24	15	8	5	176
Single woman	—aged 60–74	40	30	12	9	9	519
	—aged 75+	55	32	8	3	2	273
Single man	—aged 65–74	33	36	14	10	7	111
	—aged 75+	53	19	12	7	9	68
All households		42	30	12	9	7	1703

the household head has an important influence on living standards. In all three household types a considerably higher proportion of those headed by a person over the age of 75 is to be found in the lowest quintile. Single-female pensioner households, as a group, are poorer than married couples partly because a higher proportion is over the age of 75 years. Many of these single-female households are the surviving spouses of a married-couple household, reflecting the lower average age of wives compared with husbands and the longer life expectancy of women.

Some of the reasons for these differences in living standards are evident from Tables 6.10, 6.11 and 6.12 which show the various component parts of gross money income in percentage terms

Table 6.10

Percentage components of gross income for married–couple pensioner households classified by equivalent income

Components	Equivalent income quintile					All households
	1	2	3	4	5	
Earned income	1	11	26	40	37	22
Investment income	2	6	11	11	27	12
Pensions, annuities	6	14	18	18	20	15
Social security benefits	84	59	39	25	11	45
Imputed rental	4	6	5	5	4	5
Rent and Rate Rebates	3	3	1	0	0	2
Other income	0	1	1	0	0	0
Gross income (100 per cent) £/week	26·97	36·97	51·03	70·54	143·54	46·84

although the substantial under-recording of investment income should be kept in mind: to avoid small sample numbers the earlier age classification is omitted. In married-couple households the flat-rate Retirement Pension and Supplementary Pension account for the fact that social security benefits contribute over four-fifths of gross income in the lowest quintile but only one-tenth in the top quintile. Earned income is the main factor making these richer households better-off, although private pensions and annuities also make an important contribution while investment income plays a limited role in all but the top quintile. A similar pattern is evident in Table 6.11 for single women, the main contrast being that earned income is much less important only contributing 8 per cent of the gross income of single-female pensioner households compared with 22 per cent in married-couple households. This is partly due to the lower labour

Table 6.11
Percentage components of gross income for single-woman pensioner households classified by equivalent income

Components	Equivalent income quintile					All households
	1	*2*	*3*	*4*	*5*	
Earned income	1	5	15	20	15	8
Investment income	3	6	14	20	32	12
Pensions, annuities	2	4	15	15	26	10
Social security benefits	89	74	43	33	17	59
Imputed rental	4	7	9	10	8	7
Rent and Rate Rebates	2	4	3	1	0	2
Other income	1	1	1	2	2	1
Gross income, £/week (100 per cent)	16·84	21·69	30·96	41·03	68·67	24·92

force participation of older women (*see* Table 10.1), lower wage rates for women and the larger proportion of older individuals in this category. Pensions and annuities also contribute less in female households whereas social security benefits account for 59 per cent of gross income compared with 45 per cent in married-couple households. For single male pensioner households the sources of gross income are very similar in importance to married-couple households. The main difference arises with earnings which only contribute 11 per cent to gross income, again reflecting the larger proportion of older men in this category. Compared with single-female pensioner households both investment income, pensions and annuities are more

Table 6.12
Percentage components of gross income for single-man pensioner households classified by equivalent income

Components	Equivalent income quintile					All households
	1	*2*	*3*	*4*	*5*	
Earned income	2	2	17	33	13	11
Investment income	3	6	11	19	36	16
Pensions, annuities	3	13	21	16	34	18
Social security benefits	86	67	41	26	13	47
Imputed rental	4	5	9	6	5	5
Rent and Rate Rebates	2	6	2	1	0	2
Other income	0	1	0	0	1	0
Gross income, £/week (100 per cent)	16·07	22·29	30·08	43·91	96·17	28·47

important while the contribution of social security benefits is correspondingly reduced.

In conclusion, pensioner households composed of a married couple are, on average, better-off than single-pensioner households. This arises from the older average age among the latter group and the reduced opportunities for earned income. In Section 10.3 the factors influencing the retirement decision will be considered, as clearly it has an important bearing on the living standards of households headed by people over pension age. Investment income, pensions and annuities also make a small, but important, contribution to the incomes of pensioner households. The level of pre-retirement saving will influence this source of retirement income and the relationship between retirement and saving is examined in Section 10.4. Among the poorest pensioner households social security benefits provide the main source of income, earned income contributes an increasing proportion among the middle equivalent income quintiles while investment income, private pensions and annuities are most important in the top quintile.

6.7 Conclusions

Adjusting money income for household circumstances to yield equivalent income leads to a very considerable difference in the shape of the distribution, as Figure 6.1 has shown. The distribution of living standards is much more peaked and has a shorter upper tail than the distribution of money income—although this comparison embodies an implicit assumption that the marginal utility of money income and equivalent income are constants. Living standards, or equivalent incomes, also vary considerably between different household types. Pensioner households and one-parent families are typically poor, families are generally better-off, while adult households without children are on average the richest group in the population. Some of the reasons for this broad pattern of living standards are evident from the more detailed analysis of the three groups.

Two important conclusions can be drawn from the results presented in this chapter. First, the determinants of living standards are exceedingly complex. Taking household behaviour as it is actually observed in the FES we have shown that there is no single factor which is closely associated with living standards. Nor is there any simple explanation even within a narrowly defined and reasonably homogeneous household type like single female pensioners or one-parent families. Although a majority of both categories may be poor a substantial minority are not.

The second conclusion follows from the first. In view of the complexity of factors associated with variations in living standards there is no simple categorization, like household type, which can be used to identify the poor or the rich. Household income and circumstances are the only means of distinguishing poverty. Prior to the introduction of the National Insurance scheme the Beveridge Report (HMSO, 1942, Cmd 6404) identified eight primary causes of need—unemployment, disability, loss of livelihood, retirement, marriage, bereavement, parenthood and physical incapacity. Given the existing social security system our analysis has shown that, while retirement and childhood remain important attributes of the poorest quintile, substantial numbers of both categories are found throughout the rest of the distribution. The adage that the poor are born into poverty, grow out of it and eventually die in poverty only holds as a very broad generalization—substantial numbers of adult households experience poverty too.

This second conclusion is important because it means that under present arrangements effective income transfer mechanisms cannot be based on household type categorization. For example, if the object is to transfer income to the poorest quintile then categorical measures based on the poorest household types which we have identified, like pensioners or one-parent families, would be, at most, 50 per cent effective. More efficient measures would require a different way of identifying the poor. Given that roughly one-tenth of national income is devoted to social security transfers (Section 2.3), and that for a variety of reasons large changes in this proportion are unlikely, greater emphasis on the distributional objective of social security inevitably suggests either non-categorical income support measures or more income-related categorical programmes. We return to this issue in Chapter 11.

7. Distributional Impact of Transfers

7.1 Introduction

It was shown in the previous chapter that benefits constitute an important source of income in poor households. Yet benefits cannot be considered in isolation: social security expenditure is financed from NI contributions and general tax revenue to which personal taxes make an important contribution. The initial effect of the main income transfers—direct taxes, NI contributions and social security benefits—is examined in this chapter.

Quite aside from the fact that taxes are used to finance part of social security spending, and both bear directly on personal sector incomes, there is another good reason why taxes and benefits should be examined together. Ability to pay is an important principle used in formulating tax measures. The poor are not taxed or taxed less heavily than the rich, while large families bear a smaller tax burden than smaller families with the same money incomes. Thus tax rates increase with incomes and the tax threshold varies with certain household circumstances. The Tax Credit proposals discussed in Section 11.3 go even further and provide those below a certain income with positive payments (negative taxes) which increase as gross income declines. These features of the tax system reflect aims which are similar to the objectives of social security discussed in Section 2.8—the provision of a minimum standard of living and the associated requirement of horizontal equity. Since the tax and benefit systems share some common objectives it is logical that they should be considered together.

This chapter will focus mainly on the vertical distributional impact of income transfers. Horizontal equity is taken into account by dealing with the equivalent income distribution. It can be considered more explicitly by comparing the relativities embodied in transfers with the equivalent income scales summarized in Table 5.8. In looking at the vertical impact of measures in this and the next three chapters the terms progressive and regressive will be utilized. A measure which reduces inequality or makes the distribution of living standards more equal is progressive, whereas if it promotes inequality it is described as regressive. Thus a benefit which accounts for a declining proportion of income as we move from the lowest to the highest equivalent income quintile is progressive since it reduces inequality. A tax which absorbs an increasing proportion of income as households become better-off is also progressive. The converse holds for regressive benefits and taxes.

Table 7.1

Percentage sources of net income, 1975

Source	*Equivalent income quintile*					*All*
	1	*2*	*3*	*4*	*5*	*households*
Earned income	42	81	105	112	116	101
Investment income	3	2	3	3	8	5
Pensions and annuities	2	3	3	3	3	3
Other income	8	6	4	4	3	4
Social security benefits	56	26	11	6	3	13
Gross income	111	118	126	128	133	126
NI contributions	3	4	5	5	4	5
Income tax	8	13	19	23	29	21
Net transfers[1]	+45	+9	−13	−22	−30	−13
Net income (100 per cent) £/week	26·58	42·71	59·26	73·36	103·32	61·06

[1] Social security benefits minus NI contributions and income tax

Income transfers are placed in perspective in Table 7.1, which shows sources of gross income and statutory deductions as a percentage of net income for each equivalent income quintile (although it should be remembered that investment income is substantially under-recorded). Social security benefits contribute over half of net income in the poorest quintile while NI contributions and income tax amount to 3 and 8 per cent respectively for these households. Net income transfers therefore amount to 45 per cent of disposable income in the poorest households and fall to 9 per cent in the second quintile. Thereafter net transfers are negative, amounting to 13, 22 and 30 per cent of disposable income in the third, fourth and fifth quintiles. Transfers as a whole are highly progressive and play an important role in redistributing income in the personal sector. The three broad categories of income transfer—direct taxes, NI contributions and social security benefits—will be examined in more detail in the next three sections.

7.2   Direct taxes

Before considering direct taxes (which are defined as income tax payments less refunds) in more detail, some differences between the social security and tax systems need to be noted. The social security sector, for both contributions and benefit purposes, operates mainly on a weekly basis. In contrast, the tax system makes use of an annual accounting period. Most taxes are in fact deducted from weekly or monthly earnings but cumulative annual assessment and the progressive structure of the average tax rate mean that in some cases tax repayments exceed deductions. Moreover, the tax unit is smaller than the household and while it does not correspond exactly with the family unit utilized in Table 6.1 there will be a greater concentration of multiple tax unit households in the top three quintiles. For these two reasons the conventions adopted in this study are not entirely suitable for analysing the tax system. Nevertheless taxes on income perform similar functions to NI contributions and benefits, providing a justification for considering them within the same framework as other income transfers.

Table 7.1 showed that income tax is highly progressive: it accounted for 8 per cent of net income in the poorest quintile and 29 per cent in the top quintile. Not all households pay income tax, however, and such payments will impose a greater burden on taxpayers. Less than one-third of the first quintile made positive tax payments (Table 7.2), over two-thirds paid taxes in the second quintile and thereafter the proportion is 95 per cent or more. Some of these non-taxpayers will in fact reflect repayments offsetting tax deductions, others will be households with a high income in the survey week but a low annual income, while in some cases allowances (or tax expenditures) for items like mortgage interest or insurance premiums will reduce or eliminate tax liability. On an overall basis almost four-fifths of households pay income tax. The bottom panel in Table 7.2 shows average tax payments in taxed households as a percentage of average net income in each quintile. On this basis the tax system appears much less progressive. Income taxes probably account for less than 25 per cent of net income in the lowest quintile since the average income of taxpayers will tend to exceed the quintile average for all households. Nevertheless, the proportion paid in the

Table 7.2

Per cent of households in each quintile paying NI contributions and income tax, and average amounts as a proportion of average net income

Per cent of households paying:	*Equivalent income quintile*					*All households*
	1	*2*	*3*	*4*	*5*	
NI contributions	28	61	86	91	92	71
Income tax	31	71	95	97	98	78
Average payment as per cent of net income:						
NI contributions	9	7	6	6	5	6
Income tax	25	18	20	23	30	27

top quintile is only about 1.7 times the percentage in the second quintile.

Clearly the degree of progression in the tax system depends crucially on whether it is measured for all households or for taxpaying households. Since the object of tax thresholds is to reduce the burden on the poor the presentation in Table 7.1 in terms of all households may be preferable for many purposes. But it obscures the fact that some poor households do face quite a high tax liability and in instances where importance is attached to equitable treatment of all households in similar circumstances the approach adopted in Table 7.2 will be more relevant.

7.3 NI contributions

National Insurance contributions in Table 7.1 increased from 3 per cent of net income in the lowest quintile to 5 per cent in the third and fourth quintiles, falling back to 4 per cent in the richest group. Thus they appear to be mildly progressive in the bottom part of the distribution and regressive in the top half. But as with tax payments this measure averaged across all households in the quintile conceals the fact that not all households pay NI contributions. Table 7.2 shows that only 28 per cent of the bottom quintile make NI contributions, whereas 92 per cent contribute in the top quintile. This reflects the disproportionate number of pensioners (Table 6.2) and other beneficiaries in the bottom quintile, a smaller concentration in the second quintile, with the remainder scattered through the rest of the distribution. If NI payments by contributing households are expressed as a percentage of average net income in the quintile they appear to be quite regressive in effect.

This result will be due, in part, to the structure of NI contributions during 1975. For the first three months contributions were on a flat-rate basis with a graduated addition for gross earnings in the range £9 to £62 per week. For the remainder of 1975 employee contributions changed to the structure described in Section 2.4 at a rate of 5·5 per cent on gross earnings in the range £11 to £69. Class 2 and 3 contributions were also on a flat-rate basis during this period. The change from a flat-rate structure made NI contributions less regressive for those households making such payments, although they remained regressive since beyond the ceiling the proportion of net income going on contribution declines.

7.4 Cash benefits

Social security benefits are highly progressive in effect, accounting for 56 per cent of net income in the bottom quintile and only 3 per cent in the top quintile (Table 7.1). From the description of the main benefits in Section 2.5 it is apparent that some benefits will be more progressive than others: means-tested SB is focused on the poor, whereas Child Benefit is paid to all families with children. However, the benefits are too numerous and complex to be considered individually so five broad categories are distinguished in Tables 7.3 and 7.4. Retirement and Old Persons' Pensions account for a major part of social security spending (Table 2.4). Other long-term benefits include most of the remaining long-term benefits with the exception of long-term SB. This second category embraces Widows' Benefits, Disablement, War and Invalidity Pensions, all of which are paid at the long-term benefit rate (Section 2.6). Unemployment and Sickness Benefits and Maternity Allowance are all paid at the short-term benefit rate. Supplementary Benefit covers both Supplementary Pensions and Allowances: Supplementary Allowances can be paid at either the ordinary or at the long-term rate. In Table 7.4 average payments in the five benefit categories are shown for all households in each equivalent income quintile and for recipient households. As most benefits were uprated twice, and Family Allowances were increased once, in 1975 they are expressed in terms of December 1975 prices for the reasons discussed in Section 6.2.

Half of the poorest quintile receives Retirement or Old Persons' Pensions (Table 7.3); a further 14 per cent are on either other long-term or short-term benefits. Although 36 per cent of households in the bottom quintile are on SB and a further 25 per cent receive Family Allowances, in both cases there is considerable overlap with other benefits (Section 2.5 and Table 2.5). Looking across the equivalent income distribution the proportion receiving Retirement Pension falls more rapidly than the percentage on either short-term benefits or other long-term benefits. Unlike NI benefits in the first three rows of Table 7.3 which are contingency based, SB is means-tested and this is reflected by the higher concentration in the bottom quintiles. Family Allowances were universal for families with two or more children and the distribution mirrors the proportion of households with children in each quintile. Since the introduction of Child Benefit and the extension of payments to the first or only child in April 1977 child support has become slightly more regressive given

Table 7.3

Percentage of households receiving social security benefits in each equivalent income quintile, 1975

Social security benefits	*Equivalent income quintile*					*All households*
	1	*2*	*3*	*4*	*5*	
Retirement and Old Persons' Pensions	51	40	21	16	12	28
Other long-term benefits	7	8	8	8	5	7
Short-term benefits	7	4	3	4	3	4
Supplementary Benefit	36	16	4	3	1	12
Family Allowances	25	34	36	22	12	26

the somewhat higher standard of living of one-child families (Table 6.3).

Although SB is means-tested, 16 per cent of households in the second quintile and a minority in better-off groups nevertheless receive payments. This arises for several reasons. First, SB requirements are determined by the appropriate scale rate plus housing costs and where these are high entitlement can arise, despite the fact that the household falls in the second quintile. This treatment of housing involves a problem of equity which will be considered more fully below. The second main reason why SB payments are made to households not in the bottom quintile is that the SB unit is smaller than the household unit. Table 6.1 showed that over one-fifth of households contained multiple family units which correspond more closely to the SB unit than does the household. Some of these multiple units have very low incomes and are eligible for SB although household equivalent income is quite high. Whether these SB units are really poor or not depends on the extent of involuntary and voluntary income distribution within the household (Section 3.5). Voluntary sharing is very difficult to measure but the estimated commodity scales in Chapter 5 suggest substantial joint consumption or involuntary sharing.

Average payments of the five benefit categories are recorded in Table 7.4. The top panel shows payments averaged across all households in each quintile and so reflects the combined effect of the proportion of recipients and the actual benefit payments: average

Table 7.4

Average social security benefit payments (£/week at December 1975 prices) for all households and for recipient households

Social security benefits	Equivalent income quintile					All households
	1	*2*	*3*	*4*	*5*	
All households in group						
Retirement and Old Persons' Pensions	7·97	6·32	3·44	2·28	1·75	4·35
Other long-term benefits	1·13	1·11	1·20	1·03	0·59	1·01
Short-term benefits	1·45	0·73	0·49	0·51	0·45	0·73
Supplementary Benefit	3·26	1·31	0·28	0·19	0·10	1·03
Family Allowances	0·76	0·81	0·71	0·40	0·21	0·58
Recipient households in group						
Retirement and Old Persons' Pensions	15·61	15·94	16·11	14·16	14·81	15·54
Other long-term benefits	15·36	13·21	14·42	13·37	11·32	13·65
Short-term benefits	20·69	17·52	16·82	14·41	17·04	18·01
Supplementary Benefit	8·78	8·17	7·21	6·37	8·46	8·41
Family Allowances	2·98	2·40	1·98	1·79	1·82	2·25

payments to recipient households are given in the bottom panel. The top part of the table confirms the picture given by participation rates: benefits, as a whole, are very progressive. However, the bottom part of Table 7.4 indicates that among recipient households average payments are roughly similar across the equivalent income distribution. Retirement and Old Persons' Pensions are largely flat-rate and variations in the average amount are mainly the result of the changing composition of recipient units—whether they are entitled to single-person or married-couple pensions or possibly two single pensions. Other long-term benefit payments generally decline with increasing equivalent income, reflecting a fall in the average number of dependants.

Short-term benefit payments are generally higher than either of the other two categories of NI benefits, mainly as a result of a higher number of dependants, although Earnings-Related Supplements also make some contribution to the differential. Variations in average family size account for the fluctuations in Family Allowance payments.

Average SB payments to recipients are influenced by a number of factors. Table 2.6 showed that the long-term scale rate is higher than the ordinary rate so the balance of beneficiaries between the two categories is one important factor. The proportion of SB recipients also in receipt of a NI benefit is a second factor of considerable importance since average payments vary greatly (Table 2.5) due to the 'topping-up' nature of the scheme. Third, Exceptional Circumstance Additions also lead to variations in payments. Finally, the inclusion of housing costs when determining SB requirements is a fourth factor contributing to differences in benefit payments.

The treatment of housing, which is unique to the SB scheme, raises a number of interesting economic questions. It is, in effect, a benefit-in-kind which differs from the three types of merit good considered in Section 9.2 where either price or quantity is controlled. In the case of housing services for SB recipients the cost is met in full for nearly all beneficiaries: the price of housing services is zero and the quantity consumed is unlimited. The Beveridge Report (HMSO, 1942, Cmd 6404) argued that housing was unlike other items of expenditure in three respects. Rents differed markedly between regions, they also varied greatly for identical households in the same area and housing costs could not be easily reduced in the short-run. Variations in rents may be due to true price differences in the cost of a unit of housing services; alternatively, they may stem from the consumption of different quantities and qualities of housing services. If variations in housing costs are mainly due to true price fluctuations the payment of rent in full will promote greater equity. On the other hand if differences in housing costs arise from quantity and quality variations it will foster inequality. Coverdale (1977) has analysed housing costs using proxies for quantity, quality and true price factors: quantity and quality factors are found to be important, especially in the private rented sector. While the major part of variations in rents remained unexplained this empirical work suggests that, although reducing inequity in some respects, payment of housing costs also contributes to inequality. A similar analysis applies to other items of expenditure which are allowed in full in income transfer measures.

While the overall effect of social security benefits is progressive, the degree varies between different schemes. And within the NI scheme, Retirement Pensions are more progressive than other long-term or short-term benefits (although they will become less progressive as the new pensions' scheme matures). This pattern is the outcome of two factors—benefit participation and average payments. Average payments are determined by factors discussed in Chapter 2, among which household composition and relationships with other benefits are important. Some of the ways in which the take-up of benefits can be influenced will be considered in Section 10.7 below.

7.5 Summary

The analysis in this chapter has shown that income transfers, as a whole, are quite progressive in their impact. NI contributions are regressive for contributing households, taxes on income are mildly progressive for taxpayers and benefits are highly progressive in effect. As an increasing proportion of households make NI contributions and pay taxes with increasing equivalent income both appear to be more progressive when measured in terms of all households in each quintile. In looking at income transfers as a whole some inter-relationships between them are important. NI beneficiaries are generally exempt from NI contributions. Most long-term benefits are taxed, whereas short-term benefits, SB and compensation benefits are not subject to taxation. Family Allowances were taxed and clawed back so that their net value declined with increasing income and became negative for some higher rate taxpayers whereas Child Benefit is tax-free.

This evidence on the distributional impact of transfers does not entirely support Buchanan and Bush (1974), who argue that under majority voting at least half of the population should benefit from transfers. Family Allowances, and to a much lesser extent NI benefits, are quite widely spread across the equivalent income distribution. But there is no evidence that middle income groups, rather than the poor, are the main beneficiaries of income transfers.

It must be stressed that these conclusions relate to the initial incidence of income transfers. They take no account of the behavioural response which transfers may induce of the kind discussed in Chapter 4. It may be that for some groups of earners taxes and NI contributions reduce the supply of labour and impose large resource costs on the economy. Alternatively the supply of labour may be inelastic, in which case both employer and employee NI contributions are passed back on to labour in the form of reduced earnings.

In these circumstances NI contributions would be two and a half times the magnitudes shown earlier. The transfer system can influence behavioural response in areas other than the choice between labour and leisure. Tax allowances for insurance premiums will encourage saving, mortgage interest relief promotes house purchase, transfer relativities influence household formation, the type of benefit affects take-up, and so on.

8. Equity and Prices

8.1 Introduction

Income and household circumstances are not the only factors which influence living standards. Even if these two variables are held constant Section 3.2 showed that a rise in the general price level or a change in relative prices could make households worse off. Furthermore, changing relative prices would not have the same impact on different household types (Section 3.3). A rise in the price of food would have a greater adverse effect on families since they devote a larger share of their budgets to this commodity, whereas single-person households would be more vulnerable to higher housing and fuel prices. In general, for household circumstances where the commodity scale exceeds the income scale the budget share will, at the same standard of living, tend to be larger for that household type: the converse holds where the commodity scale is smaller than the income scale. Thus from Table 5.1 higher food, clothing, durables, miscellaneous goods and transport prices will bear more heavily on households with older children provided the composite commodity scales do not differ greatly from the direct effects. The larger budget shares for fuel and housing in Table 5.5 reflects in part the high commodity scales for these items in single-pensioner households.

Within a given household type budget shares also vary with living standards. Moving from poor to rich necessities become less important and luxuries more so. Thus relative price changes will also have a differential impact on living standards at various equivalent income levels. If the price of necessities increases relative to the price of luxuries the living standards of the poor will fall by more than those of the rich.

Households will also respond to changes in relative prices by substituting the cheaper for the dearer commodity (Figures 3.4 and 3.5). Indeed Section 3.3 demonstrated that differences in household circumstances are analogous to variations in relative market prices and also result in a price substitution effect. Those goods and services for which the commodity scales relating to a given type of individual are small will tend to be substituted in household consumption for those with large commodity scales. Unfortunately the method described in Section 5.2 does not permit the direct and price substitution effects of differences in household circumstances to be disentangled. It is not suitable for examining the impact of relative price changes on living standards since the market price substitution

Table 8.1
Retail Price Index, 1967–76

Group	1967	1968	1969	1970	1971	1972	1973	1974	1975	1976
Housing	100·0	105·1	109·3	117·5	128·3	141·8	158·4	177·1	210·1	239·7
Fuel and light	100·0	107·6	110·9	117·2	129·4	139·5	143·4	168·0	223·7	276·8
Food	100·0	104·0	110·5	118·2	131·3	143·0	164·5	194·0	243·7	292·4
Alcoholic drink	100·0	101·4	108·7	114·8	121·9	126·9	131·0	145·3	179·1	211·0
Tobacco	100·0	103·9	112·2	112·8	114·7	115·5	116·9	136·4	173·8	201·6
Clothing and footwear	100·0	101·5	105·4	110·8	118·3	126·9	138·9	163·2	187·5	208·0
Durable household goods	100·0	103·9	108·5	115·6	124·2	128·9	136·4	156·7	190·5	209·4
Miscellaneous goods	100·0	109·5	116·4	125·6	139·9	147·8	151·8	178·3	222·2	258·6
Transport and vehicles	100·0	106·1	110·4	117·7	131·2	138·9	147·0	173·2	224·5	259·0
Services	100·0	104·7	112·7	121·7	134·1	142·8	160·1	179·7	228·0	268·4
RPI	100·0	104·7	110·4	117·4	128·5	137·6	150·3	174·4	216·7	252·5

Source: *Department of Employment Gazette*

components cannot be isolated from the composite scales. In consequence, the commodity scales will only be used qualitatively in this chapter and all quantitative estimates will be based on actual expenditure weights.

This chapter will focus on the impact of changing relative and absolute prices on both horizontal and vertical equity. In the period 1967–76 the General Index of Retail Prices (RPI) increased by over 150 per cent, much of the rise taking place in the last few years of the period (Table 8.1). The prices of food and fuel, which are of greater importance in the budgets of poor households, increased more rapidly than the general price level, while tobacco, alcohol, clothing and household durable prices fell in relative terms. The

Table 8.2

Average budget shares, total expenditures and equivalent incomes by household type, 1975

Commodity	Single adult	Two adults	Other adult households	One-parent families	Two adults 1–2 children	Two adults 3+ children	All other households with children	Single pensioner	Two pensioners
Housing[1]	0·17	0·12	0·08	0·14	0·13	0·11	0·09	0·17	0·11
Fuel, light and power[1]	0·05	0·05	0·04	0·08	0·05	0·05	0·04	0·11	0·09
Food	0·19	0·23	0·24	0·29	0·25	0·29	0·27	0·29	0·29
Alcohol	0·05	0·05	0·07	0·02	0·05	0·04	0·07	0·02	0·05
Tobacco	0·03	0·04	0·04	0·03	0·03	0·03	0·04	0·02	0·04
Clothing and footwear	0·07	0·08	0·10	0·09	0·09	0·09	0·11	0·07	0·07
Durables	0·06	0·08	0·09	0·06	0·08	0·07	0·07	0·06	0·05
Other goods	0·07	0·08	0·08	0·08	0·08	0·07	0·08	0·08	0·07
Transport and vehicles	0·15	0·16	0·16	0·08	0·15	0·13	0·14	0·06	0·11
Services	0·14	0·11	0·10	0·11	0·09	0·09	0·09	0·12	0·12
Miscellaneous	0·00	0·00	0·00	0·01	0·01	0·01	0·01	0·00	0·00
Total expenditure[1] (£/week = 1·00)	35·21	55·39	79·82	38·40	61·24	67·22	89·57	18·56	32·88
Average equivalent income (£/week married couple = 1·00)	65·57	67·08	61·22	37·79	49·77	40·95	49·23	38·40	41·47

[1] Amended to exclude the imputed rental of owner-occupied housing and slot meter rebates

average budget shares of the 11 commodity groups in the 9 household types are shown in Table 8.2 for 1975. Although these variations mainly reflect horizontal factors they are partly due to vertical differences in expenditure patterns since the average equivalent income varies considerably by household type. The budget shares for housing and fuel are much larger in small households, reflecting the considerable extent of joint consumption which was identified from the commodity scale estimates in Chapter 5. The budget shares for food and clothing are more important in larger families due to the limited extent of joint consumption in such items. The focus is

Table 8.3

Average budget shares by equivalent income, 1975

Commodity	Equivalent income quintile					All households
	1	*2*	*3*	*4*	*5*	
Housing[1]	0·13	0·12	0·11	0·11	0·11	0·12
Fuel, light and power[1]	0·08	0·07	0·06	0·05	0·04	0·05
Food	0·33	0·29	0·27	0·24	0·20	0·25
Alcohol	0·04	0·05	0·05	0·06	0·05	0·05
Tobacco	0·05	0·04	0·04	0·04	0·03	0·04
Clothing and footwear	0·08	0·09	0·09	0·09	0·09	0·09
Durables	0·05	0·06	0·07	0·08	0·09	0·08
Other goods	0·08	0·08	0·08	0·08	0·08	0·08
Transport and vehicles	0·09	0·11	0·14	0·15	0·17	0·14
Services	0·07	0·08	0·09	0·09	0·13	0·10
Miscellaneous	0·01	0·01	0·01	0·01	0·01	0·01
Total expenditure[1] (£/week = 1·00)	30·38	41·67	55·14	63·44	77·64	53·65

[1] Amended to exclude the imputed rental for owner-occupied housing and slot meter rebates

on vertical variations in expenditure patterns in Table 8.3, although, since Table 6.2 shows that the household type make-up of each quintile varies, part of the difference stems from horizontal factors. The importance of food, fuel and housing declines between the first and fifth quintile, whereas durables, services, transport and vehicles have increasing budget shares.

Some of the price changes embodied in Table 8.1 are influenced by government measures. Indirect taxes (local authority rates, customs and excise duties, Value Added Tax, car tax and licence charges) yield revenue which is used, in part, to finance social security benefits: they also add to market prices. The initial incidence of indirect taxes will not be considered here, as it is covered in detail in an annual series of which the latest is HMSO (1976), *Economic Trends*. Assuming that indirect taxes are passed on fully in prices (which is unlikely for reasons similar to those discussed for NI contributions in Section 4.4) this evidence shows that they account for about one-fifth of net income in all household types. Some indirect taxes like rates are regressive, whereas others such as VAT are progressive in their initial impact. However, for alcohol or tobacco duties the incidence depends on whether consuming or all households are considered. This is an important point which is often overlooked when considering the effect of indirect taxes, and it will arise again in subsequent sections.

8.2 Subsidies

Relative prices and the overall price level are also influenced by subsidies. This section will concentrate on food subsidies, since they represent the main consumer subsidy which is operated solely through the price mechanism. Housing, the other important subsidy identified in Table 2.3, will be considered in Chapter 9. It chiefly influences local authority rents and so only affects the price of housing services as a whole indirectly by reducing the demand for housing in other sectors of the market.

The importance of food in the household budget increases with family size (Table 8.2) and falls with income (Table 8.3). The variation is greater if household type and equivalent income are considered together (Table 8.4). While the overall budget share for food is 25 per cent of total expenditure it amounts to 37 per cent for poor one-parent families or as little as 15 per cent for a single adult in the richest quintile. These differences in budget shares reflect the food commodity scales in Chapter 5, which are lower than the income scale in one-adult households and larger than the income scale for older children or additional adults. It is clear that a 10 per cent increase in the price of food will have a very different impact by household type and standard of living: to consume the same amount of food a large, poor family would need to spend 3·3 per cent more, whereas a single adult in the top quintile would only have to spend an additional 1·5 per cent. Thus the 26 and 20 per cent increases in food prices in 1975 and 1976 respectively shown in Table 8.1, which were greater than the rise in prices as a whole, had a very different impact on living standards, depending on household type and equivalent income. Small households at a given standard of living will benefit least from food subsidies, while larger families with older children and multi-adult households will benefit most.

During 1975 food subsidies amounting to £652m at current prices were paid on bread, butter, cheese, milk, tea and household flour. These commodities are necessities which, for a given household type, decline in importance with increasing equivalent income. Table 8.5 shows average expenditure on subsidized goods by equivalent income quintile. The amount spent increases from £2·00 per week in the lowest quintile to £2·56 in the middle group and £2·10 in the top quintile. The proportion of the budget allocated to subsidized food fell from 6.6 per cent in the bottom quintile to 2·7 per cent

Table 8.4

Budget shares for food in households of different type classified by equivalent income

Household type	Equivalent income quintile					All Households
	1	*2*	*3*	*4*	*5*	
Single adult	0·291	0·268	0·222	0·202	0·149	0·186
Two adults	0·295	0·283	0·251	0·243	0·197	0·225
Other adult households	0·313	0·288	0·266	0·253	0·202	0·238
One-parent families	0·368	0·303	0·277	0·186	0·211	0·295
Two adults 1–2 Children	0·303	0·282	0·263	0·236	0·206	0·252
Two adults 3+ children	0·326	0·311	0·293	0·256	0·205	0·292
All other households with children	0·331	0·292	0·273	0·252	0·213	0·265
Single pensioner	0·339	0·298	0·255	0·248	0·185	0·286
Two pensioners	0·352	0·311	0·278	0·266	0·198	0·294
All households	0·326	0·293	0·267	0·244	0·197	0·252

in the top quintile (Table 8.6). Increasing expenditure on subsidized food in the first three quintiles partly reflects changing household composition. The bottom quintile is dominated by one- and two-person households and larger households become more important in the second and third quintiles. Higher expenditure is also due to the fact that although the income elasticity of demand is low for subsidized items it is nevertheless positive. Thus higher living standards lead to a small increase in consumption although the budget share falls considerably.

In conclusion, changes in the price of food relative to other prices have a distributional impact which varies considerably both horizontally and vertically. Comparing the final row of Table 8.4 with the first row of Table 8.6, the budget share for subsidized food

Table 8.5

Average expenditure (£/week) on subsidized and nationalized industry commodities by equivalent income, 1975

Commodity	Equivalent income quintile					All Households
	1	*2*	*3*	*4*	*5*	
Subsidized food	2·00	2·32	2·56	2·43	2·10	2·28
Telecommunications	0·27	0·41	0·53	0·63	0·85	0·54
Postage	0·10	0·13	0·16	0·17	0·21	0·16
Rail fares	0·09	0·17	0·28	0·40	0·80	0·35
Bus fares	0·44	0·59	0·70	0·83	0·54	0·62
Electricity[1]	1·12	1·39	1·50	1·52	1·58	1·42
Gas[1]	0·54	0·65	0·77	0·82	0·93	0·74
Coal and coke	0·71	0·52	0·56	0·47	0·44	0·54

[1] Excluding hire and maintenance charges

declines much more rapidly with increasing living standards than for food as a whole. In consequence food subsidies are quite progressive in their initial impact. Unlike some means-tested cash or in-kind benefits where there are problems of take-up, food subsidies help all poor households. And they do so in a way which is more progressive than some other measures which have a redistributional objective: Table 7.2 showed, for example, that among taxpaying households income tax was only mildly progressive. In a situation where importance is attached to the welfare of all poor households subsidizing the price of some basic foods may be a more effective redistributional measure than many traditionally accepted alternatives.

Table 8.6

Budget shares of subsidized and nationalized industry commodities by equivalent income, 1975

Commodity	Equivalent income quintile					All households
	1	*2*	*3*	*4*	*5*	
Subsidized food	0·066	0·056	0·046	0·038	0·027	0·042
Telecommunications	0·009	0·010	0·010	0·010	0·011	0·010
Postage	0·003	0·003	0·003	0·003	0·003	0·003
Rail fares	0·003	0·004	0·005	0·006	0·010	0·007
Bus fares	0·014	0·014	0·013	0·013	0·007	0·012
Electricity[1]	0·037	0·033	0·027	0·024	0·020	0·026
Gas[1]	0·018	0·016	0·014	0·013	0·012	0·014
Coal and coke	0·023	0·012	0·010	0·007	0·006	0·010

[1] Excluding hire and maintenance charges

8.3 Nationalized industry prices

In addition to the subsidy on food, during 1975 £468m was paid to nationalized transport undertakings and a further £285m was transferred from public funds to nationalized industries for price restraint (Table 2.3). These payments contributed, in part, to holding consumer prices for telecommunications, postage, rail and bus travel, and fuel at a lower level than would have otherwise prevailed. Thus, like income transfers, indirect taxes and subsidies, these items of public expenditure will have both horizontal and vertical distributional effects. In view of its greater importance in household budgets, and the sharp rise in the price of fuel in recent years (Table 8.1), energy will be dealt with in more detail than the other commodities.

(1) *Telecommunications*. From Table 8.5 it can be seen that expenditure on telecommunications and postage increases quite rapidly with equivalent income. The proportion of the budget devoted to telecommunications also goes up with living standards, whereas for postage it remains constant at 0·3 per cent: thus a subsidy on the former is regressive while for postage it is neutral. Both are part of the services group and the commodity scales in Chapter 5 are generally the same size as the income scale or somewhat larger, being greater for single females than for men. This element of public expenditure may therefore be of rather greater benefit to larger households and more advantageous to single females. Not all households have telephones, however, the proportion increasing with living standards (Table 8.7). So in the lowest quintile the benefits from reduced prices will be concentrated on about two-fifths of households compared with over four-fifths in the top quintile. In terms of households consuming telephone services the impact is much less progressive because the rental constitutes the major element in total expenditure. Thus among telephone users average expenditure only increases by 50 per cent between the bottom and the top quintiles. This tariff structure has distributional implications similar to those of fuel tariffs, which are discussed more fully below.

(2) *Rail*. Rail fares account for 0·7 per cent of total expenditure (Table 8.6), the average weekly amount in the top quintile being almost ten times that in the poorest (Table 8.5). These figures are in agreement with another study using different data which show that 70 per cent of expenditure on rail fares is in the top two quintiles, HMSO (1976), *Transport Policy: A Consultation Document*. This arises partly because utilization of railways is negligible in the bottom quintile and much higher in the top group (Table 8.7). As

a result of this pattern of rail usage quite substantial benefits in terms of lower fares are conferred on a relatively small number of households concentrated at the top end of the distribution. The horizontal variations are also considerable, expenditure being chiefly among non-pensioner households and exhibiting a close relationship with the number of adults.

(3) *Bus.* Bus fares are almost twice as important, on average, as rail fares and account for 1·2 per cent of the budget (Table 8.6). Unlike rail fares, the budget share declines with increasing living standards, falling from 1·4 per cent in the lowest to 0·7 per cent in the top quintile. Use of bus services is much more widely spread than rail travel with at least half of each quintile incurring expenditure and a rather higher frequency among the middle equivalent income groups (Table

Table 8.7

Percentage of households consuming nationalized industry and related commodities, 1975

Commodity	Equivalent income quintile					All households
	1	*2*	*3*	*4*	*5*	
Telecommunications	8	11	13	15	17	63
Rail fares	1	2	3	4	6	16
Bus fares	11	12	13	13	12	61
Electricity	19	20	20	20	20	98
Gas	12	12	12	13	13	62
Coal and coke	5	4	3	3	1	17
Central heating	6	8	10	11	13	47

8.7). Expenditure is roughly proportional to the number of adults in the household with children involving a small addition. This reflects the fare structure which incorporates lower rates for children but cannot be rationalized in terms of the commodity scales in Chapter 5, which relate to all forms of travel: one would expect considerable joint consumption of private transport but marked economies of scale are unlikely in public transport.

(4) *Fuel.* The price of fuel almost doubled between 1973 and 1976, the greatest increase being for electricity and the smallest for gas (Figure 8.1). This massive rise in fuel prices had a very uneven impact on households of different type and at various standards of living. Table 8.8 shows that the budget share for fuel varied from 13 per cent in poor single-pensioner households to 4 per cent for households in the top quintile. Ignoring the effect of household composition the final row of Table 8.8. indicates that the fuel budget share fell by roughly half between the bottom and top quintiles. And within the

bottom quintile it was twice as great for single-pensioner households as for large families. These variations reflect the substantial joint consumption evident from the commodity scales for fuel in Chapter 5, and the considerably greater need for fuel among older households (Table 5.7). They are also due to the low equivalent income elasticity of fuel expenditure—the three main items of fuel in Table 8.5 only go up by 24 per cent between the bottom and the top quintile although equivalent income increases almost fourfold.

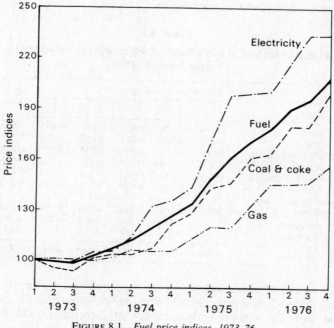

FIGURE 8.1   *Fuel price indices, 1973–76*

At a given standard of living or for a specified household type the marked change in relative fuel prices depicted in Figure 8.1 will not have the same impact simply because households make use of different types and combinations of fuels. Table 8.7 shows that although most households were electricity consumers, fewer than two-thirds consumed gas. The proportion of better-off coal and coke users will be understated since they are more likely to make larger, infrequent, purchases which are not recorded during the two-week FES survey period. For households as a whole utilization of solid fuel is roughly double the level shown in Table 8.7, although the budget shares in Table 8.8 should be an accurate reflection of average expenditure. Choice of fuel and combination of fuel types will be determined by a host of factors including the presence of central heating. Fewer than one-third of the lowest quintile have full or partial central heating, whereas about two-thirds of the top quintile make use of space heating. Type of accommodation, historical decisions about fuel-using appliances, location close to a gas main, region, season, tariff structures, and a range of similar considerations will also influence fuel expenditure.

Table 8.8

Budget shares for fuel in households of different type classified by equivalent income, 1975

| Household type | Equivalent income quintile | | | | | All households |
	1	2	3	4	5	
Single adult	0·086	0·071	0·056	0·046	0·043	0·050
Two adults	0·080	0·061	0·064	0·053	0·042	0·050
Other adult households	0·066	0·054	0·051	0·046	0·036	0·044
One-parent families	0·100	0·074	0·060	0063	0·064	0·079
Two adults 1–2 children	0·069	0·061	0·055	0·051	0·043	0·054
Two adults 3 + children	0·060	0·052	0·050	0·049	0·036	0·052
All other households with children	0·057	0·048	0·042	0·036	0·034	0·041
Single pensioner	0·133	0·110	0·091	0·078	0·076	0·108
Two pensioners	0·107	0·095	0·068	0·067	0·077	0·087
All households	0·084	0·065	0·055	0·049	0·042	0·055

The extent of variations in fuel expenditure can be appreciated from Figure 8.2, where the distribution in the bottom quintile is compared with the remaining households at December 1975 prices. While total fuel expenditure is, on average, 20 per cent lower in the first quintile there is a very wide range of expenditure within each group. A minority of the poor spend over £7 per week on fuel although some spend less than £1. Table 8.8 has demonstrated that household composition is one important source of variation. Figure 8.3 depicts the effect of household type on both the bottom and the combined top four quintiles. Fuel expenditure increases gradually with household size in line with the commodity scales in Chapter 5: it is higher for the retired and within any household type is usually higher in the top four quintiles than in the bottom quintile. Expenditure also varies with type of fuel used and Figure 8.4 shows the

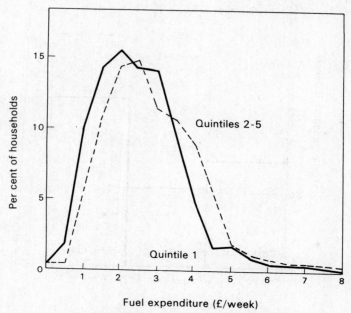

FIGURE 8.2   *Distribution of household fuel expenditure, 1975*

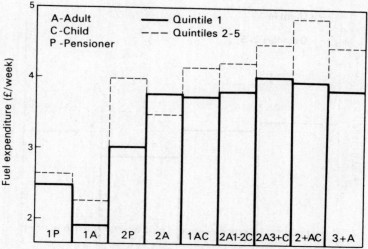

FIGURE 8.3   *Variations in fuel expenditure by household type*

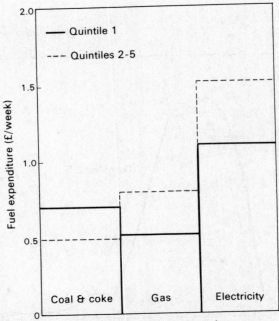

FIGURE 8.4 *Fuel expenditure by fuel type*

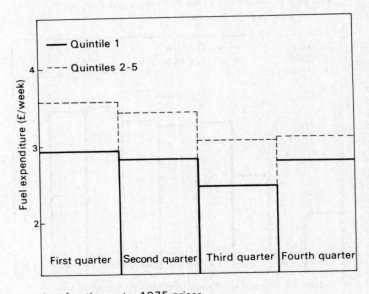

1 at fourth quarter 1975 prices

FIGURE 8.5 *Seasonality of fuel expenditure*

average expenditure on the three main fuels by the two groups. The bottom quintile spends more on solid fuel, and less on gas and electricity, than other households. Thus higher prices for coal and coke would have a greater adverse impact on the poor, although from Table 8.7 it would be confined to a sub-set of such households.

The relative importance of the three fuels influences the seasonality of expenditure. Gas and electricity bills are mainly paid

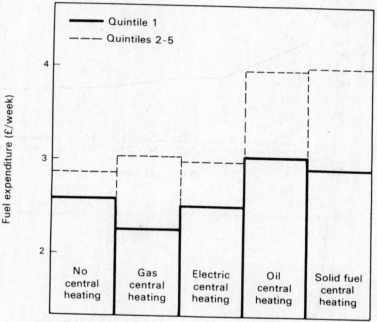

FIGURE 8.6 *The influence of central heating on fuel expenditure*

quarterly, which results in an averaging of weekly expenditure, while the poorest quintile relies more heavily on solid fuel and is less likely to benefit from reduced summer prices for coal. The overall effect is that fuel expenditure is more seasonal for the first quintile (Figure 8.5). Although one might expect the presence of central heating to be associated with higher fuel expenditure, Figure 8.6 indicates that the variations are small in the case of gas and electrical central heating but where oil or solid fuel are used spending is considerably greater. This probably reflects a higher utilization of gas and electricity for partial central heating, lower unit prices for off-peak

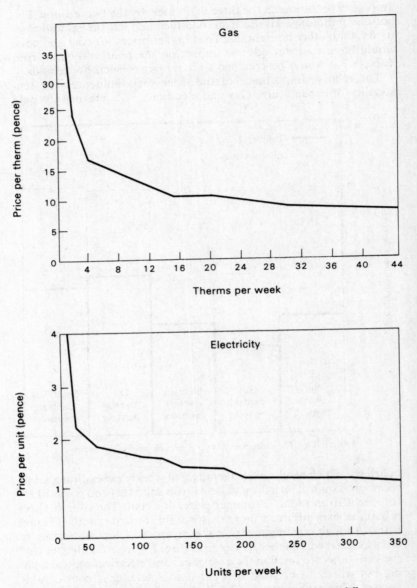

FIGURE 8.7   *The effect of gas and electricity tariffs: average price at different consumption levels*

consumption of electricity, and the tariffs for these fuels whereby the average price declines with increasing consumption.

The effect of the tariffs is depicted in Figure 8.7. Although standing charges or the equivalent vary for different types of tariff like ordinary or off-peak electricity, and are not the same between regions, the broad structure is the same (Department of Energy, 1976). The average price is higher for the smaller consumer so that for each £1 expenditure a lower volume of fuel is obtained. To the extent that small consumers are also poor, and fuel expenditure is of greater importance in smaller households, gas and electricity tariffs have vertical and horizontal distributional effects on living standards.[1] This has led the National Consumer Council (1976) to recommend flat-rate tariffs for both gas and electricity.

The economic analysis of tariff structures is essentially a matter of balancing the equity and efficiency considerations discussed in Section 4.5. The efficiency argument for standing charges is that each consumer imposes certain costs on the gas and electricity industries irrespective of the amount of fuel consumed. Efficient allocation of energy resources requires each household to be charged for the costs which it imposes on the industry. However, it is unclear what effect, if any, electricity standing charges have on resource allocation within the household sector when it is universally consumed. As the majority of households with access to a gas supply are also consumers it would seem that a similar situation holds for gas tariffs. The equity argument against standing charges is that they are simply lump sum taxes which have a greater adverse effect on living standards in smaller and poorer households. Weighing the two considerations is made more difficult by the fact that tariff restructuring, while helping the majority of the poor, would harm some larger consumers in the target population (HMSO, 1976, HC 353). But aside from this difficulty the essential questions are the costs, if any, stemming from resource misallocation and the distributional improvements from tariff restructuring together with the relative importance attached to efficiency losses and distributional gains. Other methods of helping poor consumers offset the reduction in living standards stemming from higher fuel prices—inverted tariffs, concessionary tariffs, special fuel allowances, fuel vouchers or higher social security benefits (Department of Energy, 1976)—can be analysed within a similar framework.

[1] Traditionally these effects are referred to the distributional arm of government—*see*, for example, Posner (1973). But Feldstein (1972a) and Wilson (1977a) have shown that distributional considerations modify the usual pricing rules: the adverse distributional effect of tariffs is examined in Wilson (1976).

In conclusion, subsidized rail, bus and fuel prices can have a considerable initial distributional impact. The measurement of such effects depends to some extent on the importance which is attached to whether the benefits are evenly spread within a target population like the poorest quintile. This is an important issue, for it can have a large effect on how progressive or regressive a measure is deemed to be. The other main conclusion to be drawn from this section is that tariff structures also have distributional effects.

8.4 Price indices

The focus so far in this chapter has been on the horizontal and vertical impact of changes in the price of a limited number of commodities over a short period of time. But for many purposes a wider perspective is required. In uprating benefits, for example, we are interested in the extent to which living standards of beneficiaries have been reduced by changing prices. Or studies of inequality are usually concerned with the distribution of living standards over longer periods of time.

Price indices, like the General Index of Retail Prices (RPI) used in Table 8.1, provide a means of converting cash benefits or money incomes into series which show the volume of goods and services which they will purchase. Essentially they consist of two components: price indicators and weights. The weights determine the importance attached to the individual price indicators and are usually derived from expenditure surveys like the FES. Ideally the price indicators should cover all the individual commodities purchased by consumers.

An extensive discussion of the principles and applications of index numbers is given in Allen (1975). The object is to show the change in expenditure which would be required to obtain the same standard of living given changing prices. The indifference curve analysis in Sections 3.2 and 3.3 provides the theoretical basis for price indices. In terms of Figure 3.5 for a homogeneous household type the weight for food would be OF_1 while for housing it would be OH_1. Under a new price regime the same standard of living is achieved by consuming OF_3' units of food and OH_3' units of housing services. Given the change in prices and quantities consumed the increase in expenditure required to obtain the same standard of living can be calculated. Goldberger and Gamaletsos (1970) demonstrate the application of this approach in providing the constant utility index suggested by Klein and Rubin (1948), while Muellbauer (1974) has extended it to the heterogeneous household case assuming that all the commodity scales are identical to the income scales used by Stark (1972).

The difficulty with this approach is that it requires a knowledge of the shape of the indifference curves and associated utility function. These are not directly observed but have to be estimated from price and quantity data. This estimation problem is avoided in a base-weighted Laspeyres index which uses weights derived from expenditure patterns in a previous period. A base-weighted index will tend to overestimate the impact of price changes on living standards since it does not allow for price substitution by households in response to changes in relative prices. In the case of the RPI this problem is minimized by using a chained Laspeyres index where the weights for most commodities are based on expenditure in the previous year (HMSO, 1975, Cmnd 5905).

In obtaining the weights for the RPI both high and many low income households are excluded, the latter being defined as those where at least three-quarters of total income is derived from social security benefits. The expenditure patterns of such low income households with at least one person over pension age are averaged over a three-year period to provide the weights for the One-Person Pensioner Index (1PPI) and Two-Person Pensioner Price Index (2PPI) (HMSO, 1969, *Employment and Productivity Gazette*). Although the weights for the 1PPI and 2PPI are based on smaller samples of households, and are less responsive to changes in expenditure behaviour stemming from variations in relative prices, the expenditure patterns of these groups are more homogeneous than for the wider based RPI.

Similar price indicators are mainly used in constructing the RPI and PPIs on the grounds that an analysis of food prices showed that for pensioner households they were not significantly different from prices paid by all households. However, evidence for the US suggests that the poor do purchase different types of food (Donaldson, 1976); and where commodities are bought through different outlets they often pay higher prices (Caplovitz, 1967; Kunreuther, 1973; and Reinhardt, 1974). And in the UK Piachaud (1974) cites evidence that low income groups pay higher prices. These higher prices may arise for a number of reasons: a tighter budget constraint and less storage space can necessitate more frequent purchasing in smaller amounts, poor transport facilities limit access to cheaper sources, higher risk credit facilities are needed for durable purchases, and so on. Quality variations create a major problem in comparing prices. Low income households will tend to purchase cheaper, lower-quality goods while more frequent purchases or the provision of credit facilities represent additional services or different qualities of goods. If any additional costs faced by poor households increase more rapidly over time than average commodity prices, then indices based on typical price indicators will tend to underestimate actual price increases.

Table 8.9

The General Index of Retail Prices, One- and Two-Person Pensioner Household Price Indices, 1967–76

Index	1967	1968	1969	1970	1971	1972	1973	1974	1975	1976
Retail Price Index (excluding housing)	100·0	104·6	110·5	117·3	128·5	137·0	149·0	173·9	217·3	254·1
Two-Person Pensioner Price Index	100·0	104·5	110·3	117·7	129·4	138·9	153·1	177·9	223·0	264·9
One-Person Pensioner Price Index	100·0	104·6	110·2	117·8	129·7	139·7	153·1	177·8	223·7	266·5

Source: *Department of Employment Gazette*

The RPI, 1PPI and 2PPI are compared for the period 1967–76 in Table 8.9. As many pensioner households are on SB where housing costs are mainly paid in full this element is excluded from the pensioner indices and the comparable RPI, which excludes housing, is therefore shown. During the decade the pensioner price indices increased by 7 to 8 per cent more than the RPI. Adopting a rather different approach which focused on households at different points in the income distribution, Tipping (1970) found that in the previous decade the index for the lowest 5 per cent of households increased by 6 per cent more than the index for the top 5 per cent. Extending this method to cover the period 1956–74 Piachaud (1976) records a difference of 11 per cent between the same two groups. Using a constant utility index Muellbauer (1974) has shown a similar effect over the period 1964–72.

These various studies show consistently that in the period up to 1974 the expenditure patterns of poorer households and pensioner households caused price increases to have a greater adverse effect on their living standards than in households generally. This arose mainly because the price of groups like food in Table 8.1, to which the poor devote a larger proportion of their budgets, increased more rapidly than durables or vehicles, which are more important in better-off households. During 1974 and 1975 the introduction of food subsidies and higher nationalized industry deficits helped to stop the differential from increasing, but it widened again in 1976. The divergence between price indices for various household types at different standards of living up to 1974 may not appear to be large from year to year. But the cumulative effects over a period of years, especially during an era of greater changes in relative prices and between extremes on the equivalent income distribution, can be considerable.

8.5 Summary

Prices, like income transfers, can influence living standards. Although the effects are perhaps less obvious than for other more explicit distributional measures, this chapter has demonstrated that they can have a considerable impact both horizontally and vertically. The horizontal influence depends crucially on the commodity scale in question: if it is large relative to the income scale then at a given standard of living the household budget share for the commodity will tend to increase. Thus food subsidies have a greater impact on larger families with older children, whereas fuel subsidies are of more importance to smaller households. There are two main differences between transfers and prices. First, with transfers the horizontal effects can be controlled by the equivalences embodied in benefits, whereas in the case of prices it depends on the commodity scales. Second, problems of defining the recipient unit or income accounting period which occur with transfers do not arise with redistribution through the price mechanism. However, Section 9.2 shows that if other factors like administrative costs are the same then in general a cash benefit involving the same amount of public expenditure will contribute more to the household's standard of living than a subsidy. But factors other than the living standard of the recipient may be involved and further discussion of this point is deferred until the next chapter.

The vertical influence of price changes depends on the equivalent income elasticity of demand, whereas in the case of transfers it is determined more directly by marginal tax rates. If consumption increases rapidly with living standards, as with durables, services or transport and vehicles, then the budget share tends to increase. Conversely, fuel and food have a relatively low elasticity and declining budget shares. Thus higher prices for food and fuel impose a greater burden on poorer households while increases for durables, services, transport and vehicles bear more heavily on the better-off. The examination of telephone and fuel expenditure showed that tariff structures can have distributional effects which are often over-looked. Traditionally the analysis of price changes and tariff structures has concentrated on resource allocation and efficiency: this chapter has demonstrated that both can have important distributional consequences.

The analysis of initial incidence has raised an important practical issue which is seldom considered in studies of distribution. Some measures like food subsidies benefit all households, whereas others such as rail or telecommunication subsidies are very uneven in their impact. Section 8.3 demonstrated that the degree of progression or regression could vary considerably, depending on whether it was calibrated in terms of the affected households or averaged over all households. The previous chapter indicated that this problem is not unique to prices but arose with transfers too: the next chapter will show that it occurs in an equally acute form with some benefits-in-kind.

When dealing with changes in living standards over time, especially in periods of rapid price change or during a longer run of years, the differential impact of inflation can be sizable. These influences are of some importance in monitoring the living standards of different groups of the population and in studies of redistribution which tend to focus on the upper and lower tails of the income distribution where the differential price effects are greatest.

The discussion throughout has been in terms of the initial impact of prices although Section 4.4 stressed that this will not always be a good guide to the ultimate effect. Where large changes are involved, or households are highly responsive to the stimulus of small changes, initial and final incidence may differ considerably. Rail subsidies may be very regressive if viewed as pure consumer subsidies but if they allow the earnings of some lower-paid workers to be higher than would otherwise be the case then their final incidence would be less regressive. Higher fuel prices are also regressive and bear more heavily on small households. But if account is taken of the influence of fuel prices on other commodities the effect is less regressive (Wilson, 1977b).

9. Non-Market Commodities

9.1 Introduction

The various factors influencing household living standards which were considered in Section 3.3 have now been examined. The effect of household type and income was discussed in Chapter 6; the role of income transfers was analysed in more detail in Chapter 7. The impact of market prices, especially for those commodities where prices are partly determined by government measures, formed the subject of the previous chapter. Yet this picture is incomplete. The household sector also benefits from a range of goods and services which are allocated by non-market mechanisms. The impact of these non-market commodities on living standards will be considered in this chapter.

*9.2 Theory

The analytical framework presented in Chapter 3 ignored non-market commodities and needs to be extended to incorporate them. Basically they fall into two categories—merit and public goods.

Public or collective goods have two basic attributes: they are characterized by indivisibility and non-excludability. Like jointly consumed items within the household such as a bathroom, television or refrigerator they cannot be independently varied but are supplied in the same quantity to all. Moreover, collective goods tend to be of an all-or-nothing variety. While it is possible to have rather more or less of a defence system or legislature the scope for variation is limited. Half of either is little better than none and twice of each is little better than one. Associated with this property of indivisibility is the fact that individual households cannot be excluded from the benefits of the collective good. This means that since consumption

*The general reader may wish to proceed to Section 9.3.

is collectively financed any household has an incentive to underplay the benefit which it derives from the commodity in order to limit its contribution. Consumption is also non-rival in that, unlike private goods, consumption by one household does not detract from the consumption of others. The aggregate demand function for a collective good is therefore obtained by vertical summation of individual demand curves, rather than by horizontal summation as in the case of private goods.

Merit goods are essentially private commodities which generate externalities beyond the markets in which they are traded. It may be an external benefit like a better-educated or healthier labour force or an external cost such as alcoholism or lung cancer. Typical merit goods, as the term implies, reflect a desire on the part of the community to provide a minimum standard of nutrition, housing and health care, or to curb the conspicuous consumption of luxuries. Often the externality will be a collective good, but it need not necessarily be so. Thus in many cases the difference between merit and collective goods is a question of degree rather than a more fundamental difference. None the less the conceptual distinction is useful and will be followed in this section.

(1) *Merit goods*. The provision of merit goods can take several different forms. Like food subsidies it may involve a reduction in price, but be limited to a distinct sub-group of the population. Rent and Rate Rebates, Rent Allowances, charges for some personal social services and grants for higher education are essentially of this type: they reduce the price by a variable amount depending on the income, rent and composition or other characteristics of the household. In other cases, like prescription and dental charges, a nominal payment is required which is waived for the poor and certain other categories such as pregnant women and children. Where the price is reduced consumption is still rationed by the price mechanism but in cases where it is zero some other allocative mechanism like the medical, dental or social work profession is involved. A second form of merit good is rationed by providing a minimum quantity free of charge to certain groups of households. Free School Meals give a single meal per day to the children of poor parents during the school term. The education and primary health care systems provide education and hospital care of a given standard free of charge to all children between the ages of 5 and 16 years and to all patients referred by the general practitioner service respectively. A third type of merit good makes use of both pricing and rationing. Housing subsidies result in reduced rents for local authority tenants but the quantity supplied is also fixed, since units are constructed according to

national standards and are indivisible. The three forms of merit goods are considered more fully below: a fourth was mentioned in Section 7.4.

By reducing the price of privately consumed goods and services the first type of merit good contributes to household living standards. Making use of the concepts developed in Section 3.2, Figure

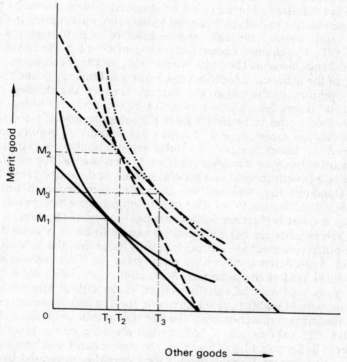

FIGURE 9.1   *The effect on household living standards of a merit good at a reduced price*

9.1 depicts household consumption of a merit good on the vertical axis and all other commodities on the horizontal axis. Under the market price regime the solid budget line shows the combination of the two goods which can be purchased with the fixed household income. Living standards are maximized when OM_1 of the merit good and OT_1 of the other goods are purchased. If the merit good price is reduced by half the household can now purchase twice the quantity of the subsidized good, or more of it and the other goods as shown by the broken budget line. Optimum consumption changes to OM_2 of the merit good and OT_2 of the other goods on a new, broken, indifference curve which denotes a higher standard of living. The cost of the merit good in terms of public funds is OM_2 times the subsidy rate: the reduced price has a price and income effect on both the merit good and all other goods.

However, with the same level of public expenditure on a cash grant a higher standard of living could be obtained. This is shown by the chained budget line which is parallel to the solid market price budget line and passes through the subsidized equilibrium point OM_2OT_2. The chained budget line is tangential to a higher, chained indifference curve at the point where OM_3 of the merit good and OT_3 of the other commodities are consumed. Drawing a line from this optimum to the origin, the distance between the chained and broken budget lines yields a measure of the extent to which the household would be better-off given the same amount of public expenditure on a cash benefit: 1 minus this proportion is sometimes termed the 'benefit weight'. A similar analysis applies to a straightforward subsidy on a market commodity like food. While expenditure on a benefit-in-kind or a general subsidy both contribute to living standards they will add less than the equivalent cash benefit (Tobin, 1952; Settle, 1976). This may be important when measuring living standards (Section 6.2) or marginal tax rates (Section 10.2).

Cash benefits are not universally superior to benefits-in-kind. If the other commodities are perfect substitutes for the subsidized good, if indifference curves are rectangular, or if all commodities are subsidized at the same rate, Schmundt *et al.* (1975) show that the household may be equally well off under either. Moreover, if the household is able to resell the merit good at market prices without incurring transaction costs the two will also be equivalent. And Little (1957) shows that if behavioural response of the type considered in Section 10.2 occurs then the cash benefit will not necessarily be superior. Finally, there is the externality generated by the merit good: we will return to this point below.

The second type of merit good, by providing a fixed quantity of a commodity, will also increase household living standards. The solid budget line in Figure 9.2 represents the situation prior to the introduction of the free allowance OM'. For a household consuming more than the free supply of the commodity, as depicted by the solid indifference curve, relative prices are unlikely to be affected. The merit good will simply allow the attainment of a higher standard of living by consuming OM_2 units of the merit good and OT_2 of the other commodities. Thus it will be identical to an equivalent cash benefit. But where the free allowance exceeds the existing level of consumption, as indicated by the dotted indifference curves, a higher standard of living could be obtained from the same expenditure on a cash benefit. The previous analysis for a subsidized price therefore applies equally to this case with one modification. Under a

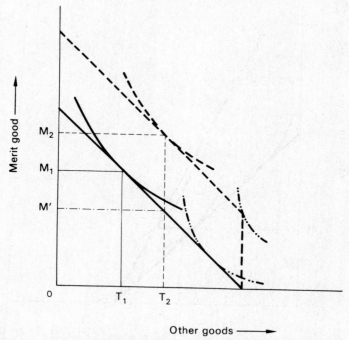

FIGURE 9.2   *The effect on household living standards of a merit good where a fixed quantity is provided free*

subsidized price the benefit weight will lie in the range 0 to 1, whereas in the fixed quantity case it may even be negative: Schmundt *et al.* cite free education and a minimum school-leaving age as an example where this may be so.

Third, a price subsidy combined with an absolute quantity restriction may also lead to enforced underconsumption as well as the overconsumption described in the previous case (Peskin, 1976). In Figure 9.3 exactly OM units of housing services are supplied at, say, half the market price. If the quantity was variable the new, broken, budget line would become applicable. But as the quantity is fixed the solid budget line remains with a horizontal segment at M' and clearly households with the solid indifference curve would be better-off: prior to the merit good they could only consume OT_1 of the other good which can be increased to OT_2 with its introduction. But in

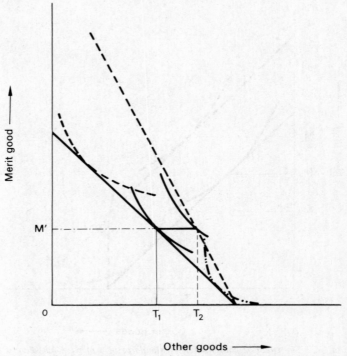

FIGURE 9.3   *A fixed quantity of a merit good provided at a reduced price*

general, as with a price subsidy, most households would be even better-off with the same expenditure on a cash benefit. However, where household preferences are reflected by consumption of the merit good which differs from OM' the conclusion that they would be better off with the merit good does not necessarily hold. The household with the broken indifference curve which preferred a considerably greater amount of housing services would be better-off not participating. Similarly for the household represented by the chained indifference curve which preferred a smaller volume of housing services. Differences in preferences would be manifested by low take-up under this type of benefit-in-kind.

The discussion of all three types of merit good has implicitly focused on the contribution which these benefits make to the living standards of a homogeneous household, Clearly the equivalent commodity and income scales developed in Chapter 3 can be used to measure the impact on households differing in composition. Where the benefit-in-kind is in the form of a price subsidy ideally the direct price substitution and income terms are required rather than the composite scales estimated in Chapter 5. In the absence of these three components, however, for small subsidies the composite scales should give an indication of the order of magnitudes involved. In the case where a free allowance is supplied which is below pre-benefit consumption of the merit good the composite commodity and income scales are appropriate. They could also be used to determine horizontally equitable allowances for households in different circumstances. For services like health care or education, which are almost entirely provided free through non-market mechanisms, it may be necessary to resort to complex indirect methods or expert judgement in obtaining equivalent commodity scales (McClements, 1977a).

So far we have been solely concerned with the contribution which benefits make to the living standards of the recipients. By definition merit goods involve external benefits or costs which should be taken into account in an overall evaluation. These externalities can be of two types: they may either be redistribution *per se* or they could stem from other considerations like economies of scale in public provision, higher labour productivity, and so on. This second category essentially stems from behavioural response of the type considered in Chapter 10, although it goes much wider than the six specific areas considered there to embrace production relationship, factor substitution, technology and similar aspects which are part of the wider effects mentioned in Section 4.4 and touched on again in Section 10.8. Such non-distributional externalities would be dealt with using those techniques like cost and production functions which have been developed in other branches of economics and need not be considered further here.

Distributional externalities, on the other hand, are central to the economics of social security. Section 4.5 showed how by applying distributional weights to households with different standards of living equity objectives could be traded-off against efficiency with the aid of a social welfare function. The distributional weights may be based on a range of alternative assumptions or, following Le Grand (1975), on the weights implicit in existing distributional instruments. Viewed in this way distribution is essentially a public good which will be considered more fully below. However, it is implicitly assumed there, as it was in Section 4.5, that distribution is a utility externality. That is, society as a whole is only concerned about living standards assuming household sovereignty: the households will be made better-off by their own choices than by the paternalistic decisions of the community. Tobin (1970) and Daly and Giertz (1972; 1976), have stressed that the externality may in fact be goods-specific. Society is concerned that households have an adequate diet, reasonable housing, health care, schooling and so on. In this case the individual household's consumption of the various externality-generating commodities would enter the social welfare function rather than a single index of its standard of living like equivalent income.

(2) *Public goods.* The distributional impact of public goods has been largely ignored in studies of income distribution: where taken into account the benefits have been allocated according to arbitrary rules like equal per capita or per household amounts, as a proportion of original or disposable income and by similar devices. Aaron and McGuire (1970) show that given a number of assumptions a superior method can be devised. It involves both the demand for and supply of public and private goods but the supply side will be ignored here. On the demand side a knowledge of household preferences for private and collective consumption is required (Maital, 1973), as depicted in Figure 9.4. Although households will have an incentive to understate their true preferences for public goods it is assumed that these can be determined. Gross earned income could be entirely devoted to the consumption of private goods OP but by collective decision OP–OP_1 is given up in taxes to finance collective consumption OC_1. Thus OP_1 represents disposable income plus the value or imputed value to the household of market and non-market private goods. In some cases disposable income will be entirely made up of transfers and, although the household has not contributed as such to the financing of collective consumption, by definition it will still benefit from OC_1 units of public goods.

The basic problem is to evaluate the benefit conferred by collective consumption OC_1 to households of different composition and varying standards of living as measured in terms of private consumption. Following Aaron and McGuire (1970), Maital (1973) shows that the imputed benefits of public goods should be allocated in inverse proportion to the marginal utility of income. Given cardinal measurement of utility this means that in Figure 9.4 successive indifference curves yielding a fixed increase in living standards will be increasingly close together. An extra £1 will add more to a poor household's standard of living than to a rich household's welfare: it will add more to a large family's welfare compared with a small family. It follows that to make the same monetary contribution towards collective consumption a rich household will have to make a small sacrifice in

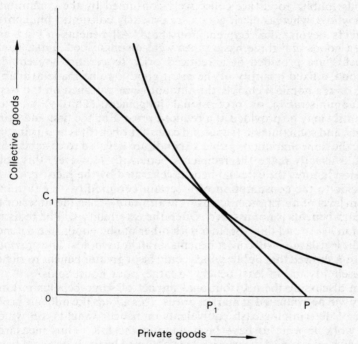

FIGURE 9.4 *Household preferences for public and private goods*

terms of private consumption and hence living standards, whereas a poor household or large household will have to make a large sacrifice. Thus OC_1 units of public goods confer a larger benefit on richer households and a smaller benefit on poorer or bigger households.

The practical implementation of this result in measuring the distributional impact of public goods poses many difficulties. Not least of these is the problem of differentiating between private and public goods, since many items of public expenditure have attributes of both categories. Measuring the externalities associated with merit goods will also be difficult: the next two sections look at the empirical evidence in more detail.

9.3 Benefits-in-kind

The previous section distinguished between public goods and merit goods: public goods are collectively consumed by the community as a whole, whereas merit goods are privately consumed but confer benefits beyond the recipient household. All benefits-in-kind are merit goods and three basic types were distinguished. First, some benefits are provided at a reduced price to certain households. Second, a fixed quantity of the merit good may be made available free or at a nominal charge, the amount being rationed on the basis of administrative or professional judgement. Thirdly, a fixed quantity may be provided at a reduced price. For the first and third types, and sometimes in the second case, if the benefit is non-transferable the same amount of public expenditure devoted to cash benefits would usually make the recipients better-off. However, this conclusion ignores the external benefit generated by the merit good: if specific to the consumption of a certain commodity—e.g. a minimum level of nutrition, housing or health care—then the superiority of cash benefits is not assured. Often the externality will be redistribution *per se* and this, together with other public goods like defence or the legislature, will confer benefits on all households. The previous section showed that public goods could be of greater benefit to richer households and of least benefit to large, poor households.

In discussing the distributional impact of some benefits-in-kind they will be evaluated at market prices. This avoids the difficult problem of determining cash equivalents or benefit weights, on which no work appears to have been done in the UK. Thus measured benefits may exceed the true benefits obtained by the household from consumption of the item as a private good. However, to the extent that the community as a whole is better-off from increased consumption of a specific good, or simply from the redistribution of living standards, the overall benefits will be understated. Table 9.1 shows the proportion of households in each quintile receiving certain benefits-in-kind: the average market value to all households and to recipient households is given in Table 9.2, although in the case of school meals the market price reflects a sizable general subsidy.

(1) *Reduced price.* Rent Rebates and Allowances and Rate Rebates illustrate the first type of merit good in which the price of a specific

Table 9.1
Percentage of households receiving benefits-in-kind by equivalent income

Benefit	Equivalent income quintile					All households
	1	*2*	*3*	*4*	*5*	
Rent Rebates and Allowances	2·4	2·4	0·9	0·3	0·1	6·1
Rate Rebates	5·1	6·0	5·2	4·5	4·3	25·0
Free School Meals	2·9	3·8	4·6	3·7	1·9	16·9
Other Benefits	2·3	2·1	2·4	1·6	0·7	9·1
Local Authority Housing	8·9	8·1	6·0	5·8	3·0	31·8

commodity is subsidized for certain households. The target population is defined in terms of rent and rate liability, household composition and income, the benefit being reduced with increasing income, although entitlement is not extinguished for larger households until about average gross earnings. Table 9.1 shows that those households receiving Rent Rebates and Allowances are mainly in the bottom two quintiles: Rate Rebates are less concentrated in the lower quintiles with the highest proportion of recipients in the second quintile. Some richer households receive these benefits because the definition of the benefit unit and income accounting

Table 9.2
Average market value (£/week) of benefits-in-kind to all households (A) and recipient households (R), 1975

Benefit		Equivalent income quintile					All households
		1	*2*	*3*	*4*	*5*	
Rent Rebates and Allowances	A	0·31	0·31	0·09	0·03	0·01	0·15
	R	2·63	2·60	2·06	1·80	1·60	2·47
Rate Rebates	A	0·14	0·17	0·10	0·07	0·07	0·11
	R	0·55	0·57	0·38	0·31	0·33	0·44
Free School Meals	A	0·35	0·36	0·33	0·24	0·13	0·28
	R	2·41	1·87	1·45	1·30	1·35	1·65
Other Benefits	A	0·03	0·02	0·02	0·01	0·00	0·02
	R	0·26	0·19	0·16	0·13	0·00	0·22
Local Authority Housing Rents	A	2·29	2·37	1·76	1·73	0·97	1·82
	R	5·14	5·88	5·87	6·01	6·37	5·73

period differs from the household and weekly basis respectively utilized in this study. SB recipients are also excluded, in the main, from these benefits since housing costs are counted in determining requirements (Section 2.5). As the majority of SB households are located in the bottom quintile (Table 7.3), both housing benefits would appear much more redistributive if SB recipients were included. Although the average values of benefits appear small for all households, they are sizable for recipients and account for 12 and 7 per cent of average income in the first and second quintiles respectively. Thus they are progressive, and highly so when measured in terms of all households in each equivalent income quintile (Table 9.2).

(2) *Fixed quantity.* Free School Meals and Other Benefits, which include school milk and welfare milk for nursing mothers, are examples of the second type of merit good where the quantity is fixed. Free School Meals for larger families are not withdrawn until well up the money income distribution, while school milk is available to all children under the age of 7. The low concentration of families with children in the lowest quintile (Table 6.2) partly accounts for the small proportion of recipients in this group (Table 9.1). The benefits of Free School Meals to recipients are sizable, the amount depending on number of children attending school and income. SB and FIS act as 'passports' to Free School Meals and welfare foods: for the reasons discussed in Section 10.7 we would expect take-up to be higher among these categories. Braley and Nelson (1975) also demonstrate that an increase in the price of school lunches led to a substantial increase in the take-up of free meals in a US city: participation is influenced by the market value of the benefit.

As the quantities of school meals and welfare foods which are supplied free are less than consumption in most households the average amounts in Table 9.2 should be a good indication of their value to recipients. The problem of valuation is especially difficult for educational and health services which are by far the most important benefits-in-kind. Both are supplied free in fixed quantity but unlike the benefits considered so far they are available to the entire population. Private provision of education and health care is therefore on a very limited scale and differs in many ways from the corresponding non-market commodities. The distributional impact of education and health care is included in HMSO (1976), *Economic Trends*, by valuing benefits at cost, and using some available information on utilization or making reasoned judgements about use by different demographic groups. In so doing, commodity scales of the type discussed in Section 3.3 are implied (McClements, 1977a).

Clearly the distributional effects of educational and health services represent a very important area in studies of living standards, where much further work needs to be done.

(3) *Reduced price and fixed quantity.* Housing subsidies on local authority or other public housing illustrate the third type of merit good. Table 9.2 shows that nearly half of the poorest quintile and almost one-third of all households live in subsidized accommodation. The subsidy is substantial: during 1975/76 it accounted for half of local authority housing costs (HMSO, 1976, Cmnd 6393). Although new housing units are constructed to national standards the total stock is composed of different vintages and other attributes like locality vary. An analysis of factors associated with variations in local authority rents (Coverdale, 1977) indicates that differences in quality and quantity are substantial and equally prevalent among poorer households. In order to determine the subsidy per unit, and hence its distributional impact, a measure of housing quality and quantity is required. This is not readily available, but if it is assumed that the subsidy is proportional to the rent, then the final row of Table 9.2 suggests that the average subsidy increases with equivalent income. Alternatively, if a fixed subsidy per unit is assumed the measure appears to be neither progressive nor regressive. On the other hand if the lower average rent paid by poorer households reflects a larger unit subsidy for a given quantity and quality of services housing subsidies could be quite progressive. To go beyond these qualitative statements on the basis of alternative assumptions requires empirical evidence on the unit subsidy, together with information on quality and quantity variations.

Despite the fact that the quantity (and quality) of housing services embodied in an individual unit is fixed, as assumed in the theoretical discussion in Section 9.2, a range does exist in the local authority sector. Thus take-up may be higher than the earlier analysis might suggest if different requirements on the part of households can be matched with variations in the available housing stock. The dynamic considerations discussed in Section 3.6 are of special importance in the case of housing expenditure. As well as information and adjustment costs, the tenancy of subsidized accommodation may confer non-transferable property rights which inhibit the matching of housing requirements with the available housing stock. Housing subsidies are also in marked contrast with food subsidies in that they are confined to a relatively small number of households, whereas food is universally consumed. The allocation of expenditure between housing and food subsidies therefore poses the dilemma discussed in Section 8.5 in an especially acute form.

In summary, the examination of the three categories of benefits-in-kind has indicated that they can have quite marked distributional impacts. This conclusion is based on evaluations at market prices which, as the previous section showed, may exceed the value which households would place on benefits. Peskin (1976) provides a good review of the US literature on this question and concludes that the cash equivalents of in-kind benefits can vary markedly. In the case of Food Stamps, for example, estimates vary from 27 to 100 per cent of the cost of providing the benefit-in-kind and the proportion increases with income. Murray (1975) finds that the cash equivalent of housing subsidies varies with household composition, tending to be highest for single-adult and large households. For some benefits, however, and Free School Meals is a case in point, market valuation may accurately reflect the cash equivalent. Even if households value benefits-in-kind lower than the same expenditure on cash benefits it does not necessarily follow that cash benefits are to be preferred. Section 7.4 showed that some cash benefits are not target efficient so that benefits-in-kind may provide an equally effective means of providing a minimum standard of living. Moreover, society may attach importance to the consumption of certain commodities in which case benefits-in-kind could be more effective than cash. And finally, whether transfers are in the form of cash or commodity-specific, redistribution itself may be a public good and contribute to collective welfare.

9.4 Public goods

It was argued in Sections 4.5 and 9.1 that redistribution is a public good. Consider a highly simplified situation in which the population is divided into two groups, 'rich' and 'poor', the latter being defined as, say, the first quintile of the equivalent income distribution. For every £1 paid in taxes by the rich £4 can be transferred to the poor. Thus if the rich are concerned about the welfare of the poor they derive satisfaction (donor benefits) from the collective tax payment: redistribution is indivisible. Moreover, no rich person can be prevented from deriving satisfaction so redistribution possesses the second basic characteristic of a public good, non-excludability.

Within this general framework Zimmerman (1975) shows that the transfer rate, defined as the benefit required for a specific household type, will be determined by several economic variables. It will tend to increase as the proportion of rich to poor increases and fall as the non-transfer income of the poor increases. Orr (1976) also argues that transfers will increase with the incomes of the rich, with a higher absolute number of poor given a fixed ratio of rich to poor and with the level of federal matching grants for state welfare payments. Both authors test the collective choice model as an explanation of AFDC (Aid to Families with Dependent Children) payments in the US. Using 1969 cross-sectional data for states Zimmerman (1975) finds that, despite measurement problems, the estimates are consistent with the theory of public goods. Orr (1976) makes use of a more detailed, longitudinal, cross-sectional data base drawing on state information over the period 1963–72. Higher per capita income, a higher proportion of rich to poor and a higher absolute number of poor are all associated with higher AFDC benefits. The average share of federal matching grants has a negligible effect, however, simply displacing state funding, although the marginal share is significant. The first factor is interpreted as an income effect which is unimportant due to the small proportion of AFDC beneficiaries in the population, whereas the marginal federal share represents a proxy for the price effect of the public good. This more detailed empirical study also supports the argument that income transfers are a collective good.

Due to the centralized nature of social security in the UK benefit levels do not vary regionally and the application of a collective choice model could only be tested using time-series data. This is less true of the health services. But education, housing, protective and the personal social services are partly financed by local authorities: in consequence there is considerable variation in provision between areas (HMSO, 1976, Cmnd 6453). To the extent that these and other services provided by local authorities have a collectively consumed element, they could be analysed within the framework of a public choice model.

The satisfaction derived from collective consumption, and hence the distributional impact of public goods, will depend on household composition and the level of private consumption. Section 9.2 showed that a given volume of public goods would contribute more to the welfare of a rich household than to a poor household, and more to a small than to a large family. Aaron and McGuire (1970) investigate the vertical impact of public goods with the aid of a utility function for private goods which underlies the indifference curve in Figure 9.4. Using two utility functions and making two assumptions about the extent of collective consumption they find that, contrary to earlier studies, the benefits may be regressive, i.e. increase with income. Maital (1973) reconciles several different approaches yielding the marginal utility of private consumption and comes to the same conclusion. The distributional weights in Section 4.5 imply that the social marginal utility of income varies and Le Grand (1975) has demonstrated how this information can be derived from existing distributional measures. Thus the judgement embodied in current practice provide an alternative method to the direct estimation of utility functions and in policy analysis it has the advantage of promoting consistency among instruments being used to pursue the same objective.

In summary, income transfers, like many other items of public expenditure, may be viewed as a public good. There is some empirical evidence to support this approach, but a major difficulty arises in determining the proportion of expenditure which is publicly consumed. This represents an important area where further research is required. The limited work which has been done on the distributional impact of public goods suggests that they may be regressive. While this research involves a number of assumptions, these are more plausible than those implicit in earlier studies which allocated the benefits of collective consumption using arbitrary formulae. If the distributional effects of public expenditure as a whole are to be analysed the approach outlined in this section provides a coherent conceptual basis for dealing with public goods.

9.5 Conclusions

Living standards are not only influenced by private consumption out of disposable income, but by the consumption of non-market goods and services both privately and collectively. Studies of the distribution of living standards should therefore incorporate measures of the benefits stemming from non-market goods and services. It was demonstrated how this could be done in principle in Section 9.2, which extended the model developed in Chapter 3 to include both benefits-in-kind and collectively consumed commodities.

The conclusions drawn in this chapter are much more tentative than those in earlier parts of the study. Most of the material which has been covered is at a very early stage of development and a lot of further research is required before a clearer picture will emerge. Given the extent of public expenditure it represents an important area in its own right as well as being central to the economics of social security.

10. Behavioural Response

10.1 Introduction

The earlier discussion of the vertical and horizontal distribution of living standards focused on the existing situation, as did the examination of income transfers, prices and publicly provided goods. Thus the household population observed under the economic environment prevailing in 1975 provided the basis for the analysis in Chapters 6 to 9. There are several justifications for dealing with the *status quo*. First, the existing population represents the situation with which social security measures must deal. Second, it also forms the basis from which all change must proceed: in deciding where we wish to go it is necessary to know the present position. Third, it is very much easier to determine the prevailing state of affairs than to show how things might change under different conditions. Yet a full understanding of how the existing situation arose requires a knowledge of how the social security sector influences household behaviour. Such information is also essential for the better comprehension of the initial and ultimate impact of any new measures.

If it is assumed that there is no behavioural response on the part of households to any aspect of the social security sector then our examination of the prevailing situation is adequate. However, the size of the sector and the seven potential behavioural influences of measures discussed in Chapter 2 provide grounds for thinking that this assumption is untenable. The purpose of this chapter is to review the available evidence on the magnitude of the behavioural responses induced by social security measures. Much of the work is of US origin and therefore not directly applicable to the UK. Yet there are many similarities between the two countries and in the nature of the problems faced by their social security sectors. US studies of behavioural response may therefore provide a very broad guide to the orders of magnitude which prevail in Britain.

10.2 Labour supply

The description of the social security system in Section 2.7 showed that the sector may influence the work decision by increasing or decreasing income in a way that is unrelated to work effort. Child Benefit or NI contributions above the ceiling are examples of this type of effect and will be termed unearned income for convenience. Alternatively, or in addition, social security measures may affect the return from an additional hour of work—the marginal 'tax' rate. Means-tested SB and FIS, or the interaction between these, means-tested benefits-in-kind and the tax system, provide examples of work-related benefits. However, many categorical benefits are also work-related although this may not be immediately apparent: unemployment, sickness and many similar contingencies are conditional on withdrawal from the labour market. The analysis in Section 4.2 indicated that labour supply influences could be decomposed into income and substitution effects. The income effect is relevant when considering measures which change income irrespective of work effort, but both income and substitution effects are important when dealing with measures which are work-related.

At least two dimensions of work can be identified. First, there is labour force participation—the choice between working and not working. If the decision is taken to work then there is the secondary question of the number of hours to devote to work and leisure. Other aspects of work like job satisfaction and work intensity may also have an important influence on work decisions, although they present major problems of measurement. For the most part this section will focus on hours worked: labour force participation can be regarded as a limiting case of the choice between work and leisure. At some points the two sequential stages provide a useful distinction for analysing the impact of social security measures, but different categories of worker form the main basis for organizing the discussion. The labour supply response of husbands, wives, female single parents and younger workers is examined in this section while aged workers are dealt with under the retirement decision in the next section.

Some practical difficulties arise in unscrambling income and substitution effects of a change in income. Typically, the two components are obtained by estimating the relationship between hours worked, the hourly wage rate, unearned income and a range of socio-economic factors like age, region, income of spouse or similar variables. The influence of unearned income on hours worked yields the income effect while the impact of wage rates on hours worked incorporates both income and substitution effects. By deducting the income effect obtained using the first relationship from the combined effects of the second the substitution effect can be calculated (Greenberg and Kosters, 1973). In some studies work-related transfers like Unemployment and Sickness Benefits have been included in unearned income, introducing a bias into the estimates of both income and substitution effects.

A second difficulty arises in calculating the appropriate net wage rate from the gross wage—the effective marginal tax rate. Barr and Stein (1974) show that awarding benefits for fixed periods brings about short-term marginal tax rates which are lower than the long-term rates. FIS is awarded for a 12-month period irrespective of changes in earnings or other circumstances, so the high marginal tax rates discussed in Section 2.7 only apply in limited circumstances.

Disregarded income, various similar administrative devices and administrative discretion will also reduce the effective tax rates below the nominal rates. Thus although the nominal rate in the US scheme Aid to Families with Dependent Children (AFDC) is 66·7 per cent, Lurie (1974) found that the effective rate seldom exceeded 50 per cent. Unreported income, which is very difficult to measure accurately, will involve zero tax rates.

Moreover, Settle (1976) has shown that where means-tested benefits-in-kind are involved the effective rate on the benefit-in-kind will in general be lower than its monetary value. This arises for exactly the same reason that a household would prefer the cash value of a benefit-in-kind: by allocating cash according to their own preferences consumers will generally be better-off with the cash value in lieu of a benefit-in-kind (Section 9.2). A number of other difficulties which arise in estimating the income and substitution effects of a change in unearned income or marginal tax rates are considered by Garfinkel and Masters (1976).

(1) *Husbands*. This category covers most male workers in the 20 to 60-year age range and constitutes the largest single group in the labour force. The cross-sectional estimates for the US reported by Hall (1973), Boskin (1973) and Garfinkel (1973b) are compared with a number of similar studies in the summaries by Cain and Watts (1973b) and Garfinkel and Masters (1976). While the results vary considerably they generally show a small positive substitution effect, indicating that an increase in wage rates will, if living standards are held constant, bring about a small increase in hours worked. But if wage rates increase living standards are not held constant: there is also an income effect which is negative and somewhat larger than the substitution effect in most studies. The net effect of these two

offsetting influences is a small reduction in hours worked with an increase in wage rates—the labour supply curve has a slight backward slope.

The New Jersey NIT experiment also indicated a small decrease in husbands' labour supply (Watts *et al.*, 1974; Rees and Watts, 1975) which is consistent with cross-sectional estimates of substitution and income effects. Most of the labour supply adjustment occurred in hours worked rather than in labour force participation (Garfinkel, 1974), which accords with the cross-sectional estimates of Boskin (1973). In the UK Brown and Levin (1974) conclude, on the basis of a survey of overtime work and attitudes, that on balance taxation has made men work more: Brown *et al.* (1976) analyse hours worked and wage rates to obtain estimates which agree with this survey evidence. These results are consistent with a negative income effect outweighing a smaller positive substitution effect.

Some indirect evidence for the UK is provided by MacKay and Reid (1972) on the basis of a sample survey of male engineering workers made redundant in the period 1966–68. They found that the length of unemployment had a small positive relationship with the magnitude of lump sum redundancy payments, while there was a more definite and somewhat larger relationship with the level of Unemployment Benefit plus Earnings-Related Supplement. Maki and Spindler (1975) on the other hand calculate that the introduction of Earnings-Related Supplements in late 1966 was associated with a sizable one-third increase in the level of unemployment. However, only a minority of the unemployed receive Earnings-Related Supplements and these results may be due to a structural change in labour markets which occurred around the same time. Taylor (1977) shows that in recent years much of the increase in UK unemployment can be explained by a fall in demand as reflected by growing spare capacity. Alternatively, Cubbin and Foley (1977) find that if changes in permanent income are taken into account increases in unemployment benefits had a negligible or even negative effect. Thus it seems most unlikely that higher benefits caused a substantial increase in unemployment. In contrast, Grubel *et al.* (1975) found a large increase in Canadian unemployment with higher benefits. For the US Marston (1975) estimates that unemployment insurance induces a small increase in duration of unemployment while Ehrenberg and Oaxaca (1976) show that this is associated with higher wages on re-employment.

(2) *Wives*. In the post-war period wives have accounted for a growing share of total labour supply although the proportion of women in the labour force has remained relatively stable until recently: the

increase in working wives has been offset by a decline in single women. Labour supply estimates from cross-sectional data in the US are more variable than for husbands (Hall, 1973; Boskin, 1973; Cain and Watts, 1973b; Garfinkel, 1974; and Garfinkel and Masters, 1976). Nevertheless most of the studies suggest that wives are very responsive to economic stimuli if other factors like the presence of preschool children are controlled for. This arises mainly from a larger positive substitution effect than for husbands and a similar or more negative income effect of a wage rate increase. Boskin (1973) finds that the adjustment is mainly in terms of hours worked rather than in labour force participation rates. In the New Jersey NIT experiment, on the other hand, most of the adjustment occurred in terms of participation rates in the case of white wives (Cain *et al.*, 1974), while more recent cross-sectional analyses by Cain and Dooley (1976) suggest that both labour force participation and weeks worked are responsive to wage rates. Using cross-sectional data for Great Britain, Greenhalgh (1975) finds evidence of substantial substitution effects for married women in terms of labour force participation.

(3) *Female heads of households.* One-parent families, mainly headed by a female, represent a large group on SB (Table 2.5) and are one of the fastest-growing categories of beneficiaries. Using cross-sectional data for the US, Hall (1973) finds that hours of work for this group are as responsive to economic stimuli as for wives. In a study of labour force participation by US mothers receiving AFDC Garfinkel and Orr (1974) found that employment rates were responsive to tax rates, deductions for work and other expenses and income disregards—the amounts of earned income which are disregarded in determining entitlement. However the employment rates were so low that very large changes in these factors would be necessary to bring about a marked increase in labour force participation.

(4) *Younger workers.* The work decision of younger people is tied up with the question of education and training: like wives and single parents they have good alternative uses of their time outside the labour market. Garfinkel and Masters (1976) find that younger workers are more responsive to economic stimuli than older workers, and if students are included a very high response is obtained. These results are probably of limited application in Britain in view of the greater prevalence of full-time education in the UK and the extensive provision of free educational services by the state.

In summary, the available evidence, much of it for the US, indicates that husbands in the 20- to 60-year age range are unresponsive in their work behaviour to labour market incentives. An increase in wage rates will induce a small reduction in hours worked and a negligible increase in labour force participation. A reduction in wage rates due to higher marginal 'tax' rates will bring about some increase in labour supply. Higher unearned income will be associated with a small reduction in hours worked and possibly some decline in labour force participation. In contrast, wives, single female heads and younger workers tend to be much more responsive to labour market incentives. An increase in unearned income leads to a larger

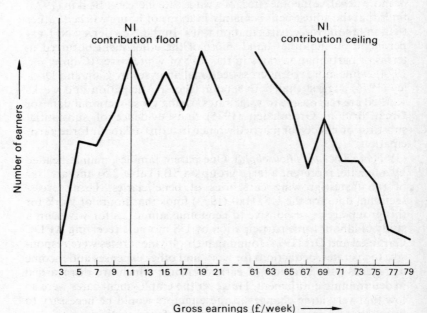

FIGURE 10.1   *Distribution of earners by gross earnings, April–December 1975*

reduction in labour supply than for husbands. Higher marginal tax rates are associated with a more sizable substitution of leisure for work (either in the form of reduced hours or a fall in labour force participation), which is only partly offset by an increase in work due to reduced income. The overall effect is a more marked reduction in labour supply. The fragmentary available evidence suggests that similar conclusions may apply to the UK.

In practical terms this means that social security measures probably have a limited impact on the labour supply of husbands but that wives, female-headed families and younger workers are more responsive. Thus NI contributions are more likely to influence the work behaviour of wives than of husbands. Figure 10.1 shows the distribution of earnings around the NI contributions floor and ceiling. As predicted in Section 4.2, there is a concentration of earners, mainly women, just below the floor, but contrary to expectation there is also a concentration at, rather than above, the ceiling. The large number of female one-parent families on SB (Table 2.5) is also consistent with the lower earnings opportunities and greater responsiveness of females to incentives. But aside from a few pieces of indirect evidence of this type we know very little about the impact of the social security system in Britain on the choice between work and leisure.

10.3 Retirement

The labour force activity rates for males and females before and after retirement age are shown for the last four decades in Table 10.1. There has been little change in male activity rates below pension age since 1931 but in the 65- to 69-year range the rates have fallen by more than half. By 1971 the proportion of males aged 70 or more actively engaged in the labour force had declined to less than one-third of the level in 1931. The picture for females is complicated by the marked increase in labour force participation in all age ranges of married women over the period. Females in the 55- to 59-year age range can be taken as indicative of this underlying trend. When the older age groups are expressed as a ratio of this baseline it is evident that activity rates for women over retirement age have also fallen dramatically.

Clearly this rapid fall in activity rates among the aged, and hence the rise in retirement, is of great importance for the social security sector. It occurred during a period when the NI scheme was introduced and Retirement Pensions grew to maturity: various other measures like Supplementary Pensions were also provided for retirement. This raises the question of the extent to which the trend to earlier and longer retirement was influenced by social security measures. It is an issue of considerable importance with the introduction of the new pensions' arrangements in 1978 and the maturation of these changes over the ensuing 20-year period.

Cross-sectional studies of labour supply by the aged are complicated by the provision of social security benefits and devices like the earnings rule discussed in Section 2.7. This makes it very difficult to obtain a good measure of unearned income since these components of income are work-related. Garfinkel (1974) reports results for married males in the US aged 55 to 61 and males over 72 years which avoids this difficulty: further estimates are given in Garfinkel and Masters (1976). Married men aged 55 to 61 had a more negative income effect and a larger substitution effect than their younger counterparts. For males over 72 years a large negative income effect was estimated. This evidence suggests that an increase in unearned income could induce a considerable reduction in labour supply: an increase in marginal tax rates, which would lower the return from an additional hour of work, would have a similar effect.

Table 10.1

Labour force activity rates as a percentage of the total population in the age, sex and marital status category, Great Britain, 1931–71

Category	1931	1951	1961	1966	1971
Males: aged 60–64	87·6	87·7	91·0	88·7	86·6
65–69	65·4	47·7	39·9	37·3	30·5
70+	33·4	20·3	15·2	14·0	10·9
Females—Single: aged 55–59	54·8	63·9	75·1	75·8	76·4
60–64	44·7	34·9	39·2	39·5	33·3
65+	20·1	11·8	10·9	10·4	8·2
Females—Married: aged 55–59	7·0	15·6	26·0	38·4	45·1
60–64	5·6	7·2	12·7	21·3	24·8
65+	2·9	2·7	3·4	5·5	6·3
Females—Widowed/Divorced: aged 55–59	28·8	39·1	51·8	59·5	62·2
60–64	22·0	19·3	28·2	34·7	33·7
65+	7·9	4·9	5·6	6·5	5·7

Source: HMSO (1975), *Social Trends 1975*

In an international cross-sectional study of 15 major developed non-socialist countries, which included the US and UK, Feldstein (1974b) has examined factors associated with the labour force participation of men aged 65 and over. Preliminary and tentative results of this study indicate that a higher level of per capita income, certainly at low and medium income levels, leads to a reduction in labour force participation. Earlier findings of Pechman *et al.* (1968) also showed declining labour force participation with increasing income. This is consistent with the income effect found by Garfinkel (1974) and suggests that rising incomes alone account for part of the reduction in labour force participation recorded in Table 10.1. An increase in benefits as a proportion of income or wages also reduces labour force participation (Feldstein, 1974b), which accords with the qualitative analysis in Section 4.2 and Figure 4.5. A high level of unemployment may also be associated with an increase in retirement (HMSO, 1977, Cmnd 6721–II). Finally, the existence of a retirement condition like the earnings rule discussed in Section 2.7 will bring about a reduction in labour force participation.

Using a rich body of cross-sectional data for the US, Quinn (1977) has analysed the labour force participation of men and unmarried women employees aged 58 to 63 years. Health limitations proved to be a major determinant of early retirement and interacted strongly with economic factors. Eligibility for social insurance benefits and

Table 10.2

The percentage distribution of earnings among pensioners who may be subject to the earnings rule,[1] April–December 1975

Earner	Gross earnings					
	Less than £10	£11–£19	£20–£23	£24 to RP limit[2]	Over RP entitlement	Number (100%)
Male head aged 65–69 years in married-couple households	85·0	6·8	0·0	1·8	6·3	220
Single female aged 60–64 years	82·0	8·2	2·5	4·1	3·3	122

[1] RP was reduced by 50p for each £1 earnings in the range £20–24 and £1 for each £1 of earnings thereafter.
[2] The Retirement Pension was £11·60 and £18·50 for a single person and married couple respectively from 7 April to 16 November 1975, thereafter it increased to £13·30 and £21·20. An approximate earnings limit at which RP entitlement is extinguished of £34 for a single person and £40 for a married couple is adopted for the entire period.

private pensions exerted a much stronger downward influence on the labour force participation of individuals with a health problem than in the case of the healthy. However, these factors were still significant and important influences on the retirement behaviour of the healthy: asset income also reduced the labour force participation of unmarried women. Unfavourable job characteristics had a much greater impact on retirement among those with a health limitation, whereas labour market conditions had a more marked influence on early retirement among the healthy. Perhaps the most surprising result was that the wage rate exerted no influence on labour force participation by men, although Bixby (1976) shows that economic factors are more important among those who do not retire early.

Quinn also found a sharp increase in the participation rates of unmarried women moving from low to moderate wage rates, but little effect thereafter.

These empirical studies of retirement behaviour suggest that social security measures have contributed to the reduction in labour force participation by the elderly evident in Table 10.1. Higher long-term benefits stemming from indexation with gross earnings (Section 2.6) and the introduction of an earnings-related element under the new pensions legislation (Section 2.5) will probably bring about some further reduction in participation. The earnings rule will have a similar effect. Table 10.2 shows the distribution of male earners aged 65 to 70 and female earners aged 60 to 65 years with earnings below, within and above the earnings limits during 1975. As we would expect on the basis of the analysis in Sections 2.7 and 4.2 there is a concentration below the earnings limit and very few individuals in the range where marginal tax rates are 100 per cent. This evidence is consistent with the US estimates that older workers are responsive to economic incentives. On the other hand increased increments for deferred retirement under the new pensions legislation will encourage later retirement. The overall effect of these various influences can only be determined by quantifying the individual components.

10.4 Saving

Changes in retirement behaviour will affect the level of saving since retirement represents one of the primary motivations for deferring consumption during working life. An increase in retirement will, *ceteris paribus*, bring about an increase in saving. But where the change in retirement is induced by social security measures other things do not remain equal. Section 4.3 showed that unfunded Retirement Pensions will discourage saving in the form of funded private pensions and other financial assets. These sources of income account for between one-third and one-fifth of total income in one- or two-adult households headed by a person over pension age (Section 6.6), whereas social security benefits contribute one-half to three-fifths of the total. Thus private saving is of some importance as a source of retirement income and in relation to social security provision for old age.

Evidence on the influence of social security on private saving comes from three sources—international cross-sections, time series data and individual cross-sectional data for the US. Aaron (1967), using data for nineteen developed countries, including the UK, for 1957, finds that high levels of saving are associated with lower levels of social security expenditure. However, further analyses of data for 1960 suggested that the relationship was much weaker than in the earlier study Pechman *et al.* (1968). Feldstein (1974b) uses data for fifteen developed countries in a more elaborate model. The average level of Retirement Pensions has a very substantial negative influence on saving as do the percentage of aged and dependants in the population. These results are consistent with the qualitative analysis of Section 4.3: a highly simplified life-cycle model can be used to predict that social security will displace private saving to some extent and that the savings ratio will decline if the aged population increases. However, all of these empirical results are also consistent with the alternative hypothesis that high levels of social security spending have been caused by low levels of private saving and inadequate private provision for retirement.

Using aggregate time series data for the US over the period 1929–71 excluding the war years 1941–46, Feldstein (1974a) estimates a consumption function which includes private wealth and a social insurance wealth variable based on an actuarial calculation of future benefits. The results indicate an increase in current consumption with increasing social security wealth and hence a reduction in saving. The calculated decline in aggregate saving is substantial: the effect of social insurance implies a fall in personal saving to half of what it would otherwise be in 1971. Munnell (1974) estimated a savings function for the US over the years 1900–71, excluding the two war periods, with both social insurance contributions and labour force participation of the elderly included as explanatory variables. The results indicated that increasing social insurance contributions depressed the level of private saving over the period while declining labour force participation brought about an increase in saving. The magnitudes of the two offsetting factors differ considerably with the time period over which the savings function is estimated. As there is limited scope for a further decline in the labour force participation of the elderly both Feldstein (1974a) and Munnell (1974) conclude that the savings-reducing effect of social insurance will predominate in the future.

The relationship between social insurance and saving is further investigated by Munnell (1976) using a cross-sectional survey of US men aged 45–59 in 1966. For these older men saving for retirement will be the primary motive for deferred consumption, and the empirical evidence indicates that coverage by social insurance and private pensions is associated with a lower level of private saving. The estimated reduction in saving is substantial. For a typical individual aged 52 the results suggest that in the absence of social insurance saving would amount to an additional one-fifth of income. This of course ignores the incentive to save more which stems from the retirement-inducing effect of social insurance.

In conclusion, the available empirical evidence indicates that the provision of retirement pensions financed on a 'pay as you go' basis does lead to a reduction in private saving. This effect may be considerable in the US, but given the rapidly falling earnings replacement ratios with increasing incomes in the UK it may be smaller in Britain. Even if the reduction in private saving in Britain is substantial it does not necessarily follow that a change in the level of social security benefits or in the method of financing them is required. There may be other means of stimulating saving which are more consistent with the objectives of the social security sector.

10.5 Household formation

Social security measures may influence household formation, and Semple (1975) has shown that changes in household composition over the period 1961–73 had an important influence on the distribution of income. The discussion in Section 3.5 indicated that the definition of the benefit unit, the extent of joint consumption, benefit relativities or equivalences for different household types, the consumption requirements of various categories of individual, voluntary and involuntary income redistribution within the household may affect formation. There has been a rapid rise in the proportion of single-person households over the years 1951–71 (Table 10.3), while the percentage of multi-family units fell by half in the second decade of the period. Although there was little change in the proportion of one-parent families between 1961 and 1971, the 276,000 on SB by 1975 (Table 2.5) represented almost a threefold increase since 1964. The Finer Report (HMSO, 1974, Cmnd 5629) discusses the developments which contributed to this trend, and identifies the improvement in SB entitlement relative to female earnings as a possible factor. Ross and Sawhill (1975) also record a rise in the number of families headed by a female in the US during this period, and a sharp increase in the number receiving welfare payments.

Demographic developments and changes in societal attitudes have undoubtedly contributed to these trends in the structure of households. The number of persons over pension age increased from 14 to 16 per cent of the UK population between 1951 and 1971: by 1975 it had reached 17 per cent. This change accounted for part of the increase in one- and two-person households. Changing attitudes, as reflected by the implementation of the Divorce Reform Act in 1971, increased the number of divorced single-parent families and the greater prevalence of single parenthood probably made for greater social acceptance.

To obtain a proper perspective of the influence which social security measures may exert on household formation we would ideally require a model explaining all the dimensions of the formation process. Children leave home to set up households on their own,

Table 10.3

Percentage distribution of households by household size and type, Great Britain, 1951–71

Household size	1951	1961	1966	1971
1 person	10·7	11·9	15·2	18·1
2 persons	27·3	29·8	30·4	31·5
3 persons	25·1	23·3	21·2	18·9
4 persons	36·9	35·0	33·2	31·5
Total households	100·0	100·0	100·0	100·0
1—*Household type*				
No family households	—	16·8	19·4	22·2
One-family households:				
Married couple, childless	—	25·6	25·8	26·7
Married couple, children	—	48·1	46·1	43·0
Single parent	—	6·7	6·8	6·7
2 + families	—	2·7	1·9	1·4
Total households (millions, 100·0 per cent)	14·6	16·2	16·9	18·3

Source: HMSO (1976), *Social Trends 1976*

or with unrelated contemporaries: Hill and Hill (1976) have analysed the factors involved in this decision. Alternatively children can create a new household on marriage and subsequently have children: the marriage may end in separation or divorce, creating two new households, these in turn doubling up with other households on remarriage. Household splitting, which occurs when children leave home, may be reversed when the aged parent (or parents) subsequently doubles up with the new household. Many aspects of family formation have been incorporated in the Urban Institute's Dynasim model (Orcutt *et al.*, 1976) which provides the type of overall demographic framework required for a comprehensive understanding of the process. However, the focus here will be on evidence on the direct impact of social security measures on household formation.

The rapidly rising number of one-parent families in the US claiming AFDC has stimulated a number of investigations of whether more generous welfare payments are a cause of family instability. Honig (1973; 1974) notes that an improvement in AFDC payments will have a twofold effect. First, for a given population of female heads of household increased levels of this means-tested benefit will make more families eligible. Second, more generous payments may induce household splitting or, as Ross and Sawhill (1975) point out, increase the caseload by deterring remarriage. Using cross-sectional data for 44 standard metropolitan statistical areas in 1960 and 1970 Honig (1974) finds that the level of AFDC has a significant effect on the proportion of females who are single parents and on the ratio of recipients to females: the effect is much stronger for black than for white women. The female wage and unemployment rate also have a positive effect on both variables, while the male wage has a negative influence. It is concluded that the first or welfare-independent effect of AFDC accounts for 56 per cent of the total influence in the case of black women and 20 per cent for white women, the remainder being welfare-induced. Using state data for 1971, Minarik and Gold-farb (1976) find no evidence that AFDC induces family dissolution, which accords with Ross and Sawhill's (1975) analysis of longitudinal data for 1968–72. In the latter study the wife's earnings and the experience of unemployment by the husband both contribute to instability. The principal effect of AFDC in the longitudinal sample was to reduce the probability of remarriage to less than half of the rate for non-recipients and this effect alone considerably increased the caseload. On the other hand, further work by Honig (1976) indicates that AFDC encourages family dissolution.

The outcome of these US studies is somewhat confused. It is unclear whether AFDC induces marital break-up or not, although it appears to inhibit remarriage. This research does indicate, however, that even if SB and AFDC do induce family dissolution this is a minor source of the growth in one-parent families on benefit or of one-parent families as a whole. Of the doubling in numbers on AFDC in the period 1967–71 some 46 per cent was due to an improvement in take-up (i.e. the proportion of those eligible for AFDC actually receiving it); another 7 per cent of the increase stemmed from expanded eligibility as a result of higher benefits; while only 27 per cent could be attributed to increased numbers of families headed by females (Ross and Sawhill, 1975). If it is assumed that all benefit-induced families participate in the programme then at most 27 per cent of the increase could be caused by AFDC bringing about family dissolution.

This discussion is of limited relevance to the UK because, unlike the US, married couples with a potential male worker are also eligible for SB. Thus social security in Britain does not provide the same incentive for family instability as the welfare system in the US. Nevertheless the US research is instructive. It demonstrates that the relationship between two factors—the number of one-parent families and benefit levels—is more complex than might at first appear. Increased participation, rather than increasing family dissolution, was mainly responsible for the growing AFDC caseload. And the expansion of elderly single-person households in the UK will have been due to the increasing proportion of old people in the population as well as to more extensive and higher retirement benefits.

Given the 10 to 20 per cent economies of scale between one-and two-adult households identified in Chapter 5 the increase in single-person households identified in Table 10.3 is of some importance. Aside from limited research on one-parent families very little is known about the causes of these developments or the extent to which they may be influenced by social security measures.

10.6 Fertility

With improved birth control technology in the post-war era fertility has increasingly become a matter of household choice, although birth control remains far from complete: the Finer Report (HMSO, 1974, Cmnd 5629) notes that in 1971 only one-third of married women at risk were using reliable methods. However, completed family size has always fallen well short of the physiological maximum, which suggests that there has always been an element of discretion in this aspect of human behaviour. Section 3.7 briefly touched on the fertility models of Willis (1973) and others in which the decision to have a child involves economic considerations. On the one hand there are the costs of feeding, clothing and otherwise maintaining a child until it leaves the home. These costs include the time involved in rearing the child in terms of the mother's forgone earnings and the consequent reduction in labour force participation. On the other hand the fact that families choose to have children suggests that they derive satisfaction from them: the number and quality of children provides an index of child utility.

If fertility is viewed within this framework then measures like

Maternity Benefit, Maternity Allowance, Child Benefit, social security dependency allowances for children, food subsidies, free health care, the provision of preschool day care and free education will reduce the costs of children. We would therefore expect these instruments of policy to have a pro-natalist effect. Higher male earnings would have a similar influence.

Section 6.4 showed faint evidence of economies of scale in consumption expenditure with increasing family size. In terms of full income, where the time of husband and wife spent in the home is measured at its opportunity cost, these economies of scale will be much more marked, since with increasing family size the same amount of forgone earnings will be spread over a larger number of children. If such economies do exist then the availability of Child Benefit or child dependency allowances at the same rate regardless of the child's parity will result in an increasing child subsidy with

Table 10.4
Birth rates, United Kingdom, 1951–75

	1951	1961	1966	1971	1972	1973	1974	1975
Live births per 1000 population	15·8	17·9	18·0	16·2	14·9	13·9	13·2	12·4
Live births per 1000 women aged 15–44 years	72·5	90·0	91·1	84·2	77·5	71·8	67·6	63·5

Source HMSO (1976), *Social Trends 1976*

each additional child (Cain, 1973). On the other hand higher female earnings would have an anti-natalist effect, and Blandy (1974) has argued that the provision of pensions may have a similar influence in less developed countries as children otherwise support their parents in old age.

Birth rates are shown in Table 10.4. Fertility increased in the post-war period to reach a peak in the early 1960s and has declined thereafter. By 1975 the fertility rate for women aged 15 to 44 years had fallen below the levels which prevailed in the depression years of the early 1930s. As real disposable incomes continued to grow in the early 1970s when the birth rate was falling some factor other than income must have been responsible for the decline in fertility.

Fertility has been analysed within an economic framework by Willis (1973), De Tray (1973), Gardner (1973), Gronau (1973) and Cain and Weininger (1973) for the US, by Ben-Porath (1973) for Israel, and by Schultz (1973) for Taiwan. Although the results of these studies are mixed, they do suggest that mother's education and earnings have a negative effect on fertility. The impact of unearned income is uncertain, although on *a priori* grounds it should have a positive influence on fertility. More recent work by Cain and Dooley (1976) using US census data for 1970 finds that unearned income has a negative effect on fertility while wife's education sometimes has a positive influence.

In the light of this conflicting evidence it is not clear what effect, if any, social security measures will have on fertility. Human behaviour in this area is very imperfectly understood and while economic factors may have some influence they do not seem to be of primary importance. Yet fertility rates have fluctuated considerably in the post-war era and in the longer term demographic factors have an important influence on the social security sector. The number of births affects the dependency ratio directly through the number of children and indirectly by influencing the number of working wives. After 15 to 20 years the majority of any birth cohort enters the labour market and makes NI contributions: ultimately they retire and are mainly supported by social security benefit payments. Thus an understanding of fertility behaviour is essential for long-term planning purposes as well as for a better appreciation of how social security measures may affect birth rates.

10.7 Take-up[1]

The number of social security beneficiaries is a primary determinant of the size of the sector and will depend on two factors:

(i) the number of eligible beneficiaries,

(ii) take-up—the proportion of those eligible who actually claim.

In the case of categorical benefits the number of potential involuntary participants will depend on the prevalence of unemployment, sickness, invalidity or the age distribution of the population in the case of retirement benefits. Section 4.2 suggested that the number of voluntary participants would depend on the level of wages relative to benefit payments with the latter possibly adjusted by a stigma factor. For means-tested benefits wage rates and earnings have a direct influence on the number of eligible participants because eligibility is defined in terms of income: Brehm and Saving (1964) show how this factor influences the demand for public assistance in the U.S.

---

[1] In writing this section I have benefited from access to unpublished papers by A. G. Coverdale which examine the factors associated with changes in the FIS caseload and various categories of SB recipients.

Similarly in the UK an increase in earnings reduces the number of people eligible for FIS because a declining number have earnings below the prescribed amount. As a result the FIS caseload fluctuates, being highest after an uprating and then declining until the next uprating. A much smaller proportion of people on SB have earnings, but among those who do an increase in wage rates reduces entitlement and the numbers who are eligible. In the previous section we noted the suggestion in the Finer Report (HMSO, 1974, Cmnd 5629) that the improvement in SB rates relative to earnings may have been an important contributory factor to the rapid rise in the number of one-parent families receiving SB during the 1960s. Atkinson (1969) has shown that around two-thirds of the increase in the Supplementary Pensioner caseload in 1966 arose from the increase in SB scale rates relative to Retirement Pensions. Thus the number of eligible beneficiaries will be determined to a considerable extent by economic factors.

The great majority of people eligible for categorical benefits actually claim them: take-up is more or less complete. However, Section 2.7 noted that this was not the case for means-tested FIS and SB. Problems of take-up also arise with means-tested benefits-in-kind like welfare food, prescription charges (Blaxter, 1974), dental charges, school meals and housing benefits. In the US Boland (1973) records that take-up of AFDC increased from 56 to 78 per cent between 1967 and 1970. On the other hand Lidman (1975) calculates that take-up in the unemployed father part of this benefit is around 15 per cent while for Food Stamps MacDonald (1975) estimates that take-up is below 40 per cent. Why should behaviour differ between categorical and means-tested benefits? And why do some means-tested benefits have a higher take-up rate than others?

A number of factors may contribute to incomplete take-up. First, it may be a matter of stigma. The process of undergoing a means-test or receipt of the benefit itself may make the perceived value to the beneficiary fall short of the monetary value or monetary equivalent of the benefit. In one of the few direct studies of stigma Handler and Hollingsworth (1969) show that recipients of AFDC who feel stigmatized are likely to spend less time on benefits. Perceptions of stigma vary among beneficiaries and will tend to be lower for groups like women with a less strong attachment to the labour market (Holtmann, 1973). The stigma factor will also be lower for those who have previously claimed the benefit or are already claiming another stigmatized benefit. A higher proportion of the overall population, or of residents in a locality, claiming a benefit will reduce stigma (Weisbrod, 1970). We would also expect the stigma factor to be lower for a centrally administered means-test like FIS compared with the more detailed personal investigation of circumstances for SB. Finally, the age and socio-economic background of those eligible may influence perceptions and evaluations of stigma.

Second, there may be access 'costs' associated with benefit participation. These may simply amount to the difficulty of acquiring knowledge about the benefit. Or a certain level of ability may be required to ascertain eligibility and some scholastic attainment may be necessary to complete an application form. Physical access to a good or service like welfare food or day-care may involve travel costs.

Thirdly, take-up will be influenced by the size of the benefit and the need of the beneficiary. Allowing access and stigma costs to vary the benefit net of these elements is more likely to be positive the larger the benefit entitlement. For a given level of access and stigma costs take-up will be higher the greater the need of the beneficiary. In the case of SB and FIS where the benefit unit is smaller than the household we would expect take-up to be lower among units resident in larger households, due to what was termed voluntary and involuntary income sharing in Section 3.5. Finally, a fourth factor was suggested in Section 9.2: for benefits-in-kind where the quantity is fixed differences in preferences may account for incomplete take-up.

A few empirical studies of take-up provide support for some of these arguments about stigma, access and need. Blaxter (1974) found that it was mainly low-income people in financial difficulties who did not make use of free prescriptions to which they were entitled. In a sizable sample survey of participants in the Special Supplemental Food Program for Women, Infants and Children, Bendick *et al.* (1976) also noted that specific barriers, or access costs, declined with increasing income: on the other hand stigma costs increased with income. In a study of Food Stamps MacDonald (1975) shows that after normalizing for other factors participation was twice as high among those reporting welfare income compared with those who had no such income. Take-up also increased with the Food Stamp bonus amount which reflects the need of the participant. An increase in the market price of a benefit-in-kind may have a similar effect: Braley and Nelson (1975) record a substantial increase in take-up of free school lunches following an increase in the price of school meals.

There would appear to be no published UK studies of factors associated with variations in take-up. The means-testing aspect of take-up involves an invasion of privacy and the provision of information which is not dissimilar to that required in a sample survey.

Kemsley (1975) has provided a series of two-way tabulations of the FES response rate in 1971 and one of the most marked variations occurs with age. The FES response falls considerably as the age of the household head increases and varies with a range of other socio-economic variables. If the take-up of means-tested benefits is influenced by similar factors this study of the FES response rate provides an insight into some of the influences which may be responsible for variations in take-up.

From the limited amount of empirical work which has been done it would seem that the factors associated with incomplete take-up are very complex. Both access and stigma costs may be contributory factors, the nature of the means-test will be important and the need of the individual or family will also affect take-up.

10.8 Conclusions

The focus in this chapter has been on the initial behavioural response to social security measures. We have considered how labour supply would adjust to a change in income which is unrelated to work effort and to an increase or decrease in the marginal return from an additional hour of work. The available empirical evidence, which mainly relates to the US, suggests that men aged 20 to 60 years are relatively unresponsive to labour market stimuli while all other groups are more responsive. Although early retirement behaviour is influenced to a considerable extent by health factors, after the normal pension age there is evidence that coverage by social insurance and private pensions induces retirement. Unlike men, single women are responsive to wage rates and asset income in making early retirement decisions. Earlier planned retirement in turn encourages private saving. On the other hand the provision of unfunded social security benefits will discourage saving since it will take the place of funded private insurance.

Household formation and splitting can be affected in a number of ways by social security measures. Benefit relativities may be more generous to one household type providing an incentive for its formation, while the related issue of the definition of the unit can have a similar effect. There is evidence that in the US AFDC delays the remarriage of female heads of households and so increases the prevalence of this household type. Provisions like Child Benefit reduce the cost of children and so may encourage fertility. However, there is no unambiguous evidence that fertility behaviour is influenced to any marked extent by economic stimuli.

The problem of low take-up is greatest among means-tested benefits and there is evidence that both access and stigma costs contribute to the phenomenon. Section 2.7 also noted that social security provisions may influence the work—education decision. There is an extensive literature on the economics of education which has not been reviewed here because it is not clear that current measures play an important part in the choice between education and work. The situation may change, however, and education takes on a greater importance in a longer-term perspective. In so far as low earnings, unemployment and poverty are generally associated with poor educational opportunities then behaviour in this area has a bearing on the economics of social security. Finally, the question of migration has not been considered in this chapter because it is of limited relevance to a small, centrally administered country like Britain. The influence of social security measures on US migration has been investigated although the evidence is inconclusive. Greenwood (1975) reviews this work as part of a wider survey of migration and its determinants. Analyses which take account of these various behavioural responses to social security measures become exceedingly complex, especially when we introduce the range, diversity, and inter-relationships of the benefits described in Section 2.5. Simulation models like Dynasim (Orcutt *et al.*, 1976) become essential for a realistic analysis of policy developments and changes.

So far we have only considered the initial impact of the social security system. The various behavioural responses can, if large, lead to a series of consequential effects which need to be taken into account. Section 4.4 stressed that higher benefits involved higher NI contributions and taxes, and that we need to go beyond the initial to the ultimate incidence of such changes. For example, Wilson (1977b) has demonstrated that the indirect effect of fuel subsidies on prices as a whole differs in its distributional impact from the direct influence of lower fuel prices to consumers. Or, Golladay and Haveman (1976) have shown that the initial distributional impact of a NIT may be desirable in terms of its stated objective of reducing poverty. Yet when its influence is traced through changes in consumers' expenditure to product markets and back to factor markets the secondary distributional effects are much less favourable.

Stern (1976) and Rosen (1976) have demonstrated how the optimal taxation framework discussed in Section 4.5 can be used to analyse practical problems. Whalley (1975a) has carried out a general equilibrium assessment of UK tax changes and shown how the ultimate effects of major changes can, in principle, be analysed. Whalley (1975b) has also demonstrated that partial equilibrium analysis can lead to very different conclusions compared with a general equilibrium approach to the same questions. All this work is at a very early, pioneering, stage yet it illustrates how the wider effects of the social security sector can be pulled together and analysed in a more comprehensive and satisfactory way.

Perhaps the most striking feature of the discussion in this chapter is our lack of knowledge about behavioural response to the social security sector in Britain. In the six areas which have been considered very little research of any kind has been carried out although some work is now getting under way. It may be that all aspects of behaviour are unresponsive to social security measures. However, we really need empirical evidence to support this contention, and some of the US studies which have been cited suggest that it is not a tenable argument. Moreover, it is scarcely a defensible position when the very object of many measures is to influence behaviour. Even small changes may set in train events which in the longer term can be of great importance given the irreversible nature of many social processes.

11. Wider Issues

11.1 Review

A twofold objective of this study was specified at the outset. The first aim was to present some useful areas of economic theory and the second involved its application to practical problems of the social security sector. Chapter 1 also outlined some basic features of economic analysis and classified the various types of judgement which arise in its application to social security measures. Chapter 2 set the scene for the rest of the study by describing the main economic features of social security in Britain. It considered the population structure, a sector balance sheet, NI contributions and the main benefits. Benefit levels and relativities were discussed together with a brief outline of the main areas of human behaviour that may be influenced by social security measures and it concluded with a discussion of the main objectives of the social security sector.

The next two chapters outlined the main corpus of economic theory which could be used to analyse many of the questions arising out of the institutional description. Chapter 3 dealt with the measurement of living standards in households of different size and composition. This led on to a number of related issues like the meaning of horizontal equity, whether living standards are absolute or relative, the definition of the unit of analysis, the appropriate time period, and so on. In Chapter 4 these ideas of equity gave way to notions of efficiency. This chapter considered the choice between work and leisure, consumption and saving; it went on to look at the inter-relationship between labour, capital and output markets. With the help of distributional judgements these efficiency aspects of social security measures can be reconciled with the pursuit of equity which, as Chapter 2 indicated, is a primary objective of the sector.

The theoretical analysis in Chapter 3 showed that variations in household circumstances were associated with differences in expenditure patterns. Expenditure behaviour could, in turn, be used to provide equivalent commodity and income scales—the relative commodity consumption and incomes required by families in different circumstances to obtain similar standards of living. Household expenditure records from the 1971 and 1972 FES were therefore used in Chapter 5 to provide estimates of these commodity and income scales. The estimated equivalent income scales are central to the pursuit of the equity objective of the social security system: they can be compared with the equivalences implicit in benefits recorded in Chapter 2.

The estimated equivalence scales developed in Chapter 5 were then applied in a number of different contexts in the subsequent four chapters. The equivalent income scales were used to classify households in the 1975 FES into equivalent income, or standard of living, quintiles. Thus horizontal variations in money income which can be justified by differences in household circumstances are removed, e.g. the greater money income required by a larger family to obtain similar standards of living. This allowed Chapter 6 to focus on the vertical distribution of living standards and examine how it varied by household type. It also looked at some of the factors associated with variations in living standards. One important source of income, transfers, was considered in more detail in Chapter 7, taking the 1975 household population as it was observed under the prevailing economic environment. The initial or impact distributional effects of direct taxes, NI contributions and the main social security benefits were analysed in some detail. Chapter 8 examined the initial distributional effect of prices, especially those influenced by government action, and went on to look at prices in general. A substantial proportion of all goods and services consumed by the personal sector is allocated to consumers by non-market mechanisms. These non-market commodities were analysed in Chapter 9: they range from benefits-in-kind like Free School Meals and housing benefits to health care, education and defence.

The emphasis throughout Chapters 6 to 9 was on the initial incidence of social security benefits and related measures which influence the living standards of beneficiaries. But focusing on the *status quo* implies that either the population does not respond in any way to these instruments or that if it does the changes are minimal and can be ignored. Chapter 10 therefore surveyed the empirical evidence on behavioural changes induced by social security measures. It dealt with six areas of human behaviour—work, retirement, saving, household formation, fertility and take-up of benefits. The available information suggests that these influences are important, but more research is badly needed into aspects of behavioural response. Further work is also required on how they, and the many diverse influences identified throughout the rest of the study, can be pulled together and integrated within a more comprehensive framework.

In the earlier chapters the focus was on specific questions and the ways in which economics could be applied in analysing them. There are wider issues which draw on many of the areas which have been examined individually: the remainder of this concluding chapter will consider some of these fundamental issues and the solutions which have been advanced for dealing with them.

11.2 Fundamental issues

In the simplest economic terms a social security system can be characterized as a set of measures designed to achieve a number of objectives. In attaining the various objectives financial and resource costs are incurred. Cash transfers involve financial costs while resources are tied up in administration. As a consequence of these transfer and administrative cost elements the revenue required to finance them may include an additional resource cost in items of output forgone. Thus both transfer payments and administrative expenditures have to be financed out of NI contributions and general taxation which may in turn create a disincentive to work and lead to a lower level of national output. The balance between transfer, administrative and forgone output costs, and their absolute levels, will depend on the type of instrument used to obtain the objectives of the sector. Transfers may be in the form of cash or benefits-in-kind; they may be universal or categorical, funded or unfunded; they may be income-related or given irrespective of income. In consequence, take-up may vary and so affect the efficiency of the measures in reaching their target populations and obtaining the specified objectives.

This brief description of an income maintenance system raises a number of basic, but related, issues. What are the objectives of the system? What relative importance is attached to the various aims? Can the objectives be better obtained by cash or benefits-in-kind? Are universal benefits more efficient than categorical benefits? Are means-tested benefits more effective than benefits which are unrelated to income? What causes variations in take-up? Are some types of measure more target-efficient than others? How do the administrative costs of alternative systems compare? Do different arrangements induce different behavioural responses? Are some instruments more efficient in resource terms than others? These are important questions which are fundamental to the provision of income maintenance. They also draw on much of the earlier analysis and on both grounds merit more detailed consideration.

It is clear from Chapter 2, especially Section 2.8, that the social security sector pursues both equity and efficiency objectives. Although these objectives are fairly clear in general terms, it is important that they should be stated explicitly. Failure to do so may mean that objectives are lost sight of, leading to measures which pull in opposing directions. One instrument may partly undo the purpose of another or a feature of it may be inconsistent with other aspects of the same measure. These conflicts will be more obvious, and are more likely to be reconciled and accommodated in a satisfactory way, if the objectives of a scheme are clearly stated.

Having stated the objective of a measure in general terms, it is helpful to go even further and spell the aims out more exactly. If the objectives are to help the poor or provide a minimum standard of living then by defining a poverty line or a minimum standard of living in £ per week attainment of the goal can be quantified. This precision may be difficult to obtain for a number of reasons. First, objectives are usually advanced in general, rather than specific terms. Second, they embody value judgements of the first type discussed in Section 1.3 and it may be difficult to obtain agreement for this reason. Third, where there are multiple objectives the relative importance attached to each will open up an additional area for different judgements. Thus the objectives of a measure may be the provision of a minimum standard of living, defined as 50 per cent of average earnings for a married couple, provided the resource costs in terms of administration and lower output do not exceed 5 and 15 per cent of the transfer costs respectively. The statement of objectives in specific terms involves a number of difficult value judgements and a good deal of technical economic knowledge about the measurement of living standards, equivalence scales, labour supply and possibly other behavioural responses.

It could be argued that in view of these difficulties it is preferable to concentrate on the specification of objectives in general terms. But this argument is unsound. The implementation of objectives in concrete policy measures involves very specific rules and regulations. The benefit unit has to be defined, relativities for different types of unit set and the absolute level of payments determined. Benefit payments in turn bear a certain relationship to the earnings distribution, whilst earnings replacement ratios decline in a very precise way, and so on. If the outcome of a given set of objectives can be determined in such exact terms there is no reason why the objectives them-selves cannot be specified with equal precision. In setting detailed goals care needs to be exercised in measuring their attainment under changing conditions. If the reduction of poverty is an objective, and a poverty line is determined in money terms, then adjusting it annu-ally to reflect price changes would bring about a fall in the number of poor people with rising living standards. But this reduction in poverty would be, in part, a statistical illusion if living standards are viewed in relative terms as the available evidence suggests (Section 3.4). Similarly, attitudes and judgements will evolve and change over time, making some objectives obsolete and creating new aims.

Given clearly and exactly defined objectives, the choice between the various types of instrument can be made. Chapter 9 showed that if the consumption of a minimum amount of a good or service like food or housing was considered desirable then its provision as a benefit-in-kind or at a subsidized price would be alternative ways of attain-ing that objective. On the other hand if individual preferences alone are to count then a cash benefit will be preferable. In either case there is the difficult question of defining the benefit unit and, where horizontal equity is important, the relativities appropriate for dif-ferent types of unit. From the discussion in Chapter 2 it is evident that horizontal equity is a pivoted feature of the social security sys-tem and much of the study was devoted to estimates and applications of equivalence scales. Although these estimates and their use have many limitations they deal with a central aspect of income, transfer mechanisms which is often overlooked by economists.

Cash benefits can be provided in a number of ways. If universal and unrestricted the financial cost will be high with the inevitable corollary that benefit levels will be low. Unless the target population is very wide target efficiency (e.g. the number of poor people brought up to the minimum standard of living) will also be low. Target effi-ciency might be improved by categorization. If specific groups like the unemployed contain a disproportionate number of poor people then a categorical benefit for this contingency will be more effective at reducing poverty than a universal benefit. However, Chapter 6 demonstrated that substantial numbers of households in even the poorest categories like the retired or one-parent families are not poor. Thus categorical benefits will only be effective at reducing poverty to the extent that the households in the category are poor.

In addition to the problem of low target efficiency, categorical benefits raise a number of further difficulties. The categories have to be delineated and Section 2.5 demonstrated just how complex and involved this process could be. In some cases it is difficult for both the administrative system and the benefit unit to determine to which category, if any, it belongs. Moreover, as Table 2.5 showed, many people fall through the categorical benefit net and have to be dealt with by other means. Lurie (1975a) stresses the horizontal inequities engendered by categorization—otherwise identical cases are treated differently depending on the category into which they happen to fall. Edelman (1975b) identifies another problem associated with categorization. It helps to create and foster perceptions and beliefs which have little factual basis. Some groups like the retired or sick may come to be viewed as more worthy and deserving than others such as the unemployed or one-parent families. Yet the unemployed and single parents have probably even less control over their circumstances than the retired or sick. There is no factual evidence that they are any less willing to work or inherently less deserving than the rest of the population. And in the SB scheme, for example, both cases are entitled to the same benefits as other groups. Thus categorization can promote an ideology which does not necessarily serve the overall objectives of the social security sector.

If the target efficiency of categorical benefits is to be improved then means-testing is necessary. However, this introduces the problem of take-up and may even exacerbate the difficulty with which it is designed to deal. And when a number of measures are means-tested cumulative marginal tax rates become high, providing a potential disincentive to work. The importance attached to this factor will depend on the labour supply elasticity of the group in question, since Section 10.2 suggested that the response varied for different types of earner. Categorical benefits, individually or collectively, may induce other forms of behavioural response discussed in Chapter 10. Their sheer complexity obscures potential behavioural incentives while the interaction of different measures can have a similar effect. The inter-relationships between benefits therefore become increasingly important: the various interlocking provisions have to be considered as a whole, although the categorical framework makes this difficult. Looking at the range of benefits also highlights horizontal inequities which they contain.

Finally, administrative costs differ considerably for the various types of benefit. The cost of administering the categorical NI scheme amounts to 5 per cent of total expenditure compared with 13 per cent for the means-tested SB scheme and 8 per cent for the less detailed income return required for FIS (HMSO, 1976, Cmnd 6615). The income tax system deals with many of the same people as the social security sector and the administrative costs amount to 2 per cent of total revenue (HMSO, 1977, *Board of Inland Revenue Report*) although there are additional administrative costs imposed on tax-payers. In the US administrative costs for means-tested Supplementary Security Income and AFDC are 9.1 and 9.5 per cent respectively although the system has come in for extensive criticism, being described as 'an administrative nightmare' (Glam, 1972), and part of the 'welfare mess'. For the means-tested Food Stamp programme administrative costs absorbed 15 per cent of total expenditure (US Department of Health Education and Welfare, 1976). The administration of means-tested benefits in the UK is also a cause for concern (HMSO, 1976, Cmnd 6615). Dissatisfaction stems not only from the cost of administering what have become very complex measures, but also from horizontal inequities and adverse behavioural incentives arising out of interaction with other forms of support for low income households. This results in confusion on the part of both administrators and potential beneficiaries.

11.3 Grand reform

The problems arising out of means-testing, categorization and the complex interaction of many different measures have resulted in the proposal of some fundamental solutions. Two basic strategies have been suggested. The first involves the integration and simplification of existing income transfer mechanisms into a single scheme of the Negative Income Tax (NIT) type which is universal and non-categorical. The second strategy diagnoses low earnings as the basic cause of poverty and advances a wage or earnings subsidy as the solution. Provided the labour supply curve is not backward-bending the second option promotes work, and hence greater efficiency, compared with the first possibility (Browning, 1973). Yet the implementation of wage or earnings subsidies has not received the same detailed feasibility study as the NIT option. This may be due to the fact that it could only be a very long-term method of tackling poverty, while part of the population would always remain to be dealt with by other measures.

This section will outline two major proposals for the reform of income maintenance which have been developed to the point of administrative feasibility. The 1972 Tax Credit (TC) scheme in the UK (HMSO, 1972, Cmnd 5116) involved integration of parts of the social security system in a reform of the personal tax system: Child Benefit implemented the child credit part of these proposals. During

1974 an Income Supplement Program (ISP) was advanced in the US as a replacement for a range of income-related benefits (US Department of Health Education and Welfare, 1976). Before considering the two proposals in more detail it is helpful to look at the main features of a NIT scheme. In very simple terms it can be characterized by three parameters: a guarantee or credit, a tax rate and a break-down income. The income guarantee OG or tax credit OC is the income transfer paid where there is no gross income (Figure

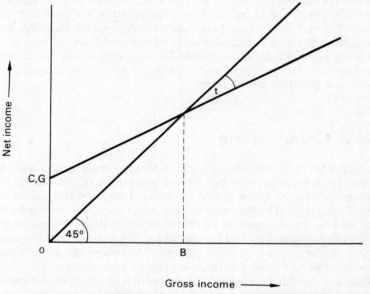

FIGURE 11.1   *The essential features of a Tax Credit or Negative Income Tax scheme*

11.1). The tax rate t determines the rate at which each £1 of gross income is taxed: together with the credit or guarantee it specifies the relationship between gross income and net or post-tax income. The break-even point indicates the gross income at which neither a negative tax payment nor a tax liability arises and is denoted by OB in Figure 11.1. Given any two of these basic parameters the third follows automatically. For example, if a tax credit or income guarantee of £15 per week is specified together with a marginal tax rate of 50 per cent the break-even income is £30 per week, whereas with a marginal tax rate of 33·3 per cent it becomes £45. Alternatively, with a given break-even income a higher guarantee or credit requires a higher tax rate. Green (1967) provides a full discussion of the origins and characteristics of negative tax schemes and a good summary of labour supply effects is given in Green (1968).

The difference between a tax credit and a negative income tax scheme is mainly a matter of emphasis rather than substance: the TC highlights the credit level while the break-even income and marginal tax rate are emphasized in the NIT. But in fundamental terms they are similar and can be characterized by the same three parameters. Unlike the existing tax systems in the UK and US they involve a 'negative' tax payment to those below the tax threshold or break-even income as well as a tax liability at higher incomes. Under the prevailing arrangements gross and net income are the same below the tax threshold as depicted by the 45° line in Figure 11.1: thereafter net income is given by the marginal tax rate applied to gross income above the threshold. However, the payment of a means-tested benefit like SB with a 100 per cent marginal tax rate would involve a horizontal segment at the benefit entitlement level in Figure 11.1 joining the 45° line. The nominal 50 or 66·7 per cent tax rates embodied in FIS and AFDC respectively would yield an upward-sloping segment with the slope depending on the marginal tax rate. Thus the introduction of a negative tax does not insert any new feature into income maintenance arrangements. Rather, it involves the integration, co-ordination and extension of a range of existing measures in a single scheme.

(1) *Tax credits.* The 1972 TC proposals, if implemented, would have integrated a small part of the social security system into a considerably simplified tax system (HMSO, 1972, Cmnd 5116). The aim was twofold. It would simplify and rationalize the tax system and income maintenance on the one hand and provide an improved level of income support for the poor on the other hand. The proposal would be easier to understand, more flexible, cheaper to administer and less of a disincentive to work: an improved level of income support for the poor would be achieved without recourse to a specific means-test. All employees with wages above a quarter of average male industrial earnings would be included in the scheme, as would the recipients of the main NI benefits, covering about 90 per cent of the adult population and their dependent children. Thus the self-employed and those solely dependent on SB would be excluded in the first instance for administrative reasons. The TC would consolidate short-term NI dependent child payments, and Family Allowances with the child credit. FIS would no longer be necessary for those in the scheme, while a substantial number of people would

be 'floated off' SB, but otherwise the social security system would not be greatly affected by the proposal.

The extent of the redistribution incorporated in the TC proposals depended on the level of the credit and the way in which the net cost of the scheme was to be financed (HMSO, 1973, HC 341–II). Simplicity was the key feature of the proposal and only three rates of credit were suggested—for a single person, married couples and dependent children. The great majority of people would be subject to a single rate of tax operated on a non-cumulative basis at weekly or monthly intervals depending on whether they were wage- or salary-earning. Only the small number of higher-rate taxpayers would need to be assessed on an annual basis with any over- or under-payment of tax corrected at the end of the year.

The tax unit would, as at present, consist of a single person or married couple with or without dependent children. A married couple could continue to file as two single-person units and a single parent would be treated as a married couple, providing a small incentive for family splitting. Unlike the prevailing arrangements whereby dependants resident overseas can be claimed for tax allowances, it was proposed that except where reciprocal agreements exist dependants should not be eligible for the payment of credits. A residence test would be applied to the members of the tax unit. Taking the married-couple credit as 1·00 the illustrative levels of credits adopted in the Green Paper embodied relativities of 0·67 for a single person and 0·33 for a dependent child. These levels are rather higher than the equivalence scale estimates summarized in Table 5.8, especially for the third or fourth adult in a household.

By integrating FIS with the tax system the high nominal marginal rates of tax noted in Section 2.7 would be reduced. With the current standard rate of tax at 34 per cent, 5·75 per cent employee NI contributions between the earnings floor and ceiling, withdrawal of Rent and Rate Rebates and Allowances and the loss of other benefits-in-kind like Free School Meals, quite high nominal cumulative marginal tax rates would nevertheless remain. However, for the reasons discussed in Section 10.2 the effective tax rates are lower than the nominal rates and Section 2.7 pointed out that under the existing arrangements a very small proportion of the labour force is subject to high nominal rates. Thus the labour supply effects of the TC proposals, while positive, would probably be small. Moreover, the available evidence on labour supply reviewed in Section 10.2 suggests that the response would differ between demographic groups. For husbands aged 20 to 60 years any reduction in marginal tax rates might lead to a small change in hours worked and possibly a fall in work effort. Conversely, for wives and for younger and older workers, a larger labour supply response would probably occur. The increase in labour supply and output would be accompanied by a reduction in education, home production and leisure with possibly a poorer matching of workers in jobs. In considering the labour supply effects of the proposals account would have to be taken of the balance between the credit level and the marginal tax rate with the former having an income effect and the latter both income and substitution effects. The impact of the method used to finance any net increase in expenditure or reduction in revenue brought about by the introduction of the scheme would also need to be included in the calculations.

It is unlikely that the TC proposals would have a marked effect on saving. Any influence would arise from the progressive tax rate structure, allowances for insurance premiums or other forms of saving and the treatment of investment income. To the extent that the credit would lead to an improvement in retirement income it might induce some earlier retirement and hence an increase or decrease in saving (Sections 10.3 and 10.4). The higher the child credit relative to the married-couple credit the lower the cost of a child, especially at low income levels, although Section 10.6 noted that there was no firm evidence of a link between fertility and economic factors. By providing a universal income-related form of support the TC scheme would provide assistance to all those who are entitled to, but do not take-up, means-tested benefits. It would also reduce means-testing to the extent that the numbers receiving SB, FIS and other means-tested benefits would decline.

The non-cumulative method of operation incorporated in the TC proposals provided an interesting departure from existing tax practice. Only a minority of taxpayers would require a cumulative, annual assessment, mainly because their income fluctuates between tax rate bands in the course of the year. This was made possible by having a single rate of tax applicable to a wide range of earnings so that weekly (or monthly) and annual assessment yielded the same tax liability. The change would therefore bring the accounting period used in the tax and social security systems more closely in line, reflecting the arguments advanced in Section 3.6 for a short accounting period in the social security sector. With the more progressive tax rate structure suggested in discussions of the proposals (HMSO, 1973, HC 341 I and II) non-cumulative assessment would be less feasible.

(2) *Income Security Program.* While the TC scheme was essentially a reform of the UK tax system which integrated some overlapping

parts of social security, the ISP proposal involved the replacement of a number of means-tested Federal benefits in the US by a single scheme which dovetailed with the existing tax system. Tax thresholds would be substantially increased and a universal non-categorical NIT introduced for all individuals or families below this break-even point. Thus the focus of the ISP scheme was on the consolidation of major parts of the welfare system into a single measure to be co-ordinated with the positive tax system, which would otherwise remain largely unchanged. Despite the emphasis on reforming welfare rather than the tax system there are many similarities between the US and UK proposals. Both involved a credit or guarantee which amounted to less than 20 per cent of average earnings. A constant marginal tax rate of 50 per cent in the US scheme and 30 per cent in the UK proposal would be applied to all earnings of lower-paid workers. As a result of these different tax rates the break-even income for the TC proposal, at over three-fifths of average earnings, would be considerably higher than the ratio of less than two-fifths incorporated in the ISP proposal. Both schemes envisaged the continuation of the separate social insurance schemes with benefits based on contribution conditions.

ISP would replace the Federal components of AFDC, Supplementary Security Income and Food Stamps although States could supplement payments to beneficiaries who would be made worse off by the change. The benefit unit would consist of all persons related by blood, marriage or adoption living under one roof, making it much closer to a household definition than the nuclear family or individual adult in the TC scheme. The guarantee and break-even income relativities are also quite different. Taking a married couple as the reference group with a value of 1·00, a single person would have a guarantee and break-even income relativity of 0·50, while for a two- or four-person household they would be 1·00 and 1·50 respectively. Thus there is no distinction between a second person who is an adult or child. Higher benefits with different relativities are applicable to households containing an aged, blind or disabled person. This benefit structure would provide some incentive for the formation of households composed of unrelated individuals; would encourage other individuals to combine with aged, blind or disabled people; and would benefit a married couple with two children who split into two separate units. In contrast, an earlier proposal (US Government Printing Office, 1974) incorporated a substantial 'marriage bonus'.

Under the ISP proposals recipients who are not aged, blind or disabled, a minor, caring for any of the previous categories, or employed would be required to register for work. And even if income was below the break-even level those with substantial assets would not be entitled to ISP payments. The income accounting period would be a retrospective 12-month period with carry-forward provisions for income exceeding the break-even level. Those participating in the scheme would be required to report income either monthly or quarterly depending on its variability. Despite the quite complex nature of ISP, administrative costs were estimated to be 4·5 per cent of total expenditure.

The ISP and TC proposals demonstrate that universal non-categorical income maintenance measures are administratively feasible. While neither scheme represents a single NIT device performing all income transfer functions, both are a move in that direction. They would reduce the amount of categorization and the associated horizontal inequities, simplify the tax and social security systems, reduce overlaps and co-ordinate the two sets of instruments, lower some of the higher nominal marginal tax rates and be cheaper to administer. One important advance stemming from the integration of tax and social security systems is that transfers can be concentrated on the poor without recourse to a means-test. While co-ordination or integration of the two sets of instruments poses many practical transitional difficulties it permits some fundamental problems of income maintenance to be dealt with.

11.4 Conclusions

While the theory in Chapters 3 and 4 was developed in terms of the social security sector the previous section has demonstrated that it is applicable to wider issues. Moreover, it has shown that in dealing with these larger problems many different economic aspects have to be dealt with together. It is not sufficient to focus on horizontal equity and the provision of a minimum standard of living. Labour supply and other behavioural incentives have to be considered at the same time while administrative feasibility and costs also have to be taken into account. As the changes become more extensive their impact on the economy as a whole increases and realistic analysis requires that a wider range of effects, including ultimate as well as initial impacts, is considered.

One important conclusion to emerge from this study is the limited nature of knowledge about the initial effects or even the objectives of the social security sector. Some general objectives of measures are evident enough—providing a minimum standard of living, an element of earnings replacement and compensation. But whether the system is intended as an instrument of income redistribution is less clear. Methods of measuring living standards have improved and the concepts developed in Chapter 3 provide the framework for understanding the effect of differences in household characteristics, changing incomes and varying prices. Recent theoretical advances have provided the basis for analysing efficiency aspects of income maintenance programmes and reconciling efficiency with equity considerations.

Much empirical work is required on the questions addressed in Chapters 5 to 10 if better guidance is to be provided on the shape of income transfer mechanisms. The equivalent commodity and income scales in Chapter 5 need to be replaced by new and better estimates. Not only are they central to the design of policy instruments, but they are also fundamental to a wide range of matters which ultimately lead to such measures. Chapter 6 demonstrated the application of equivalence scales in measuring living standards and the factors associated with poverty. It indicated that under present circumstances a categorical approach to poverty of the kind adopted in the Beveridge Report (HMSO, 1942, Cmd 6404) is unlikely to prove effective. This point was borne out by the evidence on the initial distributional effects of transfers in Chapter 7. Changes in relative prices could have a considerable impact on living standards with the effect differing both between rich and poor and among dissimilar household types at the same standard of living (Chapter 8). Those goods and services allocated by non-market mechanisms also influence living standards in an important way which varies by household type and equivalent income.

Perhaps the most pressing need for further research lies in some of the areas of behavioural response discussed in Chapter 10. Whether these reactions to measures are small or large can have a major influence on the design of income maintenance instruments. They also determine the extent to which income transfers affect the population and the entire economy, being of considerable importance in this wider context.

In conclusion, the purpose of this study was to demonstrate the application of economic analysis to the problem of the social security sector. It constitutes an important part of the national economy and the earlier chapters have shown that many areas of economics can contribute to a better understanding of the social security system. Thus economics has an important part to play in making social security and related instruments more effective and efficient in obtaining their objectives. Nevertheless, the rudimentary state of knowledge revealed by the study suggests that much further research is required if economic analysis is to make its full contribution to the solution of practical problems. In almost every area which has been considered the available information is subject to major limitations.

According to the maxim that a little knowledge is a dangerous thing it might be concluded that the contribution which economics can make should be suspended until matters are improved. However, in practical affairs a little information is almost invariably preferable to no knowledge. To assume that nothing is known often involves suppositions which are untenable or inconsistent with existing evidence and engenders uninformed judgements of the third type discussed in Section 1.3. By making use of the available information, with an awareness of its limitations, better decisions are likely to be made. Moreover, in the longer term better information will only come about through building upon existing knowledge: its use will promote improvement.

In short, economic analysis has an important contribution to make to the social security sector. Much more work is needed on many important issues if its full potential in terms of more effective policy measures is to be realized. But it is essential to remember that in the final analysis economics is subordinate to other considerations.

References

Aaron, H. (1967). 'Social Security: International Comparisons', in O. Eckstein, (ed.), *Studies in the Economics of Income Maintenance*, Brooking's Institution, Washington D.C.

Aaron, H. and McGuire, M. (1970). 'Public Goods and Income Distribution', *Econometrica*, **38**, pp. 907–20.

Albin, P. S. and Stein, B. (1968). 'The Constrained Demand for Public Assistance', *Journal of Human Resources*, **3**, pp. 300–11.

Allen, R. G. D. (1975). *Index Numbers in Theory and Practice*, Macmillan, London.

Atkinson, A. B. (1969). *Poverty in Britain and the Reform of Social Security*, Cambridge University Press, Cambridge.

Atkinson, A. B. (1970). 'On the Measurement of Inequality', *Journal of Economic Theory*, **2**, pp. 244–63.

Atkinson, A. B. (1973). 'How Progressive Should the Income Tax Be?', in M. Parkin (ed.) *Essays in Modern Economics*, Longmans, London.

Atkinson, A. B. (1975). *The Economics of Inequality*, Oxford University Press, Oxford.

Atkinson, A. B. (1977). 'Poverty and Social Security Research: An Agenda', in *Social Security Research: Papers Presented at a DHSS Seminar on 7–9 April 1976*, HMSO, London.

Atkinson, A. B. and Stiglitz, J. E. (1976). 'The Design of Tax Structure: Direct Versus Indirect Taxation', *Journal of Public Economics*, **6**, pp. 55–75.

Barr, N. A. and Stein, B. (1974). 'Income Support and the Poverty Trap', unpublished, London School of Economics.

Barten, A. P. (1964). 'Family Composition, Prices and Expenditure Patterns', in P. Hart (ed.), *Proceedings of the Sixteenth Symposium of the Colston Research Society*, Butterworth, London.

Becker, G. S. (1965). 'A Theory of the Allocation of Time', *EJ*, **75**, pp. 493–517.

Becker, G. S. (1973). 'A Theory of Marriage: Part I', *JPE*, **81**, pp. 813–46.

Becker, G. S. (1974a). 'A Theory of Marriage: Part II', *JPE*, **82**, pp. 511–26.

Becker, G. S. (1974b). 'A Theory of Social Interactions', *JPE*, **84**, pp. 1063–93.

Ben-Porath, Y. (1973). 'Economic Analysis of Fertility in Israel: Point and Counterpoint', *JPE*, **81**, pp. S202–33.

Bendick, M. *et al.* (1976). *Towards Efficiency and Effectiveness in the WIC Delivery System*, Urban Institute, Washington D.C.

Benus, J. *et al.* (1976). 'The Dynamics of Household Budget Allocation to Food Expenditures', *Review of Economics and Statistics*, **58**, pp. 129–38.

Bixby, L. E. (1976). 'Retirement Patterns in the United States: Research and Policy Interaction', *Social Security Bulletin*, August.

Blandy, R. (1974). 'The Welfare Analysis of Fertility Reduction', *EJ*, **84**, pp. 109–29.

Blaxter, M. (1974). 'Health "On the Welfare"—A Case Study', *Journal of Social Policy*, **3**, pp. 39–51.

Blinder, A. S. (1976). 'Intergenerational Transfers and Life Cycle Consumption', *AER*, **66** Proc., pp. 87–93.

Boland, B. (1973). 'Participation in the Aid to Families with Dependent Children Program (AFDC)', in *Studies in Public Welfare*, Paper No. 12 (Part I), Sub-Committee on Fiscal Policy, Joint Economic Committee, US Government Printing Office, Washington D.C.

Boskin, M. J. (1973). 'The Economics of Labor Supply', in Cain and Watts (1973a).

Boskin, M. J. (1976). 'On some Recent Econometric Research in Public Finance', *AER*, **66** Proc., pp. 102–9.

Bradford, D. F. and Rosen, H. S. (1976). 'The Optimal Taxation of Commodities and Income', *AER*, **66** Proc., pp. 94–101.

Brady, D. S. (1958). 'Individual Incomes and the Structure of Consumer Units', *AER*, **48**, pp. 269–78.

Braley, G. A. and Nelson, P. E. (1975). 'Effect of a Controlled Price Increase on School Lunch Participation: Pittsburgh 1973', *American Journal of Agricultural Economics*, **57**, pp. 90–6.

Brandt, R. B. (1966). 'The Concept of Welfare', in S. R. Krupp (ed.), *The Structure of Economic Science*, Prentice-Hall, Englewood Cliffs, New Jersey.

Brehm, C. T. and Saving, T. R. (1964). 'The Demand for General Assistance Payments', *AER*, **54**, 1002–18.

Brittain, J. A. (1971). 'The Incidence of Social Security Payroll Taxes', *AER*, **61**, pp. 110–25.

Brittain, J. A. (1972a). *The Payroll Tax for Social Security*, Brooking's Institution, Washington D.C.

Brittain, J. A. (1972b). 'The Incidence of the Social Security Payroll Tax: Reply', *AER*, **62**, pp. 739–42.

Brown C. V. and Levin, E. (1974). 'The Effects of Income Tax on Overtime: The Results of a National Survey, *EJ*, **84**, pp. 833–48.

Brown, C. V. *et al.* (1976). 'Estimates of Labour Hours Supplied by Married Male Workers in Great Britain', *Scottish Journal of Political Economy*, **23**, pp. 261–77.

Browning, E. K. (1973). 'Alternative Programs for Income Redistribution: The NIT and the NWT', *AER*, **63**, pp. 38–49.

Buchanan, J. M. and Bush, W. C. (1974). 'Political Constraints on Contractual Redistribution', *AER*, **64** Proc., pp. 153–7.

Cain, G. G. (1973). 'The Effect of Income Maintenance Laws on Fertility in the United States', *Institute for Research on Poverty*, Reprint 138.

Cain, G. G. and Watts, H. W. (1973a). *Income Maintenance and Labor Supply: Econometric Studies*, Markham Press, Chicago.

Cain, G. G. and Watts, H. W. (1973b). 'Towards a summary and Synthesis of the Evidence', in Cain and Watts (1973a).

Cain, G. G. and Weininger, A. (1973). 'Economic Determinants of Fertility: Results from Cross Sectional Aggregate Data', *Demography*, **10**, pp. 205–23.

Cain, G. G. *et al.* (1974). 'The Labor Supply Response of Married Women, Husband Present', *Journal of Human Resources*, **9**, pp. 201–22.

Cain, G. G. and Dooley, M. D. (1976) 'Estimation of a Model of Labor Supply, Fertility and Wages of Married Women', *JPE*, **84**, pp. S179–99.

Caplovitz, D. (1967). *The Poor Pay More*, The Free Press, New York.

Churchman, C. W. (1966). 'On the Intercomparison of Utilities', in S. R. Krupp (ed.), *The Structure of Economic Science*, Prentice-Hall, Englewood Cliffs, New Jersey.

Coverdale, A. G. (1976). 'Circumstances of Poor Households', (*see Social Trends, 1977*, HMSO, London).

Coverdale, A. G. (1977). 'Factors Associated with Variations in Housing Costs', unpublished, Economic Advisers' Office, DHSS.

Cox, I. (1973). 'Treatment of Families under Income Transfer Programs', in *Studies in Public Welfare*, Paper No. 12 (Part II), 'The Family, Poverty and Welfare Programs: Household Patterns and Government Policy', Sub-Committee on Fiscal Policy, Joint Economic Committee, US Government Printing Office, December 1973, Washington D.C.

Crosland, C. A. R. (1957). *The Future of Socialism*, Macmillan, New York.

Cubbin, J. S. and Foley, K. (1977). 'The Extent of Benefit Induced Unemployment in Great Britain: Some New Evidence', *Oxford Economic Papers*, **29**, pp. 128–40.

Daly, G. and Giertz, F. (1972). 'Welfare Economics and Welfare Reform', *AER*, **62**, pp. 131–8.

Daly, G. and Giertz, J. F. (1976). 'Transfers and Pareto Optimality', *Journal of Public Economics*, **5**, pp. 179–82.

Davis, H. L. (1976). 'Decision Making Within the Household', *Journal of Consumer Research*, **2**, pp. 241–60.

Denzan, A. T. and Mackay, R. J. (1976). Benefit Shares and Majority Voting, *AER*, **66**, pp. 69–76.

Department of Energy (1976). *Energy Tariffs and the Poor*, London.

De Tray, D. N. (1973). 'Child Quality and the Demand for Children', *JPE*, **81**, pp. S70–95.

Diamond, Lord (1975). *Public Expenditure in Practice*, George Allen and Unwin, London.

Donaldson, L. (1976). 'The Differential Impact of Food Inflation upon the Poor', *American Journal of Agricultural Economics*, **57**, pp. 71–5.

Donnison, D. (1972). 'Ideologies and Policies', *Journal of Social Policy*, **1**, pp. 97–117.

Easterlin, R. (1974). 'Does Economic Growth Improve the Human Lot? Some Empirical Evidence', in P. A. David and M. W. Reder (eds.), *Nations and Households in Economic Growth: Essays in Honor of Moses Abramovitz*, Academic Press, New York.

Edelman, M. (1975a). 'Language, Myths and Rhetoric', *Society*, **12**, pp. 14–21.

Edelman, M. (1975b). 'The Creation of Political Beliefs through Categorization', *Institute for Research on Poverty*, Discussion Paper, 258–75.

Ehrenberg, R. G. and Oaxaca, R. L. (1976). 'Unemployment Insurance, Duration of Unemployment and Subsequent Wage Gain', *AER*, **66**, pp. 754–66.

Feldstein, M. S. (1972a). 'Distributional Equity and the Optimal Structure of Public Prices', *AER*, **62**, pp. 32–6.

Feldstein, M. S. (1972b). 'The Incidence of the Social Security Payroll Tax: Comment', *AER*, **62**, pp. 735–8.

Feldstein, M. S. (1974a). 'Social Security, Induced Retirement and Aggregate Capital Accumulation', *JPE*, **82**, pp. 905–26.

Feldstein, M. S. (1974b). 'Social Security and Private Savings: International Evidence in an Extended Life Cycle Model', Discussion Paper 361, Harvard Institute of Economic Research, Harvard University.

Feldstein, M. S. (1975). 'Towards a Reform of Social Security', *The Public Interest*, Summer, No. 40.

Feldstein, M. S. (1976a). 'Social Security and Saving: The Extended Life Cycle Theory', *AER*, **66**, Proc., pp. 77–86.

Feldstein, M. S. (1976b). 'On the Theory of Tax Reform', *Journal of Public Economics*, **6**, pp. 77–104.

Fiegehen, G. C. and Lansley, P. S. (1976). 'The Measurement of Poverty: A Note on Household Size and Income Units', *Journal of the Royal Statistical Society*, Series A, **139**, pp. 508–18.

Gardner, B. (1973). 'Economics of the Size of North Carolina Rural Families', *JPE*, **81**, pp. S99–122.

Garfinkel, I. (1973a). 'A Skeptical Note on "The Optimality" of Wage Subsidy Programs', *AER*, **63**, pp. 447–53.

Garfinkel, I. (1973b). 'On Estimating the Labor Supply Effect of a Negative Income Tax', in Cain and Watts (1973a).

Garfinkel, I. (1974). 'Income Maintenance Programs and Work Effort: A Review', *Institute for Research on Poverty*, Reprint 118.

Garfinkel, I. and Haveman (1974). 'Earnings Capacity and the Target Efficiency of Alternative Transfer Programs', *AER*, **64** Proc., pp. 196–204.

Garfinkel, I. and Orr, L. L. (1974). 'Welfare Policy and the Employment Rate of AFDC Mothers', *National Tax Journal*, **27**, pp. 275–84.

Garfinkel, I. and Masters, S. (1976). *Income Maintenance Policy and Concerns about Work Effort*, Academic Press, forthcoming.

Glam, S. (1972). 'Issues in Welfare Administration: Welfare—An Administrative Nightmare', Paper No. 5, *Studies in Public Welfare*, Sub-Committee on Fiscal Policy, Joint Economic Committee, US Government Printing Office, Washington D.C.

Goldberger, A. S. and Gamaletsos, T. (1970). 'A Cross Country Comparison of Consumer Expenditure Patterns', *European Economic Review*, **1**, pp. 357–400.

Goldfarb, R. S. (1970). 'Pareto Optimal Redistribution: Comment', *AER*, **60**, pp. 994–6.

Golladay, F. and Haveman, R. (1976). 'Regional and Distributional Effects of a Negative Income Tax', *AER*, **66**, pp. 629–41.

Goodwin, L. (1972). *Do the Poor Want to Work?* Brooking's Institution, Washington D.C.

Gordon, R. A. (1976). 'Rigor and Relevance in a Changing Institutional Setting', *AER*, **66**, pp. 1–14.

Green, C. (1967). *Negative Taxes and the Poverty Problem*, Brooking's Institution, Washington D.C.

Green, C. (1968). 'Negative Taxes and Monetary Incentives to Work: The Static Theory', *Journal of Human Resources*, **3**, pp. 280–8.

Greenberg, D. H. and Kosters, M. (1973). 'Income Guarantees and the Working Poor: The Effect of Income-Maintenance Programs on the Hours of Work of Male Family Heads', in Cain and Watts (1973a).

Greenhalgh, C. (1975). 'Labour Supply Functions for Married Women in Great Britain', Working Paper 70, Industrial Relations Section, Princeton University.

Greenwood, M. J. (1975). 'Research on Internal Migration in the United States: A Survey', *Journal of Economic Literature*, **13**, pp. 397–434.

Gronau, R. (1973). 'The Effect of Children on the Housewife's Value of Time', *JPE*, **81**, pp. S168–99.

Grubel, H. G. *et al.* (1975). 'Real and Insurance Induced Unemployment in Canada', *Canadian Journal of Economics*, **8**, pp. 174–91.

Hall, R. E. (1973). 'Wages, Income and Hours of Work in the US Labor Force', in Cain and Watts (1973a).

Handler, J. F. and Hollingsworth, E. J. (1970). 'The Administration of Welfare Benefits: The Views of AFDC Recipients', *Journal of Human Resources*, **5**, pp. 208–21.

Harrison, B. (1972). 'Education and Underemployment in the Urban Ghetto', *AER*, **62**, pp. 796–812.

HMSO (1942). Cmd 6404. *Social Insurance and Allied Services* (The Beveridge Report), London.

HMSO (1969). 'Retail Price Indices for One and Two Person Pensioner Households', *Employment and Productivity Gazette*, June, London.

HMSO (1972). Cmnd 5116. *Proposals for a Tax Credit System*, London.

HMSO (1973). HC 341–I. *Select Committee on Tax Credit—Volume I: Report and Proceedings of Committee*, London.

HMSO (1973). HC 341–II. *Select Committee on Tax Credit—Volume II: Evidence*, London.

HMSO (1973). HC 341–III. *Select Committee on Tax Credit—Volume III: Appendices to Minutes of Evidence and Index*, London.

HMSO (1973). *Family Expenditure Survey: Report for 1972*, London.

HMSO (1974). Cmnd 5629. *Report of the Committee on One-Parent Families*, London.

HMSO (1974). Cmnd 5713. *Better Pensions: Fully Protected Against Inflation*, London.

HMSO (1975). Cmnd 5905. *Retail Price Index Advisory Committee: Housing Costs, Weighting and Other Matters Affecting the Retail Price Index*, London.

HMSO (1975). *Annual Abstract of Statistics 1975*, London.

HMSO (1975). *Social Trends 1975*, London.

HMSO (1976). Cmnd 6453. *Local Government Finance: Report of the Committee of Enquiry*, London.

HMSO (1976). Cmnd 6565. *Annual Report of the Department of Health and Social Security 1975*, London.

HMSO (1976). Cmnd 6615. *Supplementary Benefits Commission Annual Report, 1975*, London.

HMSO (1976). HC 353. *Fourth Report from the Select Committee on Nationalised Industries, 1975–76*, London.

HMSO (1976). *Transport Policy: A Consultation Document*, Volumes 1 and 2, Department of Environment, London.

HMSO (1976). *Social Trends 1976*, London.

HMSO (1976). *Parliamentary Debates*, 912, London.

HMSO (1976). *Department of Employment Gazette*, September, London.

HMSO (1976). *Family Expenditure Survey 1975*, London.

HMSO (1976). *National Income and Expenditure 1965–75*, London.

HMSO (1976). 'Effects of Taxes and Benefits on Household Income 1975', *Economic Trends*, December, London.

HMSO (1977). Cmnd 6851. *Housing Policy: A Consultation Document*, London.

HMSO (1977). Cmnd 6721–I. *The Government's Expenditure Plans*, London.

HMSO (1977). Cmnd 6721–II. *The Government's Expenditure Plans Volume II*, London.

HMSO (1977). *Social Security in Britain*, London.

HMSO (1977). *Social Security Statistics 1975*, London.

HMSO (1977). *Supplementary Benefits Handbook*, London.

HMSO (1977). *Board of Inland Revenue Report No. 119 for the Year Ending 31 March 1976*, London.

Hill, D. (1974). *Ambiguity and the Political System*, Institute for Research on Poverty, Discussion Paper 236–74, Madison, Wisconsin.

Hill, D. and Hill, M. (1976). 'Older Children and Splitting Off', in G. J. Duncan and J. N. Morgan (eds.), *Five Thousand American Families*, Volume 4, Institute for Social Research, University of Michigan, Ann Arbor.

Hochman, H. M. and Rodgers, J. D. (1969). 'Pareto Optimal Redistribution', *AER*, **59**, pp. 542–57.

Hochman, H. M. and Rodgers, J. D. (1970). 'Pareto Optimal Redistribution: Reply', *AER*, **60**, pp. 997–1002.

Holtmann, A. G. (1973). 'Time and the Economics of Welfare', *Institute for Research on Poverty*, Discussion Paper, 158–73.

Honig, M. (1973). 'The Impact of Welfare Payments on Family Stability', in *Studies in Public Welfare*, Paper No. 12, Part I, Sub-Committee on Fiscal

Policy, Joint Economic Committee, US Government Printing Office, Washington D.C.

Honig, M. (1974). 'AFDC Income, Recipient Rates and Family Dissolution', *Journal of Human Resources*, **9**, pp. 303–22.

Honig, M. (1976). 'A Reply', *Journal of Human Resources*, **11**, pp. 250–60.

Ishikawa, T. (1975). 'Family Structures and Family Values in the Theory of Income Distribution', *JPE*, **83**, pp. 987–1008.

Jencks, C. *et al.* (1972). '*Inequality: An Assessment of the Effects of Family and Schooling in America*, Basic Books Inc., New York.

Kemsley, W. F. F. (1969). *Family Expenditure Survey: Handbook on the Sampling, Fieldwork and Coding Procedures*, HMSO, London.

Kemsley, W. F. F. (1975). 'Family Expenditure Survey. A Study of Differential Response Based on a Comparison of the 1971 Sample with the Census', *Statistical News*, November.

Kilpatrick, R. W. (1973). 'The Income Elasticity of the Poverty Line', *Review of Economics and Statistics*, **55**, pp. 327–32.

Klein, L. R. and Rubin, H. (1948). 'A Constant Utility Index of the Cost of Living', *Review of Economic Studies*, **15**, pp. 84–7.

Klein, W. A. (1971). 'Familial Relationships and Economic Well-Being: Family Unit Rules for a Negative Income Tax', *Institute for Research on Poverty*, Reprint 71.

Koopmans, T. C. (1957). *Three Essays on the State of Economic Science*, McGraw-Hill, New York.

Kunreuther, H. (1973). 'Why the Poor Pay More for Food: Theoretical and Empirical Evidence', *Journal of Business*, **46**, pp. 368–80.

Lamale, H. H. (1958). 'Changes in Concepts of Income Adequacy over the Last Century', *AER*, **48**, pp. 291–9.

Lampman, R. J. (1966). 'Towards an Economics of Health, Education and Welfare', *Journal of Human Resources*, **1**, pp. 45–53.

Lancaster, K. (1975). 'The Theory of Household Behavior: Some Foundations', *Annals of Economic and Social Measurement*, **4**, pp. 5–21.

Leff, N. H. (1969). 'Dependency Rates and Savings Rates', *AER*, **59**, pp. 886–96.

Grand, J. Le (1975). 'Public Price Discrimination and Aid to Low Income Families', *Economics*, **42**, pp. 32–42.

Leibenstein, H. (1974). 'An Interpretation of the Economic Theory of Fertility: Promising Path or Blind Alley?', *Journal of Economic Literature*, **12**, pp. 457–79.

Lerman, R. I. (1973). 'The Family, Poverty and Welfare Programs: An Introductory Essay on Problems of Analysis and Policy', in *Studies in Public Welfare*, Paper No. 12 (Part I), 'The Family, Poverty, and Welfare Programs: Factors Influencing Family Instability', Sub-Committee on Fiscal Policy, Joint Economic Committee, US Government Printing Office, November 1973, Washington D.C.

Lidman, R. M. (1975). 'Why is the Rate of Participation in the Unemployed Fathers Segment of Aid to Families with Dependent Children (AFDC–UF) so Low?', *Institute for Research on Poverty* Discussion Paper, 288–75.

Lindblom, C. E. (1959). 'The Science of Muddling Through', *Public Administration Review*, **19**, pp. 79–88.

Lister, R. (ed.) (1976). *National Welfare Benefits Handbook*, Poverty Pamphlet 13, Child Poverty Action Group, London.

Little, I. M. D. (1957). *A Critique of Welfare Economics*, Oxford University Press, London.

Lurie, I. (1974). 'Estimates of Tax Rates in the AFDC Program', *National Tax Journal*, **27**, pp. 93–111.

Lurie, I. (ed.) (1975a). *Integrating Income Maintenance Programs*, Academic Press, New York.

Lurie, I. (1975b). 'Integrating Income Maintenance Programs: Problems and Solutions', in Lurie (1975a).

McClements, L. D. (1977a). 'Equivalence Scales and the Wider Analytical Framework', in V. Morris (ed.), *Distributional Effects of Public Expenditure in Social Policy*, Routledge and Kegan Paul, forthcoming.

McClements, L. D. (1977b). 'Equivalence Scales for Children', *Journal of Public Economics*.

MacDonald, M. (1975). 'Why Don't More Eligibles Use Food Stamps? **8**, pp. 191–210. *Institute for Research on Poverty*, Discussion Paper, 292–75.

MacKay, D. I. and Reid, G. L. (1972). 'Redundancy, Unemployment and Manpower Policy', *EJ*, **82**, pp. 1256–72.

MacRae, C. D. and MacRae, E. C. (1976). 'Labor Supply and the Payroll Tax', *AER*, **66**, pp. 408–9.

Maital, S. (1973). 'Public Goods and Income Distribution: Some Further Results', *Econometrica*, **41**, pp. 561–8.

Maki, D. and Spindler, Z. A. (1975). 'The Effect of Unemployment Compensation on the Rate of Unemployment in Great Britain', *Oxford Economic Papers*, **27**, pp. 440–54.

Marston, S. J. (1975). 'The Impact of Unemployment Insurance on Job Search', *Brookings Papers on Economic Activity*, pp. 13–48.

Mayer, P. A. and Shipley, J. J. (1970). 'Pareto Optimal Redistribution: Comment', *AER*, **60**, pp. 988–90.

Mencher, S. (1967). 'The Problem of Measuring Poverty', *British Journal of Sociology*, **18**, pp. 1–12.

Minarik, J. J. and Goldfarb, R. S. (1976). 'AFDC Income, Recipient Rates and Family Dissolution: A Comment', *Journal of Human Resources*, **11**, pp. 243–9.

Mishan, E. J. (1972). 'The Futility of Pareto Efficient Distributions', *AER*. **62**, pp. 971–6.

Morgan, J. N. *et al.* (1962). *Income and Welfare in the United States*, McGraw-Hill, New York.

Muellbauer, J. (1974). 'Prices and Inequality: The United Kingdom Experience', *EJ*, **84**, pp. 32–55.

Muellbauer, J. (1977). 'Testing the Barten Model of Household Composition Effects', *EJ*, **87**, pp. 460–87.

Mueller, D. C. (1976). 'Public Choice: A Survey', *Journal of Economic Literature*, **15**, pp. 395–433.

Munnell, A. H. (1974). 'The Impact of Social Security on Personal Savings', *National Tax Journal*, **27**, pp. 553–67.

Munnell, A. H. (1976). 'Private Pensions and Saving: New Evidence', *JPE*, **84**, pp. 1013–32.

Murray, M. (1975). 'The Distribution of Tenant Benefits in Public Housing', *Econometrica*. **43**, pp. 771–88.

Musgrave, R. A. (1970). 'Pareto Optimal Redistribution: Comment', *AER*, **60**, pp. 991–3.

Musgrave, R. A. (1976). 'ET, OT and SBT', *Journal of Public Economics*, **6**, pp. 3–16.

Myrdal, G. (1969). *Objectivity in Social Research*, Pantheon Books, New York.

National Consumer Council (1976). *Paying for Fuel: Report by the National Consumer Council to the Secretary of State for Prices and Consumer Protection*, HMSO, London.

Ng, Y. K. (1972). 'Value Judgements and Economists' Role in Policy Recommendation', *EJ*, **82**, pp. 1014–18.

Okun, A. M. (1975). *Equity and Efficiency: The Big Trade-Off*, Brooking's Institution, Washington D.C.

Orcutt, G. *et al.* (1976). *Policy Exploration Through Microanalytic Simulation*, The Urban Institute, Washington D.C.

OECD (1976). *Public Expenditure on Income Maintenance Programmes*, Paris.

Orr, L. L. (1976). 'Income Transfers as a Public Good: An Application to AFDC', *AER*, **66**, pp. 359–71.

Orshansky, M. (1965). 'Counting the Poor: Another Look at the Poverty Profile', *Social Security Bulletin*, **28**, pp. 3–29.

Palmer, J. L. and Minarik, J. J. (1976). 'Income Security Policy', in H. Owen and C. L. Schultze (eds.), *Setting National Priorities: The Next Ten Years*, Brooking's Institution, Washington D.C.

Peacock, A. T. (1952). *The Economics of National Insurance*, William Hodge, London.

Pechman, J. A. *et al.* (1968). *Social Security: Perspectives for Reform*, Brooking's Institution, Washington D.C.

Peskin, J. (1976). 'In-Kind Income and the Measurement of Poverty', Technical Paper VII, *The Measure of Poverty*, US Department of Health, Education and Welfare, Washington D.C.

Piachaud, D. *Do the Poor Pay More?*, Poverty Research Series 3, Child Poverty Action Group, London.

Piachaud, D. (1976). 'Prices and the Distribution of Incomes, Evidence Submitted to the Royal Commission on the Distribution of Income and Wealth', unpublished, London.

Pinker, R. (1974). 'Social Policy and Social Justice', *Journal of Social Policy*, **3**, pp. 1–19.

Plotnick, R. D. and Skidmore, F. (1975). *Progress against Poverty: A Review of the 1965–1975 Decade*, Academic Press, New York.

Pollak, R. A. (1975). 'An Intertemporal Cost of Living Index', *Annals of Economic and Social Measurement*, **4**, pp. 179–95.

Pollak, R. A. and Wachter, M. L. (1975). 'The Relevance of the Household Production Function and Its Implications for the Allocation of Time', *JPE*, **83**, pp. 255–77.

Posner, M. V. (1975). *Fuel Policy*, Macmillan, London.

Prais, S. J. and Houthakker, H. S. (1955). *The Analysis of Family Budgets*, Cambridge University Press, Cambridge.

Quinn, J. F. (1977). 'The Microeconomics of Early Retirement', *Journal of Human Resources*, forthcoming.

Rainwater, L. (1974). *What Money Buys: Inequality and the Social Meaning of Income*, Basic Books, New York.

Ramprakash, D. (1975). 'Distribution of Income Statistics for the United Kingdom 1972/73: Sources and Methods', *Economic Trends*, August, HMSO, London.

Rawls, J. (1974). 'Some Reasons for the Maximin Criterion', *AER*, **64**, Proc., pp. 141–6.

Rees, A. and Watts, H. W. (1975). 'An Overview of the Labor Supply Results', in J. A. Pechman and P. M. Timpane (eds.), *Work Incentives and Income Guarantees: The New Jersey Negative Income Tax Experiment*, Brooking's Institution, Washington D.C.

Rein, M. (1970). 'Problems in the Definition and Measurement of Poverty', in Townsend (ed.), *The Concept of Poverty*, Heinemann Educational, London.

Reinhardt, P. G. (1974). 'An Empirical Investigation of Grocery Prices Paid by High and Low Income Households', *Quarterly Review of Economics and Business*, **14**, pp. 113–16.

Rivlin, A. M. (1975). 'Income Distribution—Can Economists Help?', *AER*, **65**, Proc. pp. 1–15.

Rosen, H. S. (1976). 'A Methodology for Evaluating Tax Reform Proposals', *Journal of Public Economics*, **6**, pp. 105–21.

Ross, H. L. and Sawhill, I. V. *Time of Transition: The Growth of Families Headed by Women*, The Urban Institute, Washington D.C.

Rothenberg, J. (1961). *The Measurement of Social Welfare*, Prentice-Hall, Englewood Cliffs, New Jersey.

Russell, B. (1946). *The History of Western Philosophy*, George Allen and Unwin, London.

Ryder, N. B. (1973). 'Comment', *JPE*, **81**, pp. S65–9.

Samuelson, (1956). 'Social Indifference Curves', *QJE*, **70**, pp. 1–22.

Sandmo, A. (1976). 'Optimal Taxation: An Introduction to the Literature', *Journal of Public Economics*, **6**, pp. 37–54.

Schlenker, R. E. (1973). 'Optimal Mechanisms for Income Transfer: Note', *AER*, **63**, pp. 454–7.

Schmundt, M. *et al.* (1975). 'The Evaluation by Recipients of In-Kind Transfers', in Lurie (1975a).

Schultz, T. P. (1973). 'Explanation of Birth Rate Changes over Space and Time: A Study of Taiwan', *JPE*, **81**, pp. S239–74.

Semple, M. (1975). 'The Effect of Changes in Household Composition on the Distribution of Income 1961–73', *Economic Trends*, December, HMSO, London.

Sen, A. K. (1966). 'Peasants and Dualism with or without Surplus Labor', *JPE*, **74**, pp. 425–50.

Seneca, J. J. and Taussig, M. K. (1971). 'Family Equivalence Scales and Personal Income Tax Exemptions for Children', *Review of Economics and Statistics*, **53**, pp. 253–62.

Settle, R. F. (1976). 'Are Implicit Tax Rates for Earnings Conditioned Transfer Programs Additive?', *Journal of Human Resources*, **11**, pp. 578–81.

Singh, Balvir and Nagar, A. L. (1973). 'Determination of Consumer Unit Scales', *Econometrica*, **41**, pp. 347–55.

Stanton, D. (1973). 'Determining the Poverty Line', *Social Security Quarterly*, Spring Issue.

Stark, T. (1972). *The Distribution of Personal Income in the United Kingdom 1949–1963*, Cambridge University Press, Cambridge.

Stein, B. (1976). *Work and Welfare in Britain and the USA*, The Macmillan Press, London.

Stern, N. H. (1976). 'On the Specification of Models of Optimum Income Taxation', *Journal of Public Economics*, **6**, pp. 123–62.

Stigler, G. J. (1950). 'The Development of Utility Theory', *JPE*, **58**, pp. 307–27 and pp. 373–96.

Stiglitz, J. E. (1975). 'The Theory of "Screening", Education and the Distribution of Income', *AER*, **65**, pp. 283–300.

Suits, D. (1963). 'The Determinants of Consumer Spending: A Review of Present Knowledge', in *Impacts of Monetary Policy*, Volume 10 of Supporting Papers of the Commission on Money and Credit, Prentice-Hall, Englewood Cliffs, New Jersey.

Sussman, M. B. (1953). 'The Help Pattern in the Middle Class Family', *American Sociological Review*, **18**, pp. 22–9.

Taussig, M. K. (1973). *Alternative Measures of the Distribution of Economic Welfare*, Research Report 116, Industrial Relations Section, Princeton University, Princeton, New Jersey.

Taussing, A. D. (1973). 'Poverty Research and Policy Analysis in the United States: Implications for Ireland', *The Economic and Social Review*, **5**, pp. 75–98.

Taylor, J. (1977). 'A Note on Unemployment in the United Kingdom 1951–1976', unpublished, University of Lancaster.

Tipping, D. G. (1970). 'Price Changes and Income Distribution', *Applied Statistics*, **19**, pp. 1–17.

Titmuss, R. M. (1962). *Income Distribution and Social Change*, Allen and Unwin, London.

Titmuss, R. M. (1963). *Essays on the Welfare State*, 2nd edition, George Allen and Unwin, London.

Tobin, J. (1952). 'A Survey of the Theory of Rationing', *Econometrica*, **20**, pp. 521–53.

Tobin, J. (1970). 'On Limiting the Domain of Inequality', *Journal of Law and Economics*, **13**, pp. 263–77.

Tobin, J. (1973). Comment, *JPE*, **81**, pp. S275–8.

Townsend, P. (1974). 'Poverty as Relative Deprivation: Resources and Style of Living', in D. Wedderburn (ed.), *Poverty, Inequality and Class Structure*, Cambridge University Press, Cambridge.

US Department of Health, Education and Welfare (1976). *Income Supplement Program: 1974 HEW Welfare Replacement Proposal*, Technical Analysis Paper 11, Office of Income Security Policy, Washington D.C.

US Government Printing Office (1974). *Income Security for Americans: Recommendations of the Public Welfare Study*, Report of the Sub-Committee on Fiscal Policy, Joint Economic Committee, Washington D.C.

Ward, B. (1972). *What's Wrong with Economics?*, Basic Books, New York.

Watts, H. W. *et al.* (1974). 'The Labor-Supply Response of Husbands', *Journal of Human Resources*, **9**, pp. 181–200.

Weisbrod, B. A. (1970). 'On the Stigma Effect and the Demand for Welfare Programs: A Theoretical Note', *Institute for Research on Poverty*, Discussion Paper 82–70.

Whalley, J. (1975a). 'A General Equilibrium Assessment of the 1973 United Kingdom Tax Reform', *Economica*, **42**, pp. 139–61.

Whalley, J. (1975b). 'How Reliable is Partial Equilibrium Analysis?', *Review of Economics and Statistics*, **57**, pp. 299–310.

Willis, R. J. (1973). 'A New Approach to the Economic Theory of Fertility Behaviour', *JPE*, **81**, pp. S14–S64.

Wilson, L. S. (1976). 'Block Tariffs and Distributional Equity', unpublished, Queen's University, Kingston, Ontario.

Wilson, L. S. (1977a). 'The Interaction of Equity and Efficiency Factors in Optimal Pricing Rules', *Journal of Public Economics*, forthcoming.

Wilson, L. S. (1977b). 'The Incidence of Subsidies to the Nationalised Fuel Industries 1970–75', unpublished, Queen's University, Kingston, Ontario.

Young, M. (1952). 'Distribution of Income Within the Family', *British Journal of Sociology*, **3**, pp. 305–21.

Zeckhauser, R. J. (1971). 'Optimal Mechanisms for Income Transfers', *AER*, **61**, pp. 324–34.

Zimmerman, D. (1975). 'On the Relationship between Public Goods Theory and Expenditure Determinant Studies', *National Tax Journal*, **28**, pp. 227–39.

Index